IVAN THE TERRIBLE

IVAN VASILOVICH · EMPEROR OF RUSSIA

FROM AN OLD WOODCUT IN

"EARLY VOYAGES AND TRAVELS TO RUSSIA AND PERSIA"

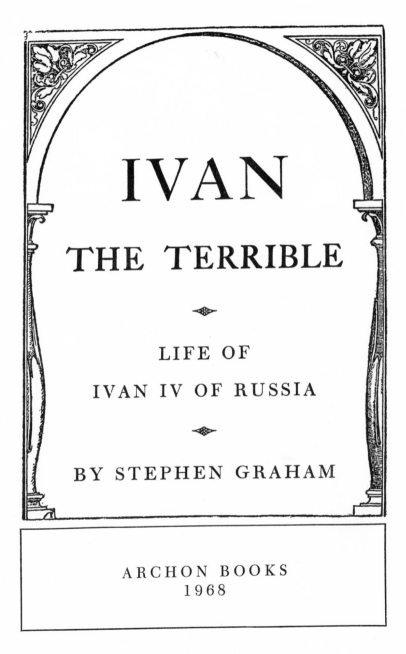

IVAN

THE TERRIBLE

❖

LIFE OF
IVAN IV OF RUSSIA

❖

BY STEPHEN GRAHAM

ARCHON BOOKS
1968

First published 1933
Reprinted 1968 by arrangement with
ERNEST BENN, LTD.
in an unaltered and unabridged edition

SBN: 208 00683 4
Library of Congress Catalog Card Number: 68-8020
Printed in the United States of America

PREFACE

BIOGRAPHY differs from History in that it diverts the interest of events to the person who had part in them, whereas History takes the interest from the personality to society at large, from cause to effect. The task, therefore, in writing a life of Ivan the Terrible, has been more to reveal his personality and character than to give a history of his reign. Perhaps now, when the Tsardom has been shattered to dust, the biography of a Tsar is more significant than the history of his reign. For History goes on and rewrites itself. It is a palimpsest, as, for instance, the history of Ivan's struggle for the Baltic, which will be rescrawled by Peter the Great. But Biography tells the story of the life of a man, and stands before us when finished, complete in itself. It can be made clearer by successive writers, brought more into perspective, but the essential story remains unmodified.

It is strange that Ivan the Terrible has, up to now, escaped the attention of the English biographer. This is the first full and detailed life of Ivan to be presented in the English language, the first attempt made to provide the psychological detail for the understanding of his character. Had all the facts been already known, it had been more fascinating to write a strongly reasoned, critical, and interpretive biography. As it was it seemed better to transcribe all the significant detail and allow the reader to use his own judgment as to the character, mental condition, and motive of the man recognised as one of the greatest and yet cruelest of the Tsars of Russia.

Now, at least, the historical novelist is provided with a true basis and a hundred colourful stories for his work, should he take Ivan the Terrible for a character. And the composer of film scenarios of this reign has surer guidance. Actually, the person most likely to be aided and interested is the student of human nature and the psychologist.

Unwilling to believe that a man in his senses could be as monstrously cruel as Ivan was, many will be apt to dismiss him as mad. But actually it will be seen that his wits did not forsake him. He murdered people in anger, but he murdered more in an icy coldness of disposition. He seldom lost his head, but remained coolly rational and sometimes witty in the midst of his barbarities.

To understand is to condone, and as it is difficult to condone it is difficult to understand. But the age itself was cruel. It was the age of Catherine de' Medici and the massacre of St. Bartholomew; the age of the Duke of Alva and his barbarities in the Low Countries; the age at first of Henry VIII and later of Mary. The three years of Queen Mary's reign when hundreds were burned at the stake for their religion belong to this time. One reads of seventy-three Protestants of Colchester dragged through the streets of London tied to a single rope. That is quite in the spirit of Ivan's doings. In Sweden, France, and Spain, not to mention other countries, deeds of fantastic cruelty were done, though in truth the narration of them would pale beside a life of Ivan the Terrible.

England in the reign of Elizabeth began to move out of the red light of cruelty. The Virgin Queen was terrible at times. There were burnings in her reign too, but the English people were moving toward a consciousness of humanity. There is little in the sayings and doings of even the worst characters in Shakespeare's plays to suggest real cruelty, and he never conceived of anyone of the temperament and character of Ivan the Terrible. He was capable of writing:

> The poor beetle that we tread upon
> In corporal sufferance finds a pang as great
> As when a giant dies.

It is strange to think that Ivan and Shakespeare were contemporaries, and that while one was working his monstrous will in Russia the other was writing plays which, in part, expressed humanity at its highest and best.

The life of Ivan the Terrible presents another strange anomaly. This Tsar, so different in character from anyone we possessed in England, was nevertheless an Anglophile. England discovered Russia during his reign and the Tsar was fascinated by the deportment of the first English travellers. He granted England extraordinary trading privileges, even monopolies, within his realm. He wished to marry the Queen, but when he realised that he could not have her to wife he was nevertheless set on having some English lady to be his consort. It may even be said he died in a frenzy to possess an Englishwoman. The refusal of the hand of Lady Mary Hastings evidently shattered his health and he became mortally ill from that moment.

As regards the greatness of Ivan, there are doubtless those who will consider that he was in no wise a great man. But he was a great Russian, and there is a difference. His barbarities were to some extent forgotten in Russia, but the strength of his personality and the legend of the fear he inspired remained. Peter the Great was one of the first to point out that Ivan was the character best worth studying in the whole of Russian history. Ivan had an instinct for the greatness of Russia; that was what Peter seized upon when he studied Ivan's reign. What Ivan started Peter furthered. He centralised the power of the throne, struck at the wealth of the Church, continued and consummated the war with Sweden. Peter was naturally a cruel monarch, but it is possible that in this also he emulated Ivan the Terrible and made himself the most feared of all men in his dominions. Strangely enough both Tsars did to death their eldest sons.

After the revolution of 1917–8 the Tsars remaining in honour in history were Ivan the Terrible and Peter the Great; not that either of them was held in great honour, but both are deemed to have done something for that progress in the destruction of an aristocracy, dear to the heart of the revolutionary. And in general to the Russian people, Ivan stands forth as a true Russian. Much of his cruelty was not intimately realised by Russians. Some stories of him everybody knew. But the legend of the fear of him has enhanced his glory through the centuries.

STEPHEN GRAHAM

CONTENTS

ILLUSTRATIONS

IVAN THE TERRIBLE

I.

THE KREMLIN

THE little Moskva river connects with the Oka
and the Volga and is the beginning of a waterway to the Caspian and the East. On a little
hill over the river, amid forested plains, Yury Dol-
goruky, Prince of Suzdal, made a stronghold in or
about the year 1147, and it was called Moskva. A clus-
ter of wooden huts soon appeared at the foot of the
fortress and that was the beginning of a great metropolis. It was a forest clearing with a village in it and its
first church was named "Our Saviour in the Wood." It
became a trading centre; it was without history and
was not ravaged for a hundred years, an obscure settlement on the ultimate border of the territory of the
princes of Suzdal.

Then Chinghiz Khan with his horde of Tartars
rolled out of Asia, burning and slaughtering to the
gates of Kief. In their first incursion, 1224, they missed
Moscow, but on their second, 1237, they burned it to
the ground, slaying the adults, but taking away the
children to sell into slavery. The reigning prince of
Suzdal was slain in battle. It was Michael, a prince of
Novgorod, brother of the famous Alexander Nevsky
who rebuilt the town. Moscow rose from its ashes and
became the appanage of the Northern princedom of
Novgorod. But fifty years after the rebuilding the Tar-

tars destroyed Moscow again. Prince Daniel of Novgorod built it for the third time.

It had nevertheless been rebuilt by permission of the
Tartars and became a Tartar protectorate. Its prince,
Daniel, did homage and paid tribute to the Tartars.
George, son of Daniel, married a sister of the great
Khan and had the use of a Tartar army for his wars on
other Russian princes. He won his battles and joined
the territories of Novgorod and Suzdal in one. Mos-
cow, his seat of power, became a great city.

Ivan I, Prince of Vladimir, brother of George, in-
herited Moscow, adding Vladimir to its potential sway.
He also acquired during his reign, Uglitch, Galitch,
and Bielozersk. The Tartar overlord required that he
regard Vladimir as his capital, but he was more drawn
to Moscow which he greatly embellished. He built the
beautiful Cathedral of the Assumption, the *Uspensky
Sobor*, and he constructed a high rampart of oak around
the Moscow Hill. Such a rampart was called in Tartar,
kreml. The wall enclosed two cathedrals, two churches,
the house of Ivan I and the houses of his friends. This
was the first Kremlin.

The wooden wall was repeatedly burned and then
rebuilt. At length, in 1367, it was replaced by a wall of
stone. The will of Russia to grow and to survive the
Tartar was shown by the change of building material.
A tired nation might have been content with a wooden
fortress. Not only did the Kremlin rise in stone, but
emplacements were made for cannon. The Muscovites
adopted gunpowder soon after the rest of Europe, but
the Tartar preferred the sword and the bow.

Tartars had become Moslems even before the Russians had become Christians, as if by fate intended for that religion. The rivalry of the Crescent and the Cross extended from Northern Africa across Asia and Europe. The Holy War which died down with the last Crusade (1271) was continued for another two hundred years in Russia. The Grand Dukes of Moscow were the vassals of the Horde, but war continued in vassaldom. One of the most notable rebels was Dimitry called "Donskoi" because of his great victory over Sultan Mamai on the Don. Dimitry was a visionary soldier trusting as much in the emblems of his religion as in force of arms, carrying the Blessed Virgin with him into the fight.

That was in 1380. The next great Grand Duke was Ivan III (1472), who extended Muscovy north-east to the mouth of the Petchora in the Arctic, took Perm, and rebelled against the Horde.

The Tartars used the Grand Dukes of Moscow as tax collectors. Moscow, despite sporadic revolt and many isolated successes against the tyrants, paid ever higher tribute for its privileges and home rule, and aided by force of arms, Tartar and Slav, exacted tribute from the other cities of Russia. From the year 1237 to the year 1487 Russia was definitely under the Tartar yoke. The year 1487 saw the first decided breakdown of the power of the Horde. The Tartars had taught the Muscovites ferocity. They had made them do their fighting and had lived on them for two centuries, but under this régime they themselves had grown tame and demoralised. Ivan III sent presents instead of regular tribute, and when the Khan expostulated the Tartar messengers were put to death. The Horde mobilised against Moscow, but when it came face to face with the Muscovite army took fright and would not fight. The Khan was put to death by his own followers.

Ivan's army then took Kazan and placed their own Tartar nominee in control of the Volga territory. The power of Moscow swelled prodigiously, and Ivan III took the double-headed eagle which looks east and west over Europe and Asia as his coat of arms. He died in 1505 and was succeeded by his son, Vasilly III.

Vasilly III was the father of Ivan the Terrible. He married a Russian, but since she bore him no son during twenty years of married life he ordained that his first wife should become a nun and he married Helena Glinski of Lithuania. She was of a Catholic family and the Orthodox Church did not approve of the union and would not, in fact, recognise the validity of his divorce. Vasilly III thereupon applied for advice to the Patriarch of Jerusalem. But neither would the Patriarch approve the union. Instead he is said to have prophesied a baleful issue if the marriage took place: "Thou shalt have a wicked son. Terror will ravage thy estate; rivers of blood will flow; the heads of the mighty shall be laid low; thy cities will be devoured by fire."

Vasilly III reigned twenty-eight years. The Tartars returned threateningly, almost to the gates of Moscow, but were bought off. The Grand Duke signed a new treaty of bondage. The Tartars plundered the land and were retiring with booty when they were set upon by the Voivode of Riazan and, being defeated, surrendered the treaty. Moscow paid no more tribute to Tartary. She became free to be European.

The city was now of considerable size. It had 100,-

ooo inhabitants and over 40,000 buildings. Above the toothed wall of the Kremlin rose the white towers and gilded domes and cupolas of cathedrals, and the flat roofs of princely houses and palaces. At the foot of this city, within a city and surrounding it, was the wooden Moscow of the people, whose outer undefended line was twelve miles about. Here were wide village streets, some of them paved with wood, most of them a river of mud in summer. Here were the open bazaar, the shops, the market, and some seventy churches, lifting purple and gold domes to the sky.

Despite the drain of wealth for centuries to the Golden Horde, Moscow had grown rich. There was great treasure of gold and gems within the Kremlin walls, especially in the safe-keeping of the cathedral and shrines there. Hangings of cloths of gold adorned all the houses of the nobles. The attire of the Grand Duke, not yet called Tsar, was extremely magnificent. A barbaric grandeur characterised the court of Muscovy, and that secular grandeur was enriched and rendered more mysterious by the Byzantine pomp of the ritual of the Church.

The nobles supped from plates of very fine gold and drank from golden goblets. Within the Kremlin, in the palaces and the cathedrals, there was probably concentrated more gold than in any other like space in the world. The love of gold and the colour of gold, as eloquently expressed in the framing of the ikons, was characteristic of the new Russia which had learned from the Tartar the price of gold in terms of blood.

With the liberation from the Tartars a new united Russia had come into being, extending from the North-

ern Volga to the Dnieper and from the Arctic Ocean
to the Don, a Russia without Siberia, without the
Volga steppes, the Caucasus, the Crimea, the Western
Ukraine, or the countries of the Baltic littoral, nevertheless a northern state of vast territory. All the petty
princes had entered the service of the Moscow Grand
Dukes and allowed their lands to be incorporated in
Muscovy. Its peoples were soldiers, peasants, artisans,
traders, priests, and monks. It bore rich harvests; its
people did not starve. It traded almost exclusively with
the Orient, even with distant Pekin, connecting with
the caravans of Central Asia by its great waterways.
The Fair of Nizhny Novgorod on the Volga and the
Oka was the commercial bridge head of the East. Its
trading laws and customs remained profoundly under
the influence of the Tartars. The peasants of the north
were free; the peasants of the centre and south were in
state of transition from freedom to serfdom, unable to
pay their taxes and their feudal dues. Laws were traditional, but little coded, and the overlord, the estate
owner, was a law unto himself as far as his underlings
were concerned. The religion of the people was an
idolatrous Christianity multiplied by an omnipresent
belief in the supernatural. The Church under the influence of the Fathers of the Desert was strongly ascetic,
preoccupied with the mystery of death and the place of
the saint in the mystical Sophia.

There was no chivalry, no French insincerity of pol-
ished manners. On the other hand there was no conscious rectitude as of the English. The people, high and
low, were crafty and talkative, sometimes subtle, social
but unsympathetic, impulsive, turbulent, capable of

uncommon barbarity in their treatment of one another.

To be Grand Duke of Muscovy was no sinecure. The Grand Duke was master of everyone. What he had he held by right, but he must protect it by force of arms, sagacity, and terror. He sat on a throne exalted above his nobles. There was no merry talk. He wore his crown as he wore his authority, with every circumstance of awe and fear.

II.

HELENA OF LITHUANIA

HELENA, a beautiful young Lithuanian virgin, was a refugee at the Russian court, the ward of her uncle Michael Glinski. She was a dark, passionate creature, educated, western, emancipated, giving herself liberties which were a novelty in Muscovy, and she attracted the desires of the old Grand Duke Vasilly who cut off his beard to please her.

The monarch had lived happily enough with his wife Salome, but she was well stricken in years and he discovered a good reason why he should put her away. Her bed was barren; she had borne him no children. One of the boyars, Simon Kurbsky, championed the unfortunate queen, but to no avail. She went under the black veil, and Helena went under the white veil—to the throne of Muscovy and the bed of the Tsars.

The wedding of Vasilly and Helena took place on the Feast of the Assumption, August 15th, 1526. Before the ceremony they were sprinkled with hops for their fertility and fanned with sables for their health. After the ceremony they went publicly to bed on a mattress laid over twenty-seven sheaves of rye, and a woman, the wife of the captain of the guard, came to them in two fur cloaks, one of them inside out, and sprinkled more hops on them. But the charms did not work then and there. The union was not fruitful within the natural space of time. Perhaps the difficulty was one more of paternity than of maternity. But various

holy men took the matter up in their prayers. We have
the anomaly of the Church disapproving of the union
and monks praying for the birth of a son. The monk
Paphnuty worked a miracle and for that reason among
others was after canonised. In the year 1530 Helena
became *enceinte* and on the 25th August of that year
bore the parlous Ivan.

The rejoicing of Vasilly III thereat was greater than
that of his court. Helena had her faction led by her
uncle, Michael Glinski, and the birth of an heir threw
the pretensions and ambitions of other princes into the
shade. Also Vasilly, being an old man, was not likely to
survive for long and the prospect of an infant Grand
Duke and a Lithuanian regency was not predictive of
peace and amity in the Kremlin.

The Grand Duke, however, pursued good fortune in
marriage and within another eighteen months Helena
was brought to bed again and bore him another son,
Yury. In his old age he began to taste the felicities and
embarrassments of a family life. He was happy and he
seemed hearty. Shortly after little Ivan's third birthday he decided to go praying and hunting and to take
his wife and family to Sergey-Troitsky Monastery
some thirty miles north of the city. On the 25th September, 1533, he set out with hounds and archers and
mounted men with forked sticks, intending to hunt on
the way and reach the monastery on the eve of the festival of its patron. The famous monastery surged with
pilgrims from all parts of Muscovy; the Grand Duke
and his consort fasted, went to High Mass, received the
blessing of the Archimandrite, and then continued on
their way in festival spirit with their hunting party

into the forest, making for a seat called Volok-Lamsky. But suddenly, on the way, he was marked with the sign of death.

He had pain in riding and there was found to be a purple boil on his groin. With great difficulty he reached the house of Ivan Podzhogin, one of his favourite courtiers, where he had been invited to a banquet. There he had a hot bath but obtained no relief. He could not join the guests, but ate in his bed-chamber, still in pain. Next day being fine for hunting, he struggled on. It is evident he had a great zest still for life. He sent for his brother Andrew, and on the day following, the two brothers went out with the hounds from the village of Kolp. But he was weaker and in greater pain. He had to return to the hunting lodge at Kolp and take to bed.

Helena sent for her uncle, Michael Glinski, and two foreign doctors practising at the Russian court. The doctors applied poultices of fresh honey, wheaten flour, and roast onion. The boil ripened and much pus was taken from it. The Grand Duke was borne by hand on a litter by his nobles from Kolp to Volok-Lamsky and there the poultice was renewed and more pus was taken from the boil. The doctors gave him a laxative of seeds after which, however, he was only the weaker. The pain had greatly increased and now his chest was in pain and he began to experience difficulty in breathing.

Then Vasilly sent a lawyer, Mansurof, and the clerk Putiatin to Moscow secretly to obtain two documents, his will, which he had made some years before, and that of his late father, Ivan III. Then the wills were read aloud to him in complete privacy and he ordered

his own will to be burned. The fact that the Grand
Duke was on his deathbed was kept secret, but the
rumour of his illness went abroad. It could not be hidden. The number of boyars arriving at Volok-Lamsky
increased, and it was with difficulty that Helena persuaded them that her husband's indisposition was trifling, a mere boil. Vasilly's brother Yury, a possible
disputant of the throne, arrived, and could not be prevailed upon to go away. The younger brother Andrew
also remained.

The crater of the boil had now become a ghastly
wound about the size of a hand. Pus was taken from it
by the cupful. But the monarch clung to life and gave
orders that he be carried on the way, first to the monastery of St. Joseph and then on to Moscow. The boyars
carried him on his bed, which was set down in the
monastery church before the altar. Here collected a
whole company, including Helena and her children,
and huntsmen and men at arms, nobles and black
clergy, in a great agitation of praying, sobbing, and
surmise.

Still Vasilly III was "an unconscionable time a-dy-
ing" and retained his consciousness and still gave orders which must be obeyed, and his mind was set on
getting to his palace in the Kremlin. The nobles must
raise his bier again and carry him on. The first snow
came down. At the Sparrow Hills the monarch was put
in a sledge with quiet horses. He had ordered a new
bridge to be built over the Moskva river so that he
might enter the city from an unusual point and thus
escape the observation of the curious. But when the
horses set foot on the new bridge it broke down. There

were many adventures in this last journey of Vasilly III, but at last on the 25th November, 1533, he reached his home within the Kremlin walls.

The apartments where the Grand Duke lived had something in common with the modern flat, three communicating rooms on the *bel étage* of his palace, an ante-chamber, the reception and banqueting hall and at the back of that the bedroom with private chapel adjoint. The kitchen and domestic offices were below; one large room little used was above. The bath was in a separate building as was also the nursery.

Vasilly called to his bedside Vasilly Shuisky, Michael Zakharin, Michael Vorontsof, Peter Golovin, and the seneschal Shigona, and in their presence dictated a new will which Putiatin wrote down. Then he called further Ivan Shuisky and Michael Tuchkof, likewise Helena's uncle, Michael Glinski. His elder brother Yury came also, unbidden. The Metropolitan Daniel arrived, and the Archpriest Alexief who brought the Holy Elements.

Then the sick man rose from his couch and got into a chair. And he rose again, and leaning on Zakharin's arms stood to receive the Bread and the Wine, and he cried. He was carried and put to bed again. The wan light of day peered through the mica windows to the nobles and the priests in the bedchamber, wreathed with incense and oppressed by the shadow of death. Vasilly, holding a cross in his hand, that he might find fortitude to bear his pain, called his brothers Andrew and Yury to his bedside and likewise the Metropolitan Daniel. The rest of the boyars stood behind and in their presence the Grand Duke made a solemn declaration of his will that the throne should descend to his son Ivan. He bound his brothers on the pledge of their salvation to uphold his testament and to regard the enemies of his child as their enemies. And he exhorted the boyars standing there in like terms. And he commended the care of his wife, Helena, to Michael Glinski, telling him that he was no longer a foreigner in Russia, but one of themselves.

He now wished, and he had had it on his heart for some time, that his crown should be taken from him and to be consecrated as a monk, that he might go to heaven as a holy man. But he was distraught with pain and still asked remedies for the disease. Zakharin wished to have vodka poured into the wound, but the doctors could not recommend it, telling Vasilly plainly that he was beyond the care of physic and commending him to the aid of prayer alone. The Abbot of Sergey-Troitsky arrived, and Vasilly commended his son Ivan to the care of the wonder-worker Sergey. Prince Michael Glinski brought the young Ivan to the father's bedside in his arms to bless. Helena, weeping bitterly, came also, supported by the young brother Andrew. When her tears had subsided for a moment the monarch told her that her son would reign in his stead, according to his testament, and that her position also had been safeguarded as mother and guardian in keeping with the established tradition of the throne of Moscow. She asked that her younger son receive the father's blessing and the infant was brought in and blessed by him. It seemed that Vasilly wished to hold longer converse with his wife, but again her sobs rent the air and it was impossible for him to make himself heard. His pain had left him now and he had that relief which is not uncommon in the hours just preceding death.

The most famous wonder-working ikon, that of Our Lady of Vladimir, was brought to him and likewise the relics of the great martyr Catherine, and after his obeisance he asked the Metropolitan Daniel to make him a monk. His brother Andrew and other boyars were opposed to that, but the dying man was most persistent, indicating his wishes even after his tongue clove to the roof of his mouth. He kissed the border of the sheet whereon he was lying, and he kept making the sign of the cross with his fingers over his face, gazing all the while at the Vladimir Madonna. Daniel sent for a black cowl and Vasilly whispered: "If you fail to make me a monk, nevertheless place the monastic garb upon my dead body when you bury me in sign of my dying wish."

Still the brother Andrew and the boyar Vorontsof were opposed to it, but the Metropolitan said to them: "A silver dish is good, but a golden is better. If you prevent me in this good work our blessing will pass from you." They then went away and left the Grand Duke Vasilly in the hands of the Church. The throne was put aside, and Vasilly III became the monk Varlaam. Shigona Podzhogin, watching at the moment of death, recounted that he saw the old man's spirit go away from his body like a light cloud. It is somewhat curious: his first wife had been made a nun against the opinion of the Patriarch of Jerusalem. She had been dead to the world these eight years. On the last day of his life the husband entered the same estate.

THE IKON OF OUR LADY OF VLADIMIR

The dead body was clad in the simple garb of a monk and the bed of his death was spread with black taffeta, and thus Vasilly III lay in state for all who wished to come and give the Christian kiss of forgiveness and farewell. Moscow showed its grief by keening and sobbing, not necessarily insincere, a passivity toward the ancient terror of death and the tradition of mourning. Helena, when she heard of her husband's death, fell into a swoon which is said to have lasted two hours. That is not to say she experienced a sorrow which would be inconsolable, but she was a primitive being, and it was safer and more becoming to fall into a faint than to develop any immediate line of action.

The boyars dug a grave. The body of Vasilly was placed in a stone coffin and was hoisted on to the heads of a number of monks from Sergey-Troitsky Monastery and borne with chanting to its final resting place in the Cathedral of the Archangel Michael. The big bell of the Kremlin yelled out its grief, drowning both the singing of the clergy and the weeping of the mourners (5th December, 1533).

Helena quickly dried her eyes and became the active ruler of Russia. Within a week Prince Yury was placed under arrest. Had there been no second marriage of Vasilly III, Yury would have been Grand Duke. He was a man of ripe years and experience, the favourite of a faction among the boyars. He had sworn to be true to the child Ivan who stood in his way, but Andrew Shuisky and other nobles wished him to break his oath and seize the government of the State. That Yury was discontented is certain; to what extent he was actually disaffected is unknown. The Regent Helena took a swift decision, and Prince Ivan Shuisky and Ivan Bielsky were shut up too.

In the normal course of events, Michael Glinski, the uncle of Helena, would have become the real ruler, and Helena the nominal ruler of Muscovy. But the death of Vasilly liberated a secret. Helena had a lover, the Prince Ivan Obolensky. Helena was wilful and high spirited, and determined not to be overborne by the counsels of her ex-guardian. That would have been like a return to childhood. So Obolensky was advanced into the open in opposition to the uncle.

Not only Glinski but Michael Vorontsof and several other boyars saw in the weak sovereignty of a woman their own opportunity. For that reason they had allowed Prince Yury to be imprisoned. He was well out of the way. But the advancement of Obolensky to the first place was an unpleasant surprise. Even Prince Andrew, Vasilly's favourite brother, was discontented. He remained in Moscow to the intercession service which takes place forty days after death, and prayed for the peace of the soul of Vasilly. He asked some extra share of lands from Helena, but was fobbed off with various keepsakes such as furs, goblets, horses, and saddles, and with these he departed to his estates at Staritsa, some distance to the north-west of Moscow, in high dudgeon. He was aggrieved by the obscurity of his position in the realm and yet apprehensive that a fate similar to that of his brother Yury might overtake him.

In the Kremlin, as indeed in the country also, there were two factions, that of Obolensky and that of Glinski. A conspiracy was soon on foot to remove Obolensky and shut Helena in a nunnery. The intrigue lost itself in words, and the coup was too long delayed. In August, 1534, Helena resolved on action. Glinski was arrested and thrown into a dungeon, whence his death was shortly reported. Vorontsof went to prison also, as did a number of disaffected boyars who were implicated in the sedition.

That same month was the fourth birthday of Ivan. He sat on the throne, with miniature crown and sceptre, and clad in silver and gold received his nobles who bowed to him as to God. Had his father lived, the child would have grown to maturity in quietude and seclusion, but Ivan from his earliest years was in the midst of men. They were his subjects, but he was the subject of their minds, the centre of dispute. In these early years the boy who was to become the terrible Tsar was quick, clever, amiable. He seems to have loved those who loved him, but was cold to all others and very observant.

Helena was a jealous mother. And jealousy breeds violence. She might have safeguarded Ivan's position with more sagacity. She could not rest while a possible pretender to the throne was at large. She could, at least, have trusted Prince Andrew, who was sympathetic and friendly, devoid of selfish ambition. In him she might have found a better guarantee of Ivan's future than in her uncle Glinski. Her lover Obolensky was not a man of much capacity. She had imprisoned the two most powerful men in the country, Princes Yury and Glinski. Now she sent spies to watch Prince Andrew and collected information about his discontents. She commanded him to come to court, but he was so apprehensive that he shammed illness, saying with pathetic lack of originality that a boil had appeared on one of his thighs. The spies reported that he was not ill. His lie might appear to amount almost to sedition. But he might yet have been won over. Ivan was being deprived of a good and friendly uncle. But Helena did not see it in that light. She saw in Prince Andrew a possible leader of revolt. For three years she conducted an angry correspondence with him and dogged his actions with spies. It was in vain that he called himself her faithful slave; she did not believe. The intelligence came at last that he was preparing to flee to some place of strength such as Novgorod or to escape altogether into Lithuania, there to wait his opportunity for a triumphant return. Emissaries of the Church were sent to him bearing the threat of anathema if he did not come to Moscow and make his peace. But in their wake they were followed by troops whose intentions were unmistakable. Andrew at once took refuge in Novgorod and rallied what friends he had there to his support.

An army of landowners and peasants mobilised for Prince Andrew. The lover Obolensky was sent with another army against him and civil war was nearly enkindled on the upper reaches of the Volga. The army of Prince Andrew was not very staunch and would not probably have stood the test of battle, but in any case its leader had no wish to fight. He was peace-loving, and doubtless for those turbulent times must be considered weak. It is said that after receiving promise on oath from Obolensky that he would be pardoned he consented to surrender. There was no battle. The prince went peacefully to Moscow. He arrived on a Thursday and on the Saturday he was thrown into prison where he was violently done to death. His followers were rounded up, beaten with the knout, and tortured. Some died in torment in the dungeon and of the others some thirty were hung on gallows placed at intervals upon the highway leading from Moscow to the city of Novgorod. Prince Andrew's wife and her little son Vladimir Andreyevitch were also imprisoned. This was in June, 1537.

The short-sighted Regent had now disposed of the possible pretenders, but the physical safeguard of her child was embodied in herself alone. She had made many enemies for Ivan. A foreigner herself, it was difficult for her to make sound friendships among the Russian boyars. The ill will toward her was great, especially after she had destroyed Prince Andrew and imprisoned his wife and heir. Within nine months of that dire act she was herself stricken and died in agony, of poison.

III.

THE TYRANNY OF THE SHUISKIES

PRINCE VASILLY SHUISKY, whom the late
Grand Duke Vasilly III had called to his bedside when he lay dying in the Kremlin, was one
of the most powerful nobles in Russia, being descended
from Alexander Nevsky and possibly of greater lineage
than the Grand Dukes themselves. He had been clever
enough to avoid the suspicion of treason into which his
kinsman Andrew had fallen, being an older man and
more crafty than most at the court of Helena. Whether
he was privy to the poisoning of the Regent is unknown, but he immediately seized the power and threw
her lover, Prince Ivan Ovchina-Telepnef-Obolensky
into prison. We finally give his full name because we
shall see him no more in this history. He died of starva-
tion and the weight of the irons with which he was
loaded.

The boyars sat in council and Prince Vasilly Shuisky
was their leader. They at once voted the release of most
of Helena's political prisoners. Not many, however,
had survived their treatment in prison; little Ivan's
uncles Yury and Andrew were both dead, as was also
Vorontsof. But the widow of Prince Andrew, Euphrosyne, and her son Vladimir Andreyevitch were set free.
His father's lands were given to Vladimir Andreyevitch, but he and his mother were obliged to live on
them and were not allowed to visit Moscow. They were
important and therefore dangerous, because in the case

of the death of Ivan, Prince Vladimir Andreyevitch was the obvious successor to the throne. However, on Christmas Day, 1541, they obtained full freedom and came to court.

Princes Ivan Shuisky and Ivan Bielsky were still alive at the death of Helena and they were released. Bielsky was a very turbulent and ambitious gentleman who claimed to be descended from Gedimin, and showed pretensions to the throne. He was far from showing gratitude to Vasilly Shuisky for his release. We have a position kindred to that of Richard III in England in 1485. It is surprising that no usurper seized the throne and that the little princes Ivan and Yury were not murdered. Possibly the rivalry of the chief boyars prevented such a consummation.

But the children were neglected. The Kremlin ceased to belong to them. It became the striding ground of men in armour with cloth of gold or taffeta over their metal breastplates, imperious nobles who passed the princes by and did not give them honour. Ivan the Terrible thus described this time, writing in after years: "On the death of our mother, Helena, we became orphans in the fullest sense. Our subjects only furthered their own desires, finding the country without a ruler. They ceased to regard us and, being their own masters, strove only for wealth or glory for themselves and quarrelled among one another. They seized my mother's treasury; they trampled on her goods. . . . As for my brother George and myself, they treated us as foreigners or rather as beggars. We lacked food and clothing, but our will counted for nothing and no one was found to provide for us as children. Once we were play-

ing with Ivan Shuisky [brother of Prince Vasilly
Shuisky] and he put his feet on my father's bed. The
children of the boyars took away our father's gold and
silver plate and wrote the names of their parents upon
it. . . ."

Ivan IV, aged eight, could hardly force a reckoning
with the boyars, but his memory was good, he was re-
markably impressionable, little escaped his observant
eyes. The day of vengeance would come.

The struggle of the Bielsky faction with the Shuisky
faction raged over the heads of the children and they
had no part or lot in it, being pawns of neither party.
The Shuiskies won and Prince Ivan Bielsky was thrust
back into prison. In this case the Metropolitan Daniel
backed the losing side. Vasilly Shuisky spared him, but
his brother Ivan removed him in the following year.
Most of Bielsky's adherents were treated with com-
parative leniency, but Mishurin, a close confidant of
the late Vasilly III, was allowed to be skinned alive by
the young princes, the children of the boyars. His
naked, flayed body was then placed upon a block and
he was beheaded (January, 1539).

That same month Vasilly Shuisky died a natural
death and was succeeded in power by his brother Ivan.
Prince Ivan Shuisky brought the Archimandrite of
Sergey-Troitsky Monastery to Moscow and made him
Metropolitan. But the new Metropolitan, Joseph, did
not remain long on his side. At least he persuaded the
infant Ivan to grant Bielsky a pardon. Apparently the
authority of the child held good, and one fine day in
July, 1540, the proud Bielsky came prancing in at a
Kremlin gate to the astonishment of Ivan Shuisky,

who for some time had ignored the existence of Ivan IV. Then a whole series of pardons were granted to all of the Bielsky faction who languished in gaol or banishment.

It is possible that Ivan Shuisky would have weakly allowed himself to be removed from power; he was not a strong character. But the Bielsky faction was intolerable to other boyars, notably the princes of Novgorod and Prince Ivan and Prince Michael Kubensky. At the turn of the year 1541–42 the insurrection came to a head. There was an army in the field ready to seize Bielsky and his adherents. Shuisky was obliged to associate himself with this mutiny which had broken out in his name. The greater strength lay with the Novgorodtsi. Ivan Bielsky was captured and bound and sent again to prison, this time to Bielozersk in the far north, and to expedite his end murderers were sent after him to despatch him in prison.

Such was the society in those times that it recked little of God or man. In the middle of the night the conspirators broke into the Kremlin cell of the Metropolitan and stoned him so that he fled for his life into the palace to the bedside of little Ivan who, wakening in alarm, was unable to protect him. He fled from the palace and getting in a sleigh with three horses set off hell for leather for his Monastery of Sergey-Troitsky, pursued by the young Novgorod princes who yelled foul words and blasphemies after him. Their intention was to kill him and he barely escaped being murdered. Afterwards he was got out of his anchorite refuge in the *lavra* and banished to the monastery at Bielozersk. Makary of Novgorod became Metropolitan in his place.

After the destruction of the Bielsky faction Ivan
Shuisky became ill and died. The chief power among
the boyars was then lodged in the cousin Andrew
Shuisky. The enemies of the Shuisky family had been
disposed of. The only menace was from the side of the
adolescent Grand Duke Ivan IV, who was now thirteen
years of age and beginning to show a temper which
would not easily be brooked. Possibly Andrew Shuisky
ignored the fact that Ivan was growing up. He still
saw in him the negligible infant whose existence had
counted for so little during the wild years since the Regent Helena had died.

Ivan kept his own counsel. He did not fawn upon
the Shuiskies although they seemed to have more power
than he had. Probably his aloofness offended them. He
had his own friend and confidant, Fedor Vorontsof,
and was more attached to him than to any other of the
boyars. Yet under his eyes Andrew and his brother Ivan
Mikhailovitch Shuisky and Prince Skopin-Shuisky set
upon Vorontsof in the palace, tore his clothes from his
back and would have killed him. What was the immediate pretext for this outrage is not chronicled. Probably some words of Vorontsof had been reported to one
of the Shuiskies. A council of state was being held at
which the Metropolitan Makary and the Grand Duke
Ivan were present. An accusation was made against
Fedor Vorontsof. The Shuiskies jumped to their feet
and accompanied by Princes Pronsky, Kubensky, Paletsky, Basmanof, rushed to take revenge. They struck
Vorontsof in the face, they knocked him down and
kicked him about, clamouring abuse. The Grand Duke
Ivan and the Metropolitan both pleaded for his life,

but the boyars were so enraged they even struck the priest and tore his mantle. But there was a dangerous light in the eyes of the young Ivan, a veiled menace. Perhaps the nobles sensed that it was the last time they would over-ride the wishes of their monarch. Fedor Vorontsof was not killed. They spared his life. They bound him and sent him into banishment in distant Kostroma.

Ivan might well have reasoned: they are striking my best friend to-day, to-morrow they will strike me. Scenes of this kind were part of the daily life of Moscow, but they did not so nearly involve the person of the young monarch. The utmost licence prevailed, not only among the elders of the State, but among their children. The hobby of the young princes was banditry and assault. The beating up of peasants and merchants is not recorded because they did not belong to history as it was then understood, but it occurred in plenty. Men were hunted and destroyed as in a wild beast chase and that was common. It was a hard and boisterous age. The almost fantastic piety of the people did not allay their barbarity and the violent satisfaction of their lusts. Sympathy, which was not encouraged, could only have been a characteristic of weaklings. To take satisfaction in cruelty was part of the education of a young prince. As young playful tigers are initiated into the mystery of blood and become fierce, so the children were taken to the torture chambers that their lust of cruelty might be awakened. Beasts captured in the chase were taken to the homes in the Kremlin and tormented to death by the children. That was not frowned upon; it was an aspect of humour. It is said that one of the early diversions of Ivan was dropping dogs from the fortress walls. According to Kurbsky, writing at the time, his teachers not only permitted this but lauded it.

Ivan at thirteen years of age was cold. He had an iciness of temperament which could be mistaken for dullness. The change of treatment which had ensued when his mother died had eaten into his soul. Up to the age of seven he had been treated with an excess of awe and veneration, but after that he was treated with neglect. The child's wrongs went inward. He stored revenge and quiet, implacable hate. Unable to obtain help from men, the child sought help in books and buried himself in Byzantine lore, the history of the Saints and the Church, Holy Writ, the histories of Byzantium and the ancient Principalities of Russia. He became very different from the rough tyrants who lorded it in the Kremlin, becoming versed in law, tradition, state-craft, and history. It is granted that he had a rare capacity for understanding. He had counterbalanced the death of his father and mother and the lack of honour into which he had fallen. He had forged an invisible weapon for the control of the Russia which was his.

While we have said he was cold, it may be urged with truth that he held the memory of his father and mother in great veneration. In his imagination he placed Vasilly III on a throne higher than the good old man actually possessed. The throne was holy, and all that Vasilly and Helena had left behind them when they died was sacred to him. The young man hoarded thoughts and memories of his parents as a miser hoards his gold, going over it secretly every night and counting it to be sure that nothing, *nothing*, has been lost. Had they lived, they would have revenged themselves, yes, they would have revenged themselves for all the insults that had been heaped upon him. This personal feeling grew to be dynastic, grew to an intimacy with God to whom alone the kings of the earth are responsible for their actions.

Puberty had arrived and that does not necessarily mean sex. It means faith. The thought was dawning upon Ivan that he had the power of God behind him, and he had but to lift his right arm to strike Prince Andrew Shuisky dead. Three months after the assault on Fedor Vorontsof he sent a party of the young fellows who tended his hounds to seize the prince. They took the proud Shuisky by surprise and beat him to death or strangled him as they dragged him toward a prison. Ivan said it was well done and no one gainsaid the act. There was a hush in Moscow as if a strange portent had been descried in the skies. Ivan the Terrible had begun to reign.

IV.

PRETENSIONS OF VORONTSOF

IVAN did not thereupon become a very active monarch. He was only fourteen years of age. He had
no cabinet in the modern sense, no council of
weighty men charged with the direction and administration of the country. The peasant tenants raised their
grain and adjusted their dues and differences with their
feudal lords. The trappers and hunters got their rich
furs which the traders bought. The merchants traded in
hides, tallow and wax, trane oil, hemp and flax, caviare, tar and salt, for gold and precious stones and cloth
and weapons. The economic organism of a vast number
of people settled in a rich land was like a tree which
without edicts of any kind brings forth fruit. Free of
the Tartar and not ravaged by any other invader, the
land grew in material wealth. In face of a robber a man
must be prepared to defend himself. There were no po-
lice. When a landowner was called upon to serve in the
army, he must bring his contingent of fellows and
equip them at his own cost and support them and himself. There was no War Office.

Russia was free and wild and lawless, and for the
time being the young Grand Duke did not stir himself
to bring it under a more systematic control. He enjoyed
holiday. He rode forth with his hounds and the gilded
youth of his time to the hunt of the white fox and the
bear; or with ger-falcon on wrist to the destruction of
the wild swan.

Or they went marauding in the villages, beating whom they wished, robbing merchants, carrying off what women they desired, drinking and making carouse. Most historians assume that what his companions did Ivan did also. But that is possibly an error and does not correspond to the psychology of the Grand Duke, nor the dignity of his position of which he was always conscious. It is more probable that he was icy and aloof, however not reproving because he was indifferent to violence.

In the Kremlin Ivan still studied his Byzantine books and was nearer to the Metropolitan than to any other man of substance in his realm. At the same time, as if some democratic strain were showing in his nature, he began to seek the company of educated commoners. He was nearer to a man of education than a man of birth. He engaged the humble clerk, the *dyak*, in converse and exchanged knowledge, or played chess. Such a relationship began to be enjoyed by Alexey Adashef, who was made a gentleman of the bedchamber in 1543. That meant in those days that he did actually superintend the making of the Grand Duke's bed. Possibly upon occasion he was commissioned to bring a lady there. Ivan was restless. Already he began to think of getting married and his envoys abroad had word to leave the rumour in foreign courts that the Grand Duke was marriageable.

Prince Fedor Vorontsof, when he returned from banishment, found Ivan somewhat changed. In the few months which had elapsed the boy had become a man. He had struck down the tyrant Shuisky and had gained self-assurance. He held himself with greater dignity.

He had made a new impression in Moscow and the
nobles treated him with respect. Of course, Vorontsof
was welcomed warmly. There was good cheer in the
palace that night and his merest whim was as law. Not
that he was revengeful. Some of those who had struck
him were there, but he did not demand their heads. He
forgave or forgot his injuries. All the blame was con-
veniently put upon the dead Shuisky and the others
who belonged to the assaulting party were glad to frat-
ernize with the returned exile. Vorontsof was evidently
the sort of man who when he gets drunk becomes in a
state of amity with everyone.

In a maudlin state he told the young Ivan how to
govern his realm and the Grand Duke listened to him
indulgently. But in the sober days which followed his
reception, he saw that Ivan had become a law unto
himself and did not consult him. He received petitions
and made decisions without the slightest regard for
Vorontsof's advice. For a while he was treated as the
most important man in the Kremlin, but it was a show
without substance, and he became deeply mortified because he had fancied that now Prince Andrew Shuisky
was dead he would occupy as powerful a position as the
tyrant had done.

Ivan's kindred, Princes Yury and Michael Glinski,
had more real power in the land. Vorontsof was on
friendly terms with them, but they warned Ivan
against him. He was also friendly with his ex-enemy,
Prince Ivan Kubensky, and it seemed as if he were trying to organize a faction to control Ivan. The Grand
Duke met that by sending Ivan Kubensky to prison for
six months. Evidently it was a light imprisonment, for

Kubensky was none the worse when he returned to court in May, 1545. Ivan, under the charitable influence of the Metropolitan Makary, was more lenient than he showed himself in after years. Still, when one of the boyars, Afanasy Buturlin, permitted himself an impoliteness toward the sovereign, Ivan ordered his tongue to be cut out so that he be relieved from the danger of committing the offence a second time. Vorontsof, learning nothing, made carouse with what was left of the Shuisky faction and fell into disgrace. Ivan was angry and had Vorontsof and all his table companions arrested. They were Prince Peter Shuisky, Prince Ivan Kubensky again, Prince Alexander Gorbaty and Fedor Vorontsof. But they were only in durance for two months. Upon the intercession of the Metropolitan, in December, 1545, they were pardoned and restored to court.

But Ivan's patience was short. Almost every one in the Vorontsof group was executed in the following year. Their fate was a surprise and an accident. In May, 1546, the Grand Duke was reconnoitring with a part of his army at Kolomna and there a misunderstanding took place. A deputation of fifty arquebusiers from Novgorod came unannounced to present some petition. They did not know how to behave in the presence of their sovereign, but threw their hats in the mud and shouted. Ivan ordered his boyars to disperse the band, and they rode their horses over them. The arquebusiers fired their arquebuses and the boyars shot at them with arrows. There was a confused engagement and Ivan became convinced that an attempt upon his person had been organised by someone.

Returning to the Kremlin, Ivan asked one of the clerks whom he trusted to investigate the affair. The *dyak*, Zakharof, perhaps prompted by the Glinski princes, declared that Vorontsof and his brother Michael and Ivan Kubensky had sent the arquebusiers to make an attack upon him. The doings of this group during the past two years being reviewed, Ivan had done with them and ordered them to be beheaded. And most of their adherents were seized and banished. This time the charity of the Metropolitan Makary did not avail.

Now Ivan allowed the greatest influence in Russia to fall to his uncles Yury and Michael Glinski, who misused their powers and continued the corrupt and disorderly government of early years. Freed from the embarrassment of Vorontsof and other intriguers Ivan followed his personal taste for the rest of the year. That was a combination of hunting and praying. He visited the monasteries of Vladimir, Mozhaisk, Tver, Novgorod, Pskof. There was no mistaking the extreme piety of the young Grand Duke. His brow was bruised by prostrations before the ikons. It was no tax on his patience or endurance to stand five hours in a service. The counterpart of this was an exaggerated wild ardour when he went on marauding parties. The adoring St. John in the desert changed at a thought to a Barabbas. At night there were roisterous drinking parties, the entertainment being at the cost of the people they dwelt among. Each community must furnish hospitality for this large pary and must bring costly gifts to give evidence of its loyalty and good will. But Ivan was prevented from receiving petitions from those who had grievances. The affair with the fifty arquebusiers of Novgorod made the courtiers wary to prevent another misunderstanding. But there was discontent. Ivan did not, at this time, seem to be shaping well as *gosudar*.

V.

THE CHOICE OF A BRIDE

IN December of that same year, 1546, Ivan being sixteen years of age, he told the Metropolitan Makary that he had decided to marry and asked his advice. The decade of violence had given Moscow an ill fame in neighbouring lands, and there was no intelligence of foreign princesses willing to enter the hymeneal yoke with Ivan IV. Nor had the eyes of Ivan lighted upon any lady in Russia to awaken in him some feeling of romance. He had decided to marry, but without a bride in view.

The Metropolitan advised that he should choose a wife in the traditional manner by assembling all possible candidates and picking the one he liked best. This pleased the Grand Duke well, and accordingly the Metropolitan called all the nobility in Moscow to Divine service in the Cathedral of the Assumption. This was on the next morning after the conversation with Ivan. The nobles must have known that the question of the Grand Duke's marriage was in the air and they flocked to the cathedral in great numbers. Even those who were in disfavour appeared there. Some announcement was expected.

From the cathedral, after the saying of the Liturgy, the Metropolitan led the way, followed by all the nobles, to the reception hall of the palace, where Ivan upon his throne awaited them. And standing facing the Metropolitan he made the following speech:

"Putting my trust in the grace of God and of His Immaculate Mother, in the grace and intercession of the great miracle-workers, Peter, Alexey, Jonah and Sergey and of all Russian miracle-workers, and with thy blessing, O father, I have thought to marry. I had at first intended to seek marriage in a foreign court in the house of some king or tsar but I have now forgone that intention because I was orphaned and left a small child after the death of my father and mother. And if I take a wife in a foreign country and afterwards we do not get on well together, it will be difficult for us. Therefore I wish to marry within my own country the one whom God will bless to be my wife, and with thy blessing, O father."

Having made this recital, the Grand Duke sat down and entered into private converse with the Metropolitan. That the boyars applauded Ivan is most probable. The chronicler states that they were moved to tears, which is a figure of speech. The men of that time did not sob so easily. But they were pleased. There was a murmur which grew to an excited clamour. The Grand Duke had made a very popular and national declaration. Moreover, he had not taken some exalted family into his confidence. For the nonce almost every boyar in the palace, even the most humble, was the potential father-in-law of the monarch. No choice had been announced by Ivan, and it was quickly noised about the assembly that no actual choice had been made, but that the young Grand Duke had decided to follow the old traditional usage and have all the virgins of rank brought to the Kremlin that he might look them over and select one. Here was a great national excitement.

Even those who were not fathers or who possessed no daughters were excited because they might at least prove to be uncles or cousins of the fortunate bride.

At various periods of his reign Ivan the Terrible was far from being unpopular, but this was his first popular decision. The foreign consorts of previous Grand Dukes, such as Sophia, the wife of Ivan III and Helena, the wife of Vasilly III, had been distasteful to the boyars. Why should our Grand Dukes search abroad for their wives? Are not our own Russian girls the most beautiful in the world? The boyars in the palace all began comparing the rival merits of their daughters, but each must have been anxious to rush home to break the great news to the women folk.

But Ivan had still another announcement to make and that was that he intended to be married not as Grand Duke but as Tsar. Here we see the first fruit of Ivan's secret studies. He would elevate the rank of the Russian throne to that of the Cæsars. The boyars were in the mood to applaud anything, and they applauded that too, though it was a step which demanded some reflection. The change of style could not prove to be a mere empty form, an embellishment of the already elaborate title of the Grand Duke.

"Before my marriage, I wish, with thy blessing, O father Metropolitan, to seek the ancestral rank, such as that of our ancestors the Tsars and Grand Dukes, and our kinsman Vladimir Vsevolodovitch Monomakh. I wish also to be invested with that rank."

But the immediate interest of the country was concentrated upon an edict which was sent far and near, to

every noble house, commanding that all eligible girls be
sent to court forthwith for the selection. Fathers were
charged upon severe penalty not to hide their daughters
for any reason whatsoever.

Such a sorting out of lace and head-dress, such a
bathing and painting and braiding then took place in
Muscovy! A universal chatter and badinage, not un-
mingled with prayer—but it has died away to silence
in the history books. A fairy tale situation, but no
wood-chopper's daughter, no Cinderella was to win the
prince. The beauty prize went to the child of quite a
well-established family, the daughter of a widow
Zakharina-Koshkina. Her name was Anastasia, she was
brought to the Kremlin by her uncle Gregory Zakharin.
There were many daughters of nobler houses, but the
press of maids and their guardians was very great. Ivan
had two thousand to choose from, and it is said that he
made no mere formality of looking them over. All his
life he had "an eye for a woman," but at this early age
he may be assumed to be looking as much for virtue and
religion as for beauty and sex. In any case Anastasia
had the advantage of being tall and striking, the sort of
girl that one sees directly one comes into a room, no
matter how many others happen to be present. She had
also a political advantage; her family had in no way
got itself compromised by the factionalism of Ivan's
majority. It had not been involved either with the
Shuiskies or the Bielskies. They were betrothed in the
presence of a large company and with the blessing of
the Church.

February third, 1547, was set as the date of the wedding, but first Ivan would be crowned as Tsar of all the

Russias. The 16th of January was the day set for the coronation. On the morning of the sixteenth all the princes, voivodes, and boyars were clad in cloth of gold and they gathered on the threshold and about the outer doors of the palace. Ivan's confessor, the Archpriest of the Cathedral of the Assumption, took from the monarch's hands a golden tray on which were placed a large wonder-working cross, the crown, and the coronation mantle. These he carried high in air, followed immediately by the Grand Duke, and escorted by the other nobility and the *dyaks*. In the cathedral there was a double throne, one seat for Ivan and the other for the Metropolitan. These two seats were at an eminence at the head of twelve steps. But before stepping upward Ivan prostrated himself before every ikon in the temple. The choir burst into the anthem of greeting for sovereigns, and the Metropolitan blessed him.

Ivan stood with Makary at the head of the steps, and then the Archimandrites brought the mantle and the crown up the steps and gave them to Makary who, with much signing of the cross, put them upon Ivan, praying in a loud voice that God would protect this Christian David with the power of the Holy Ghost. Then again when the Tsar was crowned, the choir and all the clergy and the nobles too sang their anthem wishing health and many years of grace. The Tsar Ivan then proceeded slowly out of the cathedral, treading on velvet and damask, and the nobles threw showers of gold coins over him as he walked. Still wearing his crown and accompanied by his whole court he made his way back to the palace. The common people of Moscow then crowded into the cathedral to tear strips of silk from the throne in memory of the day, and no one said them nay.

There are various legends and suppositions affording a doubtful justification for the Russian title of Tsar. One of them is that Rurik was descended from Augustus Cæsar and Ivan was descended from Rurik. Augustus gave the northern part of the world to his nephew Prus, from which, according to some, the name Prussia is derived. Others derive Prussia as meaning "bordering on Russia," vide Carlyle. But be that as it may, Rurik was supposed to be descended from Prus and thus from Augustus and God. For Augustus became divine. Ivan IV raised the eagle of the third Rome.

When Ivan III was offered the title of King he rejected it with scorn, holding that his original title of Grand Duke was immeasurably higher than that of king.

The legend of Vladimir cited by Ivan IV in making his pretension to the title is that he was the son of a daughter of the Byzantine Emperor Constantine Monomakh, who had been dead some fifty years when his nephew took the throne of Kief. Vladimir made war on Constantinople, and the Emperor in order to obtain peace sent a high priest bearing part of the wood of the actual cross of Christ and the imperial crown from his own head. The Metropolitan from Constantinople brought the crown and expressed the wish that all Orthodox peoples might be at rest under the common sway of "our Empire and of the great autocracy of great Russia." With this crown, as sent from God, Vladimir was crowned in Kief and took to himself the surname Monomakh.

It will be realised that, whether Ivan the Terrible had historical justification for his pretension or not, he was arrogating to himself a title which had not only a temporal, but a divine, character. In finding his constellation in the night of History one must pick out the pale distant star of David and then the more yellow and lustrous star of Augustus.

VI.

THE GREAT FIRE

A HOLY man, Gennady of Kostroma, hospitably entertained by Anastasia's parents, had, it is said, predicted that the girl would become the consort of the Tsar. That was perhaps because she combined unusual beauty with something of a royal mien. Perhaps pilgrims in princely houses paid that sort of innocent compliment, much as a visitor in a modern English home might say "You'll see that son of yours will be Prime Minister one of these days." The auguries for Anastasia were good and it was a happy marriage.

The wedding took place on the 3rd of February, 1547. It is not recorded that hops were sprinkled on the couple as they had been upon Vasilly III and Helena. Women had been delegated to look over the body of the bride and she was found perfect. Everything good was said of her that could be said in the Russian language, says Karamzin. The elaborate ritual of solemnization of marriage was performed in the Cathedral of the Saviour. After the ceremony the Metropolitan thus addressed the wedded pair:

"This day, in the mystery of the Church you have been united for ever, that together you might submit to the Almighty and live in virtue, virtue for you being righteousness and grace. My lord! Love and honour thy wife, and thou, Christ-loving Tsaritsa, obey him. As the Holy Cross is the head of the Church, so is the hus-

band the head of his wife. Fulfilling God's commandments, you will have vision of the blessed Jerusalem
and peace in Israel."

The Tsar and Tsaritsa then came out of the cathedral and showed themselves to their subjects gathered
in great crowds from all parts of the country. The Tsar
gave honours to his boyars present and the Tsaritsa
with her own hands gave alms to the many beggars.
The going to bed of the royal pair was accomplished
publicly, almost everyone at court having a function of
some kind. The Glinski uncles stood at the head of the
bed. Prince Shemiakin held the Tsar's nightcap. Another boyar placed a blanket under their legs.

Within the palace and without there was great festivity. While Ivan and Anastasia picnicked in bed their
health was drunk with acclamation by the princes and
boyars and all their people. The merriment lasted till
the first day of Lent, when all roistering ceased at the
tolling of a thousand bells for prayers. The Tsar Ivan
and his consort then left the feast of Hymen, and simply clad, set out on foot through the snow for the
monastery of Sergey-Troitsky. Now they were as pilgrims, not lovers, and with rigorous asceticism they remained a whole week in prayer and communion at the
grave of St. Sergey the Wonder-Worker.

Anastasia was as pious as her husband, but, if the
chroniclers are to be believed, with more humanity. She
was a simple child from a quiet widow's home. There
was not in her veins the fiery conflict which was beginning to rage in those of Ivan. Ivan, having assumed
Tsardom, saw his subjects from a higher pedestal. They

seemed smaller and less significant. In a mistaken way he felt himself nearer to God. He was God's chosen vessel. He let the Glinski do the dirty work of governing his people. They did it dirtily, but that was nothing to Ivan. The Glinski grew in unpopularity because of their oppression, but Ivan did not intervene. Many had thought that after Ivan was crowned Tsar and after he had married he would do much to better the lot of his subjects. But they were disillusioned. The Tsar was at prayer, or he was wrapped up in the delights of his consort, or he was hunting or pilgrimaging. It was known that he had a terrible temper and brooked no reminder of his duties from anyone. He was capable of falling upon a messenger or a servant and beating him to death. Pity the unfortunate peasant or merchant who got in his way!

An answer came from the common people of Moscow, who expressed the increasing odium for the Glinski by incendiarism. On the 12th of April, 1547, there was a serious fire in Moscow; it was put out, but it broke out again on the 20th. That was extinguished, but another fire started at the beginning of June, driven by a strong wind, and that one was not stopped so easily. Certain persons unknown were repeatedly firing the city.

Ivan had paid little attention to this phenomenon. Late in May a deputation of burghers from the city of Pskof sought the Tsar in a country house at Ostrovka. It is explained that the Pskovians had more hardihood than any other people because Pskof was the last of the great seats to be annexed by Muscovy. Otherwise they would not have risked the Tsar's wrath by any such complaint as that they came to make. The Glinski had put their venal nominee in control of Pskof, a certain Prince Pronsky. The delegation, supported by witnesses, had brought a table of grievances to present, seventy petitioners who prostrated themselves before Ivan. Instead of listening to them the Tsar had them bound. That he made mock of them is too light a phrase. He poured hot spirits on their heads and went about with a taper, setting fire to their beards and their hair. He ordered them to be stripped and made naked and laid in rows on the ground and was evidently thinking out some frightful doom for them when messengers rushed in from Moscow with the news that the fire had swept across the Kremlin and that the great bell of blessing had fallen with a crash to the ground. The Tsar forgot his victims, turned his horse's head around and galloped at once to Moscow.

Moscow, which grew in extent every year, was a vast area of pine cabins, wooden palings, wooden footways, wooden stalls and many wooden churches besides those of stone. It blazed with the fury of a forest on fire in a dry summer. The reason the city had not been destroyed by the earlier April fires was that the snow was not gone from the roofs. One of these was a bad fire, gutting the shops of the Kitai Gorod beside the Kremlin and blackening out a great drive from the Ilinka Gate to the walled banks of the Moskva river. But the June fire starting from the Arbat and enveloping the Kremlin was much more serious.

The fire was whipped up by a gale which sent it crackling and roaring forward. It crossed the little Moskva river as if the fosse were a mere ditch, and

blazed in a racing tempest of flame and flying ember
across the pink toothed walls of the Kremlin to the
roofs of palaces and cathedrals. The upper part of the
Cathedral of the Assumption burst into flame, likewise
the roof of the Tsar's palace and the Cathedral of the
Annunciation. In the stone churches the flames lapped
the frescoes and the ikons and burned the holy screens
and gates. The armoury was burned out and so was the
hostelry of the Metropolitan and the houses of the
boyars. The aged Makary with singed beard struggled
amid fire and smoke in the interior of the Cathedral of
the Assumption and aided by his clergy carried out a
thrice precious ikon of Our Lady. He then went along
the city wall adjacent to the Kremlin toward a secret
passage leading down to the river. There were no steps
to this passage and one had to be lowered by a rope. On
this occasion the rope broke and the unfortunate Metropolitan fell a long distance with such concussion that
it was long before he regained consciousness.

In the city below the Kremlin the oncoming fire
surged along the streets as if the God of Hosts had
come in his wrath. It was not difficult to save oneself
from a one-storeyed house, but the danger was in the
streets. There was no refuge from the widespread consuming element which was one in volume with the air
itself. The inhabitants in mobs fled toward the river
which was crowded with people standing in the water.
But their clothes burned off them as they ran. Fire like
a sword struck them. They shrivelled to death and
fell in the roadway like moths. Seventeen thousand
grown-up persons were burned to death: they did not
count the children who died.

Every tree and living shrub perished. The large vegetable gardens were scorched to dust. All provisions and goods were destroyed. Brass melted and poured on to the stone floors of the churches. The cows perished in the barns and the horses in the stables. The yard dogs and the hounds for the chase and the domestic cats were suffocated or burned to death.

The Tsar did not stay long in the zone of danger gazing at the desolation, but rode to his palace on the Sparrow Hills, where he was joined by Anastasia and many of the nobility and their families. He gave orders, however, that as soon as the fire had died down the work of repairing the buildings within the Kremlin should be commenced.

The fire burned itself out, but the embers did not get cool for some days. The fugitives returned to the ruins, and Moscow was like a vast cinder dump in which strange bent rag-pickers with black faces and hands sought their dead and their treasures in the ash. They could not stay long because there was nothing to eat, but they searched and then went out of the ruins to the villages and monasteries round about Moscow for succour. How they complained and what they said we do not know. All that has come down is the rumour that the fire was achieved by sorcery. A body-snatcher had unearthed dead men from their graves, cut out their hearts and brewed an unholy water which had been sprinkled on the streets of Moscow.

This rigmarole was taken up by the Tsar's confessor and the enemies of the Glinski princes. Someone gave the rumour a sinister complexion. It was said that Anna, the mother of the Glinski, had performed this dire act with men's hearts. The Tsar ordered an investigation, and on Sunday the 26th June, five days after the fire had died down, a mass of homeless, common people was interrogated on the Kremlin Square. The story about the Glinski had caught on and the mob repeated it. Prince Yury Glinski was present. The other, Prince Michael Glinski, was staying with his mother Anna, at Rzhev. Prince Yury Glinski listened nonchalantly if with displeasure to the absurd story of his mother's sorcery. He did not realize the extreme danger of his position. He had enemies among his fellow nobles holding the inquiry. At the same time he thought it better to slip off quietly into the Cathedral of the Assumption. A wiser, braver man would have stood with the boyars and awaited the outcome in the open. What happened was that after a parley with the mob the boyars said: "You find that this calamity was contrived by the Glinski. We hand them over to you. You can work your will with them." Then, as if led by conspirators, the crowd surged forward. The nobles stood to one side and let them go on. Then they rushed into the cathedral and strangled Prince Yury. That done, they set upon his adherents of whom there were a fair number and killed most of them. And they killed any Glinski bastards they could find and a number of other unfortunate children supposed to be connected with the family.

The blood lust of the crowd was up. It sought in blood some indemnity for its ruin. Something like a revolutionary movement was started by this lynching. The boyars did nothing to restrain it. The revenge movement gathered impetus like the fire itself. All the diggers among the ruins joined together in a howling mob and set off for the palace on the Sparrow Hills, there to demand from the Tsar the persons of Prince Michael Glinski and his mother Anna. There was a tremendous uproar. The Tsar was besieged in his own palace. The guards were ordered out. Anastasia and the Tsar retired to the innermost rooms. But the rabble, though they had the power had they known how to use it, were bolder in word than in action. The Tsar sent out and had all the noisier spirits seized and they were executed there and then in full view of the rest of the mob. This cowed them. They ceased vociferating. They slunk back to the black wilderness that had been their home.

Prince Michael Glinski fled toward Lithuania, but was arrested on the way. He was pardoned for his flight, but the great fire which had destroyed Moscow had destroyed the power of the Glinski family also. It did not raise its head again.

VII.

THE WRATH OF GOD

IT is not probable that Ivan and Anastasia believed the story of sorcery. They knew Anna Glinski well enough. She did not dabble in black arts. This brew from dead men's hearts, absurd as it sounds, had some sensible meaning behind it. The dead men in question were those whom the Glinski princes had done to death. Though dead they were still capable of revenge. The Tsar had ignored the misrule of the Glinski, but the uproar against them was now so great that it was impossible not to be impressed. The Tsar must have felt that he was to blame. The Glinski had acted in his name, and he was responsible for their misdeeds. That they were his kinsmen brought the odium nearer. When the crowd was at the gates of the palace clamouring for more victims, they might well have clamoured for the life of the Tsar himself. It was more probable that the burning of Moscow was a sign of wrath, a warning, rather than an act of witchcraft or sorcery.

Or the Tsar was scared by the demonstration outside the palace. That mob had the power to have torn him limb from limb. There is a yellow streak in most cruel people. They are generally cowards who would tremble like an aspen at receiving one hundredth part of the pain they would lightly inflict on another. There is a certain ingredient of good character which in English is called "pluck." There is no Russian equivalent for it, and Ivan did not have it. He was only seventeen years of age, but if you are going to have pluck at any time in your life, seventeen is the time when you will show it. In strict fairness, the fracas at Kolomna when the arquebusiers of Novgorod merely wanted to approach their sovereign and present a humble petition was due to lack of pluck on Ivan's part. A young Henri Quatre or Henry the Eighth would have boldly asked the petitioners what they wanted. A sovereign of merely indifferent temper like Richard II was capable under more menacing circumstances of saying to the mob: "I will be your leader." In dealing with the petitioners of Pskof who came unarmed the young Ivan showed himself as both cruel and craven. We shall see that fear was an important element in the character of Ivan the Terrible.

But Ivan feared God more than man. How, then, if the fear of the Lord is the beginning of wisdom, was he so strikingly unwise? The answer is that he had a superstitious, but not an enlightened, fear of God. He was no cynic. His faith was blind. As if somehow bewitched before birth, he was the born slave of the supernatural. The contemporary of Henry the Eighth, he had nothing in common with him on the religious side. Henry, when the Church stood in the way of his physical desires, was capable of making a complete mockery of the Popery. But for Ivan at this early period of his reign the Church was sacrosanct. Its priests, monks, and holy men were privileged. They did not stand in the same danger of torture and death as did the rest of the Tsar's subjects.

The Metropolitan Makary, who it will be realised was a good old man, wise, courageous, and dignified, a

man of God, whatever his superstitions, exercised a
beneficial influence upon Ivan. He was Ivan's father in
God and had more control over the young sovereign's
life than anyone else in the realm. But his influence was
more devotional than ethical. Makary was a peace-
maker who hated violence and cruelty but he could not
eradicate these from the character of the Tsar. Ivan
made more prostrations and grew more cruel in pro-
portion.

But the great fire was the opportunity of the Church.
The Tsar's confessor was identified with the witchcraft
story, but the Church as a whole was not. The Church
believed positively in black magic, the power of the
devil through human agents called witches, sorcerers,
and magicians, but in this case it believed plainly that
the fire was a visitation from the Almighty who had
destroyed Moscow as in time past He had destroyed
Sodom and Gomorrah, and for a like reason.

As the angry crowd melted away from before the
palace on the Sparrow Hills a humble priest from the
Cathedral of the Annunciation broke in upon the Tsar
and Tsaritsa, with a denunciatory finger upraised, calling upon them to repent. This was the Presbyter
Sylvester of Novgorod, a man, it is said, of apostolic
bearing. People sent from God always arrive at a psychological moment, so one need not be surprised that
Ivan did not have him thrown into a dungeon.

"The thunder of God has come upon thee, O Tsar,
for thy idleness and evil passions. Fire from Heaven
has consumed Moscow and the cup of God's wrath has
been poured into the hearts of the people."

Sylvester told of portents and signs he had observed and of visions which he had had of God's judgment upon the Tsar, and turning to Holy Writ, he expounded God's commandments to the Kings of the Earth, and, showing Ivan his shortcomings, bade him repent lest a worse fate should overtake him and his country.

It is probable that the Metropolitan Makary was privy to this bold speech. It seemed to succeed. The mind of the Tsar was swept by the terror of the Unknown. He made his repentance upon his knees and asked strength and wisdom of God and His saints that he might be enabled to govern his country in more righteousness and piety. With one accord, chroniclers and historians seem to regard this moment as one in the nature of conversion. At once the rule of Ivan, guided by the Church, improved. Sylvester was rewarded for his spiritual courage and his advice was asked and taken on many matters. Sylvester happened to be a friend of the *dyak* Alexey Adashef, who had been made gentleman of the bedchamber. Adashef was a religious character with the face of a young saint. These two came to have a privileged position at court.

There seems to be something holy in itself in building—not of course in building Babel, but in building homes and churches for a people. With God's blessing the rebuilding of Moscow commenced. Ivan's birthday in August passed in a clatter of axes and timbers. In a mood of contrition he addressed the architects and artisans who were taking in hand the restoration of the burned churches.

"It is impossible to describe and the tongue of man cannot exaggerate the sinful folly of my youthful days. When God took away my father, then the boyars and fine people, in the position of guardians and pastors, pretending good will toward me, in actual truth sought power for themselves and in darkness of counsel seized and killed my father's brothers. Upon the death of my mother the boyars usurped the Tsardom. Through my sin, orphandom, and youth many people were destroyed in civil strife. I grew up in neglect, without instruction, hardened to the insidious ways of the boyars, and from that time until now, how much I have sinned before God, and what chastisements He has sent upon us! Not once or twice did we endeavour to be revenged on our enemies, but always without success. I did not understand that God was sending great punishments upon me, and I did not repent, but continued to visit Christian people with all manner of violence. God punished me for my sins by flood and famine but still I did not repent. At last God sent the great fires, and fear entered my soul and trembling into my bones, I was moved and repented of my wrong-doing and asked forgiveness of the clergy, and in turn granted forgiveness to the boyars and princes."

This was certainly a new note in the life of Ivan. One sees his long association with the Metropolitan Makary bearing fruit; one sees the spiritual influence of the Presbyter Sylvester, and the sweetening influence of Anastasia. One must not leave Anastasia out of account. He was still in the first year of union with a virtuous lady who by all that has been handed down about her, added tenderness and humanity to piety and

beauty. Of course, the influence of Anastasia is surmised rather than deduced. The Tsaritsa within her
terem did not receive men of state for converse or to
give advice. She did not often dine with the Tsar in the
midst of his court. Her life was private. Apart from
Ivan and upon occasion Ivan's brother Yury, or the
aged Metropolitan, or her confessor, she had no contact
with men. In those days women at marriage entered
into what may be called a state of sacred bondage.

The time had come when another marriage should
take place. Ivan thought that his younger brother Yury
should be blessed with a happiness similar to his, and
he took him to the Metropolitan for advice and blessing. Once more the girls of Russia were bidden to court
for a marriage choice. Prince Yury could have which-
ever maid he wished whether she desired him or not.
Then when the candidates were brought Prince Yury's
eyes fell upon Princess Ulyana and he loved her at
sight. Ivan was well pleased and was very active making all the arrangements and appointments for the
wedding. Then when all was ready, on an appointed
day a dual throne was made in the reception hall of the
palace. Now was one of the rare occasions when the
Tsaritsa Anastasia made a public appearance. In a
splendour of jewels bedizening cloth of silver and gold
the young Tsar and Tsaritsa, in the presence of a full
court, entered the hall and mounted to the throne. The
Tsar wore his crown and carried his sceptre. The Tsaritsa wore a headdress studded with diamonds and
rubies. Ivan then ordered his brother to approach for
blessing. And Yury came and the Tsar and Tsaritsa
blessed him. And then the Metropolitan blessed him.

Yury then sat at the feet of the Tsaritsa and she combed his hair with wine. She sprinkled wine on his head while a servant stood holding a golden comb for her to use. Then the Princess Ulyana was blessed and sat beside Prince Yury and her hair was combed in like manner. The Tsaritsa then fanned them with sable. Breadths of embroidered linen were presented to everyone at court. Then the Tsar permitted the pair to be married. After the service there was a State banquet presided over by the Tsar and Tsaritsa, and the young wedded pair received wine from their Majesties and there was great festivity. This happened on the 3rd November, 1547.

The years which followed, 1548–1549, were the most uneventful in the domestic history of Moscow. The city was being rebuilt with rapidity. But a metropolis as large or larger than the London of those times is not rebuilt in a day. By the coming on of the winter of 1547–48 there was a city of shacks and shelters with many families under one roof. In the spring of 1548 new homes and shops began to rise from the black foundations. In 1549 the city began to look more as it was and the buildings of the Kremlin certainly were restored to pristine splendour and comfort. Trade was slow to recuperate, but the gold of the capital had not been lost and there was a great market for building materials, rugs, furs, clothing. The sister cities of Moscow brought much to its aid and, not least in importance at that time, relics and ikons to replace those which had been lost in the conflagration. Much was irreplaceable—the first family ikons handed down from generation to generation, the traditional wedding garments handed down from mother to daughter through the ages. But the shadow of tradition came to replace tradition itself.

The Tsar and his princes and boyars did not give a hand to the rebuilding. It was enough for them to give orders. As they rode in and out of the great working camp they could see Moscow rising slowly from its ashes. But there was another scene of desolation which attracted the attention of the Tsar. The Tartars had descended upon Russia again. To the south of Moscow, beginning at a point about 150 miles distant, and also to the north-east, the territory of Russia was strewn with the bones of Christians, and the villages had been destroyed. Ivan in his splendid mood of repentance and righteousness burned to go forth against the heathen, leading his army in person. So in December, 1547, he set out with his army, in deep snow. The weather soon changed; frost and snow unseasonably gave way to ceaseless rain. When the Tsar reached the Volga about the beginning of February he stayed on an island near Nizhny. The Volga was frozen and the ice presumably yards thick, but on the first morning, from his island Ivan witnessed a catastrophe on the river. It was natural to use a frozen river as a highway, but as the army and cannon came along on parade that morning Ivan saw the water burst up from the banks and great cracks appear in the surface of the ice. Part of the army was thereupon incontinently engulfed. Thus it did not seem as if Ivan had God's blessing. He saw in this happening an evil portent. He was not yet entirely forgiven for his sins and he refused to go on. Instead he returned to a life of prayer and fasting in Moscow and entrusted further military operations to Prince Dimitry Bielsky. Bielsky was sent against Kazan, not indeed, to take it, which would have been impossible for his small force, but to make such demonstration as should cause the Tartars to pause in their depredations (February–March, 1548).

A year later the ruling prince of Kazan, Sapha Hirei, being drunk, committed suicide in his palace. The throne was left to his infant son Utemish, but the inhabitants asked the Khan of the Crimean Tartars whether he would send his son to rule over them instead. At the same time they sent messengers to Ivan seeking peace with the Russians. Ivan replied that he would treat with properly appointed ambassadors if they were sent. But no such ambassadors ever came and preparations for a second campaign against Kazan went forward. On the 24th November, 1549, the Tsar set off, accompanied by his brother Yury, and his boyars and their adherents in arms. This time the Metropolitan Makary accompanied them as far as Vladimir where he blessed the Tsar and his army in the godly work they were undertaking. They set off and on the 14th February, 1550, were under the walls of Kazan. Kazan was invested and the towers of the besiegers grew up facing the walls and earth ramparts of the Tartar city. The noise of battering rams and catapults was greater than that of the artillery. Ivan, sword in hand, led his men into the city and they did great slaughter, but they could not take the actual fortress. There were sixty thousand Russians in the attack and they must have triumphed over the Kazantsi had it not been that the second day of the storming of the city there was a rapid thaw and heavy rain. The cannons would not fire, the ice on the Volga gave way again, there was fear of being cut off by flood. The Russians were in great confusion, not to say panic. The Tsar at once decided upon retreat. It was not, however, a rear-guard action. The Kazantsi waited till the enemy was well out of sight before they set out to pick up anything the retreating Russians might leave behind. Ivan, seeing he was not harassed, decided to commemorate his raid by building a town on the Volga, not far from Kazan, at the estuary of the Svyaga. This was in enemy territory and it was consecrated as a Christian fortress, a base for the next campaign against Kazan. By this positive bit of work Ivan strove to cover up his actual failure at Kazan. But there were some murmurings against him and more against Dimitry Bielsky, who was reputed to be a traitor. This prince, brother of the ill-fated Ivan Bielsky, died shortly after the return of the army to Moscow. But he had not been treacherous, only incompetent.

VIII.

IVAN AT TWENTY

IVAN at twenty had come to his full stature. He was tall, just about six foot, well formed, without physical defect. His timidity and furtiveness seemed out of keeping with his athletic frame, his good horsemanship, his fine carriage. His blood was stilled by his mind; he was always watching and listening. Suspicion had informed his mouth and the lines on his fine brow. He is usually depicted with large staring eyes, eyes that are too large, as of a startled animal. His nose was aquiline and subtle, aristocratic, sensitive. His mouth was craven, distrustful. He had long dark side hair, but the hair at the back of his head was cropped. We have a face of a Byzantine cast, marked already by mental suffering and nervousness, but awe inspiring, dangerous.

Among several paradoxical characteristics we note his growing self-pity. He had a stronger sense of his titular greatness than had any of his ancestors. He was God's anointed, the mysterious Tsar of all Russia whose word was law, but he was oppressed with melancholy by his situation. He had a growing sense that he was all-powerful and a growing self-pity side by side in his nature. Thus he will whine for a long time that he was left an unhappy orphan at the age of three and that the boyars neglected his upbringing and usurped his power. He was happiest when in converse with priests or monks on some religious or ecclesiastical theme and was capable of witticism and raillery, but when left to himself he invariably relapsed into melancholy and was for ever brooding on the wrongs of his unhappy childhood. Even at an early age his character was marked by an uncommon impulsiveness of anger and unexpected violence, as if some mad alter-ego lurked behind the religious canopy of his Byzantine face. His probable behaviour, even at the best of times, was incalculable.

But the fairest time in his life was when he was twenty years old and still under the shadow of the wrath of God, still repentant, under the influence of the old Makary and the good Anastasia. The new Moscow had grown under his eyes and the crosses had been taken down from the framework of the rebuilt houses and the priests had sprinkled Holy Water and blessed the new homes. Earth had been placed on the roofs of the houses so that sparks from the chimneys should not ignite them and start a new conflagration. But the new Moscow was not less a wooden city than the one which had preceded it. There were iron frames to some of the windows and stone foundations to a very few houses. The outsides were made draughtless with moss and often covered with birch bark, which is to some extent more dangerous than timber because it can smoulder in secret for some time and then, fanned by a breeze, break into a great flame. Moscow did not possess a fire brigade. Its water was the river. Its chief protection against fire was prayer.

The people were, however, restored to equanimity after the scourge of God. A new era had been inaugurated, and the Tsar, to better the occasion, on the ad-

vice of Adashef and Sylvester, decided upon a gesture
which would seem to make him the father of his people.
Shortly after his birthday, 1550, he called together
a representative assembly both of the gentry and the
common people to meet in the open air in the great
square of the Kremlin. For this occasion he prepared
himself with fasting and prayer and received the Holy
Sacrament, that with only the sustenance of Christ's
Body and Blood he might declare to his subjects a new
policy for Russia.

"Holy father," said he addressing the Metropolitan
after a service conducted in the open, "I know thy loving zeal for the welfare of the fatherland. Be thou my
champion in the blessed work whereunto we are resolved! Early in life God deprived me of father and
mother, and the gentry without care for me wished to
rule the land themselves. In my name they stole power
and honour and grew rich by misrule, oppressed the
people and no one said them nay. In my pitiful childhood I seemed both deaf and dumb. I did not hearken
to the wailing of the poor nor did my lips utter anything."

He then turned sharply to the assembled boyars and
addressed them. "You, you evil rebels, unjust stewards, did what you liked in Russia. What answer will
you give us now to our charge? How many tears, how
much bloodshed you have caused! I am innocent of
that blood, but you will receive judgment at the bar of
Heaven for your misdeeds."

Ivan then turned to the populace. "And you, O
people, given to me by God, I pray you to have faith in
Him and love toward me. Be magnanimous! It is im-

possible to redress the wrong which is past. Only in the future can I save you from oppression and robbery. Forget what will not be repeated! Let us put away hate and enmity and live together in Christian love. Henceforward I will be your judge and your defender."

Then to Alexey Adashef he said: "Alexey, I took you from the poor, one of the common people, having heard of your good deeds, and now am seeking of thee something more for the good of my soul, that thou wilt assuage my sorrow and protect the people whom God has given into my keeping. I appoint you to gather the petitions from the poor and the afflicted. . . ."

Adashef was charged to look over the petitions of all who felt they had received injury during the misrule of the boyars and bring to Ivan's attention such grievances as could be remedied. He was to act fearlessly. No one in the great families of Russia should have power to touch him. It is not recorded how many people were courageous enough to present petitions at the Tsar's invitation. Probably few at first. The gesture was fine. "The Tsar, God bless him, will receive our petitions!" But a man would be a fool who pushed himself forward into having an account to clear with the noble families and the Tsar. Nevertheless the industrious Adashef and Sylvester were links with the people at large. It was possible for them with the privilege extended to them to bring before Ivan a considerable number of legal anomalies and distresses. The first fruit of this invitation to general petition was the making of a new book of laws which was set in hand in this same year 1550.

Russia was a state in which titular princes and territorial lords had surrendered their independence without assimilating laws. The legal code was not well established. A law in force in Moscow might not be considered binding in Novgorod or Pskof and *vice versa*. Ivan had raised himself on to the pedestal of Tsardom high above all princes in the land. It is not altogether surprising that it fell to the lot of the first Tsar to make a new legal code for Russia. A correlation of all local laws was required and withal some cancelling out of laws that contradicted other laws.

The problem of the revision of the code was entered into by the young Tsar himself, who, albeit no lawyer, had certain definite views as to what new statutes he wished incorporated. Once more he would show that his becoming Tsar was not an empty gesture. The change of title must have its counterpart in a modification of law. Ivan wished to gather together into his own hands much of the distributed authority of the princes. Tsardom meant centralisation, and it portended a greater absolutism. Ivan, who was already making commoners his counsellors, sought to find support for the throne in some element less turbulent and powerful than the nobles.

The Russian people, it must be supposed, were pleased by the prospect of being governed by the Tsar himself rather than by factions of the nobility and having the laws of the land restated and made clear. The boyars and the court were spectacular enough, but they were not all of Russia and, despite their large estates and many serfs, they would soon have begun to look rather shabby but for the prosperity of the great trading community on which they battened.

As a preliminary to the inauguration of the better era, the worst of the boyars were banished from Moscow. Prince Michael Glinski's court titles were shorn away, but he was allowed to retire quietly to his estates. The Tsaritsa's uncle Zakharin became a member of the Council of State. Ivan's brother Yury, now married, lived in state in the Kremlin and had almost as much honour as the Tsar himself. The two brothers lived in amity and Ivan frequently headed declarations with the words "My brother and I."

Having approved the new book of civil law which had been drawn up, the Tsar turned his attention to ecclesiastical abuses, and he gave orders for a Convocation of the Church to be held on the 23rd February, 1551.

IX.

THE CHURCH

THE Metropolitans of Moscow were not raised
to the rank of Patriarch until 1589, five years
after Ivan's death. But in 1453 the Turks had
taken Constantinople and placed the whole Orthodox
East in duress, beggaring the Patriarchs and the monasteries. Incomparably the richest and most powerful nation within the fold of the Orthodox Church was that
of Russia, untouched by the depredations of the Moslem. It was inevitable that in course of time the Russian Orthodox Church should have its local Patriarch,
inevitable also that it should rise steadily in power and
grandeur.

But as a Church becomes richer its spirituality
wanes. The craven bequests of the wicked before death,
endeavouring to indemnify God for a life of sin, have
proved a dire embarrassment of Churches. In the time
of Ivan IV the Church in Russia was already too rich.
It invited spoliation by the secular arm. It is curious
that in this ultra-pious Russia of Ivan's time the ac-
cumulated wealth of the monasteries was not simply
regarded as "God's property." And it is also surprising
that the life and behaviour of those who had forsaken
the world, the "dead but not yet buried," should have
come into question.

The wind bloweth where it listeth, and it would
almost seem as if a breeze from the England of Henry
VIII had reached Russia. At the Convocation of the

Church in 1551 Ivan attacked both the morals of the
Church and the validity of its ownership of its vast estates. The storm of the Reformation had broken over
Western Europe, and the vague thunder of a spent dis-
turbance was audible over Moscow.

There was within the Church itself some demand for
reform, and it must have been at the suggestion of
Sylvester or the new Archimandrite of Sergey-Troitsky
Monastery that the Convocation was made. The Metropolitan Makary as a humble man of God was willing
to submit the Church to criticism if not to chastisement, but the inspiration was not from him. He would
much rather pray than argue, and prolonged prayer
may sometimes amount to passive obstruction. The old
man, gracious and wise as he undoubtedly was, had
nevertheless some streak of godly avarice, as if the ad-
monition "I, thy God, am a jealous God" implied a
jealousy lest anything given to God should be alienated
to man. And as regards inquiries into morals, the suggestion that the Bride of Christ could be other than
pure was hotly repelled.

There was not actually a great number of people at
the Congress of 1551. There was not in any case ac-
commodation in the Tsar's palace for a representative
all-Russian assembly of clergy. But there were nine
bishops and all the archimandrites and abbots and the
Metropolitan himself. The Tsar and his court, the
Council of Boyars, received them and it was almost as
if they had been bidden to appear before a tribunal of
the laity.

Most of the clergy must have believed that they had

been called to approve and bless the new book of laws. That was the first duty of the assembly. Ivan in a speech, most of which he had expressed publicly on previous occasions, told them of the wrongs done during his minority and of the visitation of God's wrath upon the city of Moscow. He humbly invited their condemnation of his sins, "Convict me in them, thunder the Word of God, that my soul may live!" Of course the clergy did not take his advice or do anything of the kind. But instead Ivan explained to them the provisions of the new civil code. They were gratified. They approved. They confirmed the statutes in the name of God.

Then came the surprise. Instead of receiving the Tsar's permission to disperse, they were held to consider elaborate proposals for the reform of the Church. Ivan by the aid of Sylvester and Adashef had edited a questionnaire and Ivan propounded question after question concerning the property of the monasteries, the stewardship of that property, the morals, the errors of copying in the religious books, heresies and malpractices. As if to bring the Middle Ages to an end it was agreed to cease copying the liturgical books by hand and to set up a printing press for them in Moscow. Consecrated error is better than scholarship, and it is not surprising that the populace soon destroyed that first printing press. Few ordinary priests knew even their letters, but they knew the services by heart. Ivan could not approve illiteracy; he owed too much to books himself for that. He soon persuaded the Archbishops of Novgorod and Rostof—Veliky, Theodosy and Nikander—the Bishops Trifon of Suzdal and Cyprian of Perm, and the Metropolitan Makary, to sanction the establishment of church schools in Moscow and other cities. The question of morals was shirked by the Church. In a widespread monasticism there is bound to be sexual irregularity in some institutions and it could well have been urged that there was an exaggerated counter-balancing asceticism in others. In fact there was too much irresponsible asceticism, and it was decided to forbid the making of new unauthorised hermitages in woods and caves and desert places.

As in theory the monks were dead to the world it was proposed that the lands belonging to the monasteries should be understood as belonging to the crown, the religious orders being merely tenants at the sovereign's pleasure. Naturally enough this was vigorously resisted by the clergy, and Ivan had to content himself with an agreed law that for the future, bishops and monasteries could not acquire land without the Tsar's consent.* Gifts of land made to the Church during Ivan's minority were to be restored to the original owners. It was made clear that the patrimonial estates of certain great historic families had an entail, and heirs could not legally be beggared through the religiosity of their elders. In cases where the Church was now found to be in occupation of these inalienable freeholds it was obliged to make restitution.

The declared intention to reduce the acreage of

---

* This law was not observed. The traffic continued unchecked throughout the reign of Ivan although the law was re-enacted in 1580. Ivan, however, despite his piety, confiscated at various times much Church property and enriched his treasury from the Church.

Church property was probably the most substantial fruit of the Congress. The great palaver occupied the time which could not be used in eating and drinking. The Congress lasted throughout Lent with rigorous fasting and much prayer. In those times Lent was observed without compromise or indulgence.

All that winter of 1550–51 the war with Kazan smouldered and Ivan's attention was frequently diverted from ecclesiastical and legal questions by reports from his Eastern front. In snow and ice the serfs felled the timber in the forest nearest the foundations of the new town of Svyazhsk, wood for the houses and the churches of the new town which Ivan had ordered to be raised.

The Tartars of Kazan, with the benefit of the retirement of the Russian army from their walls, at once sought reinforcements from Tartary and aid even from the Sultan of Turkey. In Moscow it was rumoured that the Crimean Khan was moving north and an army was sent to attack him, but could not find him. The Khan Saip Hirei imagined himself at least as great a potentate as Ivan was. He had lately conquered Astrakhan, which was a rich city in those days. He laid pretensions to Kazan and therefore to the whole Volga region from Kazan to the Caspian Sea. He had felt sufficiently strong to offer to sell peace to Ivan at the price of 15,000 gold pieces paid to him annually by the Russians.

"Thou wast young, but now hast reached the age of reason, declare thy wish—blood or love. If love, thou'lt send gifts worthy of a prince and 15,000 gold pieces every year. When it may be thy pleasure to fight, I'm ready to advance on Moscow, and all thy lands will be under the feet of my horses."

Ivan answered by placing the Khan's messengers in a dungeon.

Neither from the Crimean Khan nor from Usuph of Kazan were overtures for peace received with much respect. The war with the heathen was a holy war; there might be armistice, but there could be no final peace. Those who died fighting the Moslem went straight to heaven with glorious news. Those wars were conducted under a light of haloes. Priests carried their crosses and their ikons into the fray. At the sieges of Kazan pictures of the Holy Virgin were hoisted beside the rams and the catapults and lamps were kept burning while the assault of arms continued. The Moslem defenders met this show of religiosity by obscenity of various kinds, shouting words to the Virgin which the chronicler is loath to record, and lifting their frocks and showing their backsides to the enemy. Their behaviour resembled that of the degenerate Greeks who mocked the Romans from their walls.

One wonders why the defenders of Kazan did not sally forth and destroy the beginnings of Svyazhsk, whose menace grew steadily under their eyes. On the 18th of May, 1551, before dawn, the Russians from Svyazhsk made an unexpected attack on Kazan, got past the outer ramparts and killed a thousand Tartars in their sleep. Many Tartar princes and notables of the city perished in this assault, but the Russians got back to their base at Svyazhsk unscathed. Such a blow ought to have convinced the people of Kazan that they would not be able to hold out long against the Russians.

The young princess Suunbeka with her infant son were nominally rulers of Kazan. But the princess took as lover a Crimean Tartar prince, Koschak, who was thought to be capable of murdering her child, marrying her, and making himself Prince of Kazan. He was so unpopular in the city that a plot matured against him. This plot was no less than to bind him and his chief adherents and deliver the party to the Russians. Koschak and forty-five of his friends fled at night, but there was no refuge from the Russians who captured them and sent them in chains to Moscow. Ivan is said to have offered Koschak his life if he would be baptised a Christian, but he refused. All the prisoners were executed.

Overtures were made for peace and the Tsar demanded the surrender of Suunbeka and her child. The inhabitants, to save themselves, shipped her off. The chronicler says that all Kazan was in tears at the sight of the frail and beautiful Suunbeka whom they must yield, and that she prostrated herself at the grave of her husband, Sapha, envying him his peace. She was lowered on to a barque, richly dight—this partakes of the ballad as much as of history—and was slowly rowed along the little Kazan river in sight of all the population on the battlements, she and her son Utemish and her Tartar attendants. At the entrance to the river Volga she was met by the Tsar's emissary, who came aboard and greeted her with comfort in the name of his sovereign. Then they were rowed to the confluence of the Oka and the Volga and thence along the Oka to the Moskva river, and so to Moscow itself. At Moscow Suunbeka was received with honour and she embraced the Christian faith. When next year Ivan's son Dimitry was born, there was a double baptism, Dimitry and Utemish were christened together.

X.

THE CONQUEST OF KAZAN

ALL the bells of Novgorod are ringing because Kazan has been conquered" one may read in the ancient Chronicle of Novgorod. And all the bells of Moscow rang, and as each city of old Russia had the news, its bells began to ring. There was great national jubilation. Kazan had been added to Christendom. It was a triumph of the nation and the Church, of the nation in God. The ikons of Orthodoxy would soon be carried across the Volga. The conquering Russian with Destiny in his eyes was at the gate of Asia. The Crescent of Islam grew dim in the morning light of the Slavs.

The Tartar rule over Kazan was ended by Ivan. Arquebuses and cannon and the mining exploits of German engineers proved too much for scimitar and arrow. "The Tartars not using in field of any firework, but only a naked people on horseback, expert in the bow and the sword. It is most credibly reported that they be born blind, opening their eyelids on the third day, peculiar to these only, a barbarous brutish people living upon the increase and nourishment of bestial. . . . Their provision of diet at what time they invade their neighbours' territory is everyone his bag of meal, whereof in his journey taking his handful, moisteneth the same with warm blood of his horse's leg pricked with a needle to that intent."* This was their way of

* Letter of William Harbourne to Sir Francis Walsingham.

life as it had been for centuries. They were still a wild
and dangerous people, repeatedly in later years menacing Moscow, but they had become much milder. The
greatest conquerors of the earth since Alexander of
Macedon could not hold the mud banks of the Volga.
In the sixteenth century they were still capable of putting up a fight, but three centuries later they will all
have become petty traders and old clothes merchants,
without a spark of political ambition. In 1551 at least
half the inhabitants of Kazan were in favour of surrender to Ivan. "He is a merciful monarch, we can live
well under him." There had been many deserters; there
were many traitors. There was Shig Ali whom Ivan
used as a catspaw. After the removal of Suunbeka, Shig
Ali was responsible for a *pogrom* of Tartars. He made
a big feast for the best people in Kazan and with the
aid of a small band of ruffians cut all their throats.
Seventy guests perished in that set-to.

At this, with some show of indignation, Ivan the
Terrible sent Adashef to Kazan to tell Shig Ali that it
was plain to Moscow that the unfortunate Kazantsi
were unable to govern themselves and that it was the
Tsar's intention to proceed thither very shortly and to
take the city and give it and Prince Shig his august
protection. Shig was asked to become a Christian, but
proudly refused. In fact, he proved difficult and had to
be invited to Moscow to explain himself. The Tsar
made Prince Mikulinsky governor of Kazan and the
inhabitants met him and did homage on the banks of
the Volga. Mikulinsky and Adashef spent most of their
time in Svyazhsk. They were seldom admitted into the
fortress of Kazan and there were few Russian soldiers

in Kazan itself. The inhabitants needed time and so made it appear that they accepted Mikulinsky. Belatedly they were thinking of defending themselves with all the power at their disposal. Very soon Adashef and Mikulinsky found themselves shut out at the gates and the defenders of the city all making faces at them from the walls. But if the Tartars had not the courage to murder these two Russians they would not have the spirit to face Ivan the Terrible in person.

In March, 1552, in a full session of the Council of Boyars, Ivan declared his intention to deal with Kazan finally. "God sees my heart," said he. "I wish no earthly glory, but the peace of Christendom. But how can I repeat in my prayers the words 'I and the people given to me by Thee' if I do not save them from the ferocity of our age-long enemies?"

The boyars advised the Tsar to remain in Moscow in case there should be an attack from the Crimean Tartars in the south. But Ivan had decided to go with his army to the Eastern front and win in person the laurels which were to be gained there. It seemed as if for the Russians a walk-over was assured.

To make assurance doubly sure a very large army was mobilised. Here were many arquebusiers now called *strieltsi*, the ones who shoot. Here were Cossacks taking for the first time a large part in Russian wars. And there were gunners and artillery. Cannon appealed to the Russian mind and in the development of artillery the Russians were at that time ahead of most nations in Europe.

The mustering of this force took some three months and meanwhile fortune fickly smiled on the Tartars of

Kazan. In their sorties from the fortresses they caught the Russians idle and slew princes and princes' sons. They did considerable execution on the enemy and sought military assistance from the Crimea and Astrakhan. At the same time Svyazhsk was visited by a plague of scurvy. Many died and the survivors gave themselves up to sexual debauchery. The army there was so demoralised that the Metropolitan sent a missionary priest, Timothy, with Holy Water and bade him call the perverts to repentance.

The letter which Timothy brought from the Metropolitan is remarkable:

"By the grace of God, through the wisdom of our Tsar and the valour of our arms, we have been able to establish the stronghold of the Church in a hostile land. The Lord has delivered Kazan into our hands. We flourish and become famous. Germany, Lithuania, seek our friendship. In what way can we express our gratitude to the Most High, but in the keeping of His commandments? But do you keep them? The popular rumour has alarmed the sovereign's heart and my own. It is said that some of you, forgetting the wrath of God, are sunk in the sins of Sodom and Gomorrah, that many decent looking virgins and women, released from Kazan, defile themselves with debauch among you, and that men, to please them, put a razor to their beards and in shameful effeminacy pretend not to be males. But God will punish you not only in disease but in shame. Where is your glory? Once a terror to the enemy, now you serve him as a scoff. Strong men weaken from vice and weapons are blunt when virtue has gone from the heart. It has led to villainy; there has been betrayal. . . . God, Ivan and the Church call you to repentance. Amend your conduct or you will know the anger of the Tsar and you will hear the curse of the Church."

This missive was evidently composed by the Metropolitan and Tsar in collaboration. It is not clear whether the morals of the Russians wilted after the misery of the scurvy or they fell by infection from Tartar customs. At that time the Tartars were more gross than the Russians, which is saying much. We have Shig Ali who called himself Tsar of Kazan, fat, out of breath, gluttonous, mirthful, treacherous, blood-thirsty, nonchalant, quite a character. He came to no harm in Moscow. The Tsar made him presents. Instead of falling into disgrace or losing his head, he made love to the fair Suunbeka, won her, and obtained Ivan's permission to marry her. That was an event in the early summer of 1552. Shig Ali in high spirits advised the Tsar to postpone the conquest of Kazan till the following winter. But Ivan's mind was set. "All is ready," said he. "With God's help we will bring this enterprise to a good end."

Ivan handed the reins of government to his brother Yury during his absence at the front and asked the Metropolitan and the bishops to help him with their advice. He also asked them to comfort Anastasia. The Tsaritsa was *enceinte* and wept bitterly when she realised that Ivan would go to the war. She fell upon his shoulders and cried. He said to her that she should have the care of the poor and unfortunate while he was away, and the keys of the prisons, and her will should be his will if she had in mind to release anyone, no matter how serious his disgrace. In this we may discern the character of Anastasia. Had she been a callous, worldly woman Ivan would hardly have offered her the chance to be kind as a treat.

Apparently there was an official parting of husband and wife, Tsar and Tsaritsa, in the cathedral. It is recorded that Anastasia fell on her knees and prayed aloud for the health, victory, and glory of her husband. Ivan stood by her while she prayed for him. And having prayed, she rose to her feet and kissed him. Ivan passed then through a file of nobles to his waiting horse at the door of the cathedral and rode away to join his army.

It was not a moment too soon. Shig Ali's advice that he wait a few months was the worst that could have been given. For all the forces which Tartary could muster were on the move. The Horde from the south had reached Tula and laid siege to it. They approached Riazan and threatened to cut across the way to Kazan. With Turkish Janissaries and an array of cannon and several hundred camels the Khan of the Crimean Tartars made at least a great show of force. Had he advanced north-eastward instead of due north, and struck at the demoralised army at Svyazhsk the Khan might have frustrated the Tsar's great enterprise. Or had he reconnoitred the Tsar's position on the River Oka he might have avoided defeat. But the advance guard of the Russian army took the Horde unawares and, though greatly inferior in numbers, routed it completely, so that the Khan left all his camels and many weapons behind, and a large number of killed and wounded. The civilians of Tula, who had made a great defence of their city, stood on the ramparts and shouted "The Tsar, the Tsar has come to deliver us!"

Was it here that a camel was killed because it would not kneel to Ivan? But Ivan was only twenty-one and had never seen so many camels together before in his life. The booty left behind by the Tartars was enormous and it gave the monarch a childish pleasure to count it and send it back to Moscow for Anastasia to see. There was a show for the populace of Moscow, bound Tartar prisoners for the people to spit on, and camels to cause them to gape.

That was at the end of June. On the 3rd of July a general advance of the army toward Kazan was ordered. In Kolomna was preserved that picture of the Blessed Virgin which Dimitry Donskoi had carried into battle when he inflicted the great defeat on Sultan Mamai, and Ivan prayed to that same Virgin to grant him a like victory over the Tartar. Neither he nor his army missed any opportunity of intercession for victory. All good omens such as the report that the plague of scurvy had ceased at Svyazhsk and that good morals and discipline had been re-established there, were regarded as answers to prayer. There was little doubt but that God was on the side of Ivan. Messages followed him from the capital to say that all Moscow was praying for his victory and that the faith of the Tsaritsa was serene. "But be pure and chaste of spirit," admonished the Metropolitan. "Be humble in victory and courageous in grief! The Tsar's virtues are the salvation of his country."

The way of approach to Kazan, following the Oka

and the Volga, was through the towns Kolomna, Riazan, Kasimof, Murom, Nizhny Novgorod. The Tsar
went on horseback to Vladimir and thence to Murom.
That copper-faced Falstaff, Shig Ali, was sent on by
water together with Prince Peter Bulgakof and the
arquebusiers and a party of bridge-makers.

On the third night the Tsar's pavilion was put up in
the forest of Sakan; on the fourth in the open on the
bank of the Irzha; on the fifth on the Avsha; on the
sixth on the Kevsa; on the seventh by the side of a
lake at Iksha; and on the eighth in the neighbourhood
of Kasimof. The Princes of Kasimof and Temnikof
presented themselves with their bands of feudal retainers and joined the main army. July passed among forests and streams on the way to Murom. Those who
went by boat got there much ahead of infantry and
cavalry. In August a large party of princes and boyars
rode out from Svyazhsk to meet the Tsar. Deputations
of Cheremisi and other tribes arrived to demonstrate
their loyalty. With a grand equestrian flourish, the
Don Cossacks entered Russian history. All the way to
the Volga the hidden splendour of the Russia of the
sixteenth century was evoked. On 13th August the
grand cavalcade sighted Svyazhsk, the city which the
Tsar had called into being.

Ivan looked over the new town, its churches, arsenal,
forts, houses, and found that it was well built and he
added his opinion that not in all Russia had a town
more beautiful views from its walls, a quaintly modern
consideration. While he was there the axes clamoured
in wood, building a house for him while he waited, but
Ivan galloped off to his tent in a mead outside the

town. There, with the help of Shig Ali, a message in the Tartar language was indited to Kazan and its chief, Ediger, calling upon the inhabitants to surrender, whereupon they were guaranteed the clemency of Russia. As this was really a challenge to the *Crescent* to submit to the *Cross* it was not likely to be accepted. And yet the option was between surrender and the sword. Kazan stood no chance of winning.

The Tsar ordered his boyars to count the soldiers at their command, and a grand total of 150,000 men was computed. Possibly individual boyars exaggerated a little, desiring to ingratiate themselves with Ivan or to appear more important than they really were. But certainly there was a great force of men at the disposal of Ivan for the conquest of Kazan. Tempted by the tremendous business of selling to this army, merchants and hawkers and petty traders came in boat after boat to Svyazhsk, from Nizhny Novgorod, from Moscow, from Yaroslavl, and their booths were a great spectacle in the brilliant August sunshine.

On the 20th August, Ediger said "No." The reply was abusive and ironical. Shig Ali was called a traitor. Kazan spat on Ivan, Russia, and Christianity. But, "all is ready for you here; we invite you to the feast." Nevertheless a leading Mussulman with his wives and servants fled from the city at night and came to make submission to the Russians. He said that the defenders numbered 30,000 and that there was abundance of ammunition and of provisions. Ivan received the deserters kindly. Next morning he ordered the advance. He was standing in a field facing a banner on which was depicted the face of Christ, and looking steadfastly at this face he called out in a loud voice "Father, in Thy name we go forward!"

The cannons and powder were taken from the ships. The timber for the making of the siege towers was assembled, each ten infantry men carrying material for one tower. The ikons and crosses and lighted lamps and the great Cross borne in battle for centuries were lifted high. Long-haired priests in full habiliment escorted the symbols of the Church. Incense mingled with the morning air. As the sun burst through the mist and showed the high minarets over the drab battlements of Kazan, the army beat its drums and several hundred trumpets blared.

The Russians made no doubt about letting the Tartars know they were coming. The whole Muscovite army paused again for prayer ere it plunged to the assault. The Tartars had plenty of time to prepare for their enemies ere they arrived. In the preliminary stages Kazan and its besiegers kept, as it were, arranging a design for a carpet, static, woolly, colourful, barbaric.

Kazan, like Moscow, was a city with a fortress and a town, but the fortress was large enough to accommodate the whole population in time of danger. The Russian army found the town deserted and silent when they broke into it that morning. There was a stillness in Kazan as if all the inhabitants were dead or had fled in the night. The main army of the Russians invested the city while companies of *strieltsi* with their arquebuses reconnoitred within. There was a suspense which may have been greater inside the citadel than outside of it. Half the fighting force of the Tartars was waiting a signal for sortie—15,000 of the ugliest people on earth, with their facial muscles writhing with fear and blood-lust, were pent and taut behind the massive iron gates of the fortress. Suddenly the gates opened like the jaws of a monstrous dragon, and out pelted the Tartar mob, scimitar in hand, hideously screaming. There were Tartars on foot and Tartars on horse, mingled. The Russian musketeers, scared almost out of their wits by the surprise of the onslaught and the yells and the contorted faces of the foe, fled at once, and the streets soon ran red with their blood. They put up no sort of fight until they had got clear of the city and they might have stampeded the main army but for the spirit of the young princes and boyars, the subalterns and lieutenants of those days. These officers rallied the panic stricken *strieltsi* so that they fought an old-fashioned pitched battle under the walls of Kazan. Thousands of Tartar arrows sped from the battlements into the serried mass of the Russians. But now the rage of the Moslem onset had spent itself and the besieged slowly withdrew to their stronghold. The Russians attacked them as they retreated and they took some prisoners. Honours were even.

That proved to be enough fighting for the first day. The organisation of the complete investment of the city continued. There was a quiet night, but on the second day there was a great gale. It hardly looked as if God were on the side of the Russians. It was no ordinary storm, but more like a typhoon, whirling away all the tents, laying the new field-churches flat, raising great waves on the river, capsizing and sinking boats, flotillas, ruining, drowning. All the food supplies were lost, and the warm clothing for the autumn, and much ammunition. The preparations of months were undone in a few hours of tempest. Fortunately the Tartars had little imagination. A dense cloud of rushing sand and dust hid the beleaguering army from view. But there was a moment when the Kazantsi might easily have made an end of Ivan's army and perhaps of Ivan himself. The second engagement was an "act of God" by which, however, the Tartar had not the wit to profit.

On the scene of desolation Ivan called together the contractors and merchants and arranged to be re-victualled with all speed, and for abundance of warm clothing to be sent. He had found Kazan more strongly held than he had anticipated, and he decided that with his whole army he would besiege the city all through the winter should that be necessary. This is one of the occasions on which the strong will and determination of Ivan the Terrible became manifest.

At the same time, outnumbering the besieged by three to one, it ought to have been possible to storm Kazan. Its battlements were of mud and timber, and although those materials offer greater resistance to cannon balls than masonry it must have been easy to break a way through. The Russian fighting character was that of the wolf pack which waits and harasses and snarls and retreats and returns always reinforced.

The vast army of the Tsar was always on the move. The indefatigable Ivan was often visible to the defenders of the city, but just out of arrow range. The bowman was still a better long-distance marksman than the arquebusier, and bows and arrows were used in plenty in this Kazan warfare, as were also spears. And defenders still poured boiling water over enemies trying to climb their walls. The Russians invited sorties by adventuring small bands of men into unfavourable positions, whence they would retreat fighting into the forests. When the Russians captured prisoners they tied them to stakes facing the walls of Kazan and made them cry out to the defenders that it would be better for them if they surrendered. The Tartars replied by shooting these unfortunates as it was better to be killed by a Moslem arrow than done to death slowly by Christians.

The Russians never ceased to promise freedom and life to the Tartars if they would surrender the city. Ivan, though terrible in other respects, did not wish unnecessary casualties. He had men whispering under the walls all the time "Surrender, surrender." His strategy was devised to save bloodshed among the Russians. The Tartars did not trust his promises. The promise of a Russian was known to mean little. They believed they would be put to the sword whether they surrendered or were conquered. And during the first month of the siege they held the hope that the Russian army, baffled, would in course of time melt away.

But early in September the Russians dug underground passages and by dint of constant listening under the streets of Kazan, located the main source of the water supply. The Tartars had very good drinking water. A considerable amount of gunpowder was then stowed in the region of the wells and touched off in the morning at the time when most people were drawing water. Ivan was out on the Russian earth-works in time to see the mine go up. It was very successful, not only making a pleasing noise but bringing down a substantial part of the fortress wall. A storming party was at once made up and sent through the breach, but the Tartars, though stupefied by the explosion, were able to drive the Russians back.

On the following day Prince Gorbatof-Shuisky was ordered to make a descent on a protected part of the town, a villa region with orchards and pleasure gardens. This also was successful. There was a short, sharp conflict in which the Russians were the winners and then the forces of Prince Gorbatof-Shuisky broke through into what they considered a paradise of a kind, a place where much bread was stored and all the year's honey, with fruit on the trees and cattle grazing under them. The Russians burned all the homes, killed the male inhabitants, loaded carts with provisions, and returned to the main camp singing.

The Tartars had certainly much to think about in the first ten days of September. But they did not seem much daunted. They came out on the battlements and made terrible faces which the Russians considered to be part of sorcery. They also made obscene gestures and apparently as a result of the enemy's strange behaviour on the walls it began to rain. The campaign was plagued by some very unsuitable weather. The Church, however, gave its answer to that by preparing some very special Holy Water which was sprinkled all about the camp, and fine weather ensued.

Then the small siege towers were moved up closer to the walls, and in the night a huge wooden structure on wheels was moved up close to the battlements. This was over forty feet high; ten heavy guns were mounted

on it and fifty little ones together with a band of gunners and snipers. On top of this erection the *strieltsi*
dominated the streets and could pick off whom they
wished. The range was limited, but nevertheless this
wooden colossus drove a great number of the defenders
of the city to refuge in cellars and holes in the ground.
Their position was parlous, and still the Tsar offered
clemency if they would evacuate the city and betake
themselves wheresoever they desired.

Meanwhile the work of undermining sections of the
city continued, and there was a terrifying explosion on
the 30th September, followed by another on the morning of the 2nd October. The Tartars, driven out of
their holes by panic and concussion, swarmed upon the
Russians for a final encounter. The last day of September was one of bloody conflict. The boyars were of the
opinion that the time was ripe for a general encounter
and must have pressed their advice upon Ivan that he
seize the opportunity of making an end of the Kazantsi
that day. But Ivan was in no hurry. First the whole
army must confess and partake of the Holy Elements
and so prepare for death and immortality. The more
energetic spirits among the Russians were not content
to remain so religiously passive, and they spent the
time of prayer busily organising for the general engagement. Thus vast quantities of materials were mobilised
for the filling in of the fosse. The Tartars could observe unusual activity in the Russian camp. They
grasped that a storming of the fortress would be at-
tempted on the morrow and they also made their preparations.

Next morning Ivan at church was startled by a ter-

rific explosion from under the walls of Kazan. The last
mine had gone up and it was the signal for the assault.
The Tsar wiped the dust from his eyes and continued
his devotions. In a lad of such mettle it seems surprising that he should be content to be prostrating himself
in church while his army was gaining a glorious victory. By the time the Benediction had been pronounced
the Two-Headed Eagle was floating from the highest
tower of Kazan.

The army was in the fortress. The Tsar was escorted
to the scene of carnage where every Tartar was selling
his life at the cost of two Russians. The battle was
won; this was the dreadful execution. The Russians
fought their way from street to street. The dead piled
on top of one another in the roadways. There were
desperate encounters in every doorway and alley and
underground passage, the clash of swords, yelling,
moaning, shrieking, a great hubbub. It was difficult for
the princes or the Tsar to be sure what exactly the
Russian army was doing, but the assumption was that
it was winning its way everywhere. That assumption
proved to be wrong for a while. When the Moscovite
soldiers got to the bazaar wherein was a great store of
silver work and precious stones and furs and silks, they
ceased burning the homes of the Tartars, ceased the
massacre, and turned to looting. This gave the enemy a
chance to rally, which he accordingly did, and at the
twelfth hour almost changed the fortune of the day.

But there were too many Russians within the city.
The panic-stricken looters might stampede out of the
city followed by the enemy, but the main part of the
army was unaffected. The killing of the Tartars went

on. All the wives were made widows and all the children orphans. For only the women and children were spared, for the most part to be sold into slavery. In the afternoon of 2nd October the victory was complete. Ivan thanked his soldiers and told them they might keep all the loot they had obtained, except the regalia of the Princes of Kazan, which he retained for himself and his house.

Next day the streets of the city were cleared of dead. There was a great ecclesiastical procession. A *Te Deum* was sung and the Tsar raised the Life-Giving Cross in the place where had been the chief standard of Tartary. Thus Kazan was added to the territory of Russia.

XI.

BIRTH OF THE TSAREVITCH

IVAN in this war did not fire a shot or strike a blow. Nor was he at the head of his men, leading them to the assault. It does not appear that his royal person was ever in much danger. A great number of men at arms were detailed to protect him. Sometimes as much as half of the whole army was disposed uniquely for the Tsar's protection. He was not the conventional hero of war. He did not borrow disguise and go down into the trenches to see how the common soldier fared. Nor did he cheat his bodyguard to get away alone to further some romance or to find out for himself what the enemy was like. But his presence was a source of inspiration for his army. It had not been the custom for the Grand Dukes of Moscow to fight their wars in person. The young Ivan, so magnificently dressed, so unremitting in his intercessions with God and the Saints for victory, was like a star.

"Rejoice, most pious Tsar! Through thy valour and good fortune victory has been achieved and Kazan is ours. Prince Ediger is in our hands. The population is either destroyed or made captive. Untold treasure has been gathered. What dost thou order next?"

So announced the Commander-in-Chief, Prince Michael Vorotinsky.

"Let us give the glory to the Most High," answered Ivan.

The Prince Ediger was brought before the Tsar and he knelt down and made public repentance. The Tsar then forgave him for the resistance that he had made. Shig Ali and Ediger embraced. Two Tartars at least seemed to be happy on that day of massacre and victory. Ediger decided to become a Christian.

The missionary spirit of the Church at that time is exemplified by the statement of the chronicler that the signal for the onset, the great explosion, had occurred at the very moment when the words "There shall be one fold" were being read in the Divine service. "All the world shall become Christian" was still a hope and a belief in that time. Ediger's becoming a Christian was like a signal to the Moslem: "Give up your faith; it no longer serves you in battles!"

In gayer mood Ivan called his soldiers "Macedonians," called them "worthy descendants of those who served the Grand Duke Dimitry Donskoi when he defeated the great Mamai." For they had gained a victory which would be recorded in heaven.

Now there was feasting and song in camp. The army which had rifled harem and household made merry with the Tartar women and, no doubt, some who had been made widows in the fight followed the example of Prince Ediger and became Christians. They and their children became Russians and bred Russians, thus strengthening that undercurrent of Tartar which became characteristic of the race.

But Kazan itself was nothing without a population. The Tsar marked the spot where a Christian cathedral should arise. He ordered various mosques to be destroyed. He indicated his will that churches should be built in their place. But there was no Christian community to worship in those temples, unless the army should be bidden remain on the ground of its victory. A governor was appointed, an administrative staff. Merchants from Moscow and Nizhny Novgorod were granted privileges. But that was not enough to make Kazan a live city. Kazan for centuries had been a great mart of the East. From the time when it had been a Bulgarian city it had traded with China and Persia and Bokhara and Samarkand. It was known throughout Asia. One could easily become rich in Kazan. But the Russians at the disposal of Ivan the Terrible were not of the type capable of assimilating a great foreign trade. The Tsar at once found it necessary to offer a free pardon to all Tartar refugees lurking in the forests and to all the demoralised and panic-stricken Mahometans of the region. So, despite the victory of the Church, a large number of Tartars were soon to be found ready to take the homes and the stalls and the shops of the people who had been destroyed. All that Ivan asked of them was an oath of loyalty and that each man should pay to his tax-gatherers an amount similar to what he had been accustomed to pay to his prince. Kazan did not cease to be a great stronghold of Tartars, though under the acknowledged sovereignty of Russia. A substantial number of Tartars remain there to this day.

Ivan prepared to return to Moscow. He had sent couriers with the tidings of victory, and word to the Metropolitan and Anastasia and his brother Yury that he would soon be returning with his army. He left a garrison of 5,000 men at Kazan, 1,500 men of noble birth and 3,500 *strieltsi* and Cossacks. Gorbatof-Shuisky was governor and Serebranny vice-governor. It took some ten or twelve days to make the final arrangements and then Ivan set off ahead of the home-going army. Great news was to meet him on the way. A messenger had been despatched from Moscow to let the Tsar know that the Tsaritsa had given birth to a son.

On the 14th and 15th October he was rowed up the Volga to Nizhny Novgorod where a vast concourse of people were waiting for him, all on their knees. The shouts of greeting from the merchants were so loud that the voices of the clergy could not be heard. Novgorod rejoiced because its enemy and rival was ruined. For now the great fair was immune from Tartar raids, and at the same time commerce was certain to increase greatly owing to the destruction of the Kazan bazaars.

Ivan, having made the people a suitable speech, set off on horseback for the capital, and when he had ridden about a third of the distance and was nearing Vladimir, he was met by Anastasia's messenger, Vasilly Trakhanyot. When the Tsar heard that he had a son his joy was unbounded. He jumped from his horse and kissed Trakhanyot, prayed, gave thanks to God and capered about like one mad. He impulsively offered the messenger both his horse and his mantle as a present for bringing him the good news. To have a daughter was nothing; to have a son was to hear Destiny sound one's name on a trumpet.

Now curiously this news slowed down his journey home. He did not urge his horse, did not gallop post haste to his palace. He stayed at Vladimir to pray and sent tender messages of thanks and sympathy to Anastasia. And he stayed at Suzdal to pray. And finally when he was within a few hours' ride of Moscow, he stayed at the Monastery of Sergey-Troitsky to pray at the grave of St. Sergey. There he broke bread with the monks and he was visited by his brother Yury and various gentry from the Kremlin. That was on the 28th October, 1552. Next day he rode into Moscow.

The resounding significance of the victory over Kazan was testified by the popular reception which awaited Ivan in the streets as he rode in to Moscow. At times it was impossible to move because of the swarms of people pressing about him to kiss his hands or his feet. The Russians kissed their first Tsar because he gave them assurance of a great future for Russia and for their children's children. Sometimes a people appreciates the historic meaning of an event more quickly than monarch or government.

Ivan descended from his horse at the Sretenka Gate to make reverence to the ikon of the Vladimir Mother-of-God, in the presence of the Metropolitan, the Bishop, and all the priests of Moscow. He then acknowledged the power of prayer in the remission of the sins of his childhood, the power of prayer by which they were enabled to go forward against Kazan and destroy the heathen.

"And now I implore you," he concluded, "continue your zealous intercession at the throne of God, that I may be enabled to establish law and righteousness and good morals within the State, that the fatherland in peace may blossom with virtue, that Christianity may flourish in it, that those infidels, the new subjects of Russia, may recognise the true God and together with us laud and honour the Holy Trinity, for ever and ever, Amen."

The old Makary thereupon in touching language acknowledged the victory on behalf of the Church and the true religion and, as if voicing God's verdict, said "Blessed slave, thou hast been faithful in a small thing. I shall give thee charge over many things." And the Metropolitan and all the clergy bowed to the dust before Ivan.

The Tsar then took off his coat of mail and cast aside his sword. The purple was placed on his shoulders. A large cross was tied across his breast and on his brows the crown of Monomakh. The Metropolitan and all the clergy and the ikon bearers and the cross-bearers and the men with lanterns and the monks with incense formed into a procession, slow stepping and solemn, to the Kremlin, singing as they went.

Thus at last Ivan reached his palace and the bedside of Anastasia, who embraced her hero with tears of joy. Ivan put off the crown of Monomakh and kissed his Tsaritsa and his infant heir, Dimitry, with rapturous fondness. This was in the sunshine of the morning of his reign.

XII.

TRIPLE BAPTISM

THE end of the year 1552 passed in considerable festivity. After the arduous campaign the Tsar and his court relaxed. On the 8th November there was a state banquet in the large palace and everyone of dignity or consequence was bidden, the Metropolitan, Prince Yury, the recovered Anastasia, the bishops, princes, voivodes, an immense company. This was the occasion of presenting war honours and gifts. There were sables and pieces of brocade and golden cups and goblets, raiment, horses, bags of gold pieces, carpets, weapons, altogether worth a very great sum of money. And there were many who received lands in addition to these gifts. The Tsar showered his largesse. The Tsaritsa bore wine to the great nobles who had the privilege of a ceremonial kiss.

The feasting and merriment lasted three days and no doubt became more uproarious after the clergy retired from table. Apart from gluttonous eating and drinking such banquets were seldom graced by intelligent entertainment. There was no dance, no court fool, no buffoons or harlequins or mummers. Russia had no theatre. There was no staging even of religious plays. But the Tsar had his singers who came and sang to him, sang of his exploits and the exploits of his army at Kazan, new words to ancient tunes. His musicians played on the *guslyar* the natural harp-like accompaniment of the ballad. For within a month of the taking of Kazan, the story became a ballad, exaggerated with music throughout Russia till some have exclaimed in annoyance "The siege of Kazan did not compare with the siege of Troy."

And it's all one now, far away and long ago in the morning of History.

> Perchance the plaintive numbers flow
> For old unhappy far off things
> And battles long ago.

Perhaps it is not the taking of Kazan that they sing, but revenge on Tamerlane, on Chinghiz Khan, on Asia; Tamerlane with kings harnessed to his chariot—"Ye jades, what, can ye go but twenty miles an hour?" Ivan has revenged the kings of the earth on the monster out of Asia. Russia was in a grand mood. She has had such grand moments in her history, moments of self-realisation and creativeness. The picture has become faded like a fresco washed out by time, but there was a great vivid living picture, and one can but see some arm in a sleeve of gold brocade, raising a golden tankard to pledge Ivan and Russia.

From that time of national exaltation there still endures one memorial which is an architectural wonder of the ages, the Cathedral of Vasilly Blazhenny in the Red Square. It was planned then. The Tsar ordered it to be built in remembrance of God's mercy at Kazan.

Although we have suggested that the clergy retired from the feast somewhat earlier than the boyars and princes, it is not to assume that the bishops and the good old Metropolitan did not get very drunk on this occasion. If Tsar Ivan and the Metropolitan Makary were together responsible for the design of Vasilly Blazhenny it is probable that their imagination was helped by an exaltation which was enhanced by wine. No name of any architect has ever been associated with the building of this strange church. It was said a century afterwards that the Tsar had the architect's eyes put out so that he might never build anything to rival it. But that is the sort of story that grew up around the name of the Terrible and is the echo of some other western barbarity. The cathedral is unlike anything that had been built in Constantinople or in ancient Russia. But it expresses the fantasy of Ivan, the first to take the title of Tsar and at the same time a man of the most extraordinary religiosity.

The Tsar decided that the city of Kazan should defray the expense of the building of this cathedral, an indemnity of a kind. One may understand therefore that the triumph of Orthodoxy over Islam is to some extent expressed in the architectural design. The moment was one of conquest and conversion. Many Tartars were becoming Christian.

The baby Dimitry was soon taken to Sergey-Troitsky Monastery and baptised in the presence of the relics of St. Sergey. This baptism was followed by other baptisms, the most interesting of which were those of little Utemish, the child of Suunbeka, and of Ediger, the ex-ruler of Kazan. Nikander, Archbishop of Rostof, performed the ceremony on the infant Dimitry. The Metropolitan himself christened Utemish and gave him the Christian name of Alexander. What his stepfather Shig

CATHEDRAL OF VASILLY BLAZHENNY

Ali thought of this is not recorded, but the Tsar himself, remembering how he was left an orphan, took care
of the little Tartar boy and ordered that he should live
in the palace and that his education should be commenced.

The conversion and christening of Ediger took place
on the 26th February, 1553. For him the ice of the
Moscow river was broken. The Metropolitan was his
godfather, though that implied no responsibility for sin
since Ediger was of mature years. The Tsar and his
court were witnesses of the prince's abjuration of Ma-
hometanism. Moscow, in deep snow, was still in the
rigours of winter. All were fully dressed, except Ediger, and many wore sables. But the dark visaged Tartar stood among them clad only in a linen shroud. Ediger was asked if it were by any compulsion or outward
violence that he changed his faith, and he boldly af-
firmed that it was the will of his heart. "I love Jesus. I
hate Mahomet," he declared in a voice that all could
hear. Then he was dipped in the icy river and the ritual
was performed. He died as a Mahometan and was born
again a Christian with the name of Simeon.

The Tsar gave Prince Simeon a large house to live in
in the Kremlin. Somehow, although Kazan had fallen,
he had managed to preserve some fortune, but the
Tsar was his benefactor. He was given a retinue and a
status almost equal to that of blood royal. In this same
year 1553 he married Maria Kutusova . . . and was
happy ever after—at least he fades out from the records of history, which seems to mean happiness.

But this time of joyous events in Moscow was

marked by a dire calamity in north-eastern Russia, the outbreak of ulcerous plague which almost obliterated the populations of Pskof and Novgorod the Great. It broke out first in Pskof and created such a panic that Novgorod enacted that no one from the sister city should be allowed within the confines of Novgorodian territory. If anyone from Pskof was discovered in Novgorod, he and all his personal belongings should be forthwith consumed by fire. But that did not save Novgorod. The dreadful scourge soon appeared mysteriously there as from nowhere and spread from hundreds of cases to thousands in one night. Soon the dead were too numerous to be buried by the living, or the living were afraid to do the work. The streets of the towns and the open places of the forests roundabout were strewn with the bodies of the dead. The wrath of God must have seemed unreasonable after the divine good favour shown at Kazan. But the Russian did not demand a reasonable God. The wrath of man shall be unreasonable also, in humble imitation of the wrath of God.

Among those who perished of the plague was Archbishop Serapion of Novgorod the Great. He was said to have been a good man who went on ministering to the dying without a care for his own health. As the Archbishop in a sense held Novgorod in trust for God, his death was a serious blow to faith and love. In place of Serapion an unusually holy monk was found, Pimen of the Andreyanovsky wilderness. The Tsar and the Metropolitan prayed long with this Brother Pimen, and they sent him to the place of death to be Archbishop, and he carried with him a very considerable quantity of Holy Water specially consecrated to the purification of Novgorod.

It is said that within a year, half a million people perished of the plague in the cities and territories of Pskof and Novgorod the Great.

XIII.

THE TSAR FALLS ILL

THE region of Kazan proved not to be entirely pacified. The wild tribes, mostly of Mongol origin, the Cheremises, Mordvins, Chuvashes, Votiaks, and Bashkirs did not accept the change of overlord. They refused to pay tribute, although the amount had been fixed at the same as they had been supposed to pay to the Prince of Kazan. It is probable that the officials and boyars left as stewards were less honourable than their sovereign and asked more. The spoliation begun in the hour of conquest did not cease when the main army went away. The garrison still sought booty. Prince Gorbatof-Shuisky was not a success as governor, nor was Prince Peter Shuisky secure in his control of Svyazhsk.

Christmas of 1552 was marked by the melancholy spectacle of many gibbets, where hung seventy-four Mahometans convicted of banditry or militant disaffection. The Tsar in Moscow was vexed by the news from Kazan. He had hoped and believed that his victory was complete. The Governor wrote that the tribute was nevertheless coming in satisfactorily. This tribute was mainly paid in furs, which had almost the position of currency. The agents collecting this tribute were in themselves the unconscious agents of revolt. Had the tribute been in coin the tribesmen would have known definitely how much they had to pay, but the value of fur is open to argument.

An insurrectionary movement was developing. The Tartars built a fortress fifty miles from Kazan and manifestly prepared for a belated counter-attack upon the Russians. At the beginning of March there was a massacre of fur collectors. One district of Kazan rose against the Russians. The people proved to be plentifully provided with weapons. The *strieltsi* lost 350 men and the Cossacks 450. It was such a startling victory that to some it appeared that Kazan, so gloriously won, was after all untenable. Some of the boyars gave Ivan the humiliating advice to withdraw the garrison and abandon the city once more to Islam. Such pusillanimity on the part of the Council discounted Ivan's glory and prestige as a champion of Christendom. It conveyed to the Tsar's mind that behind all the adulation of which he had but lately been subject there was a hidden enmity and jealousy.

On March 10th the Tsar received the bad news: on the following day he was stricken dangerously ill. He lay in a fever which the doctors pronounced incurable. It was not plague; the pestilence had not visited Moscow. But it was almost as bad. Ivan lay helpless in bed, expecting death. The bad news spread like wildfire, and the people of Moscow crowded into the Kremlin to besiege the palace with prayer. For Ivan had become most popular. The people liked him well. They must see God's hand in this sudden blow, but they did not think the illness came to Ivan because of his sins. His piety was too marked. He had been a gift of God. He was all but a saint on earth. They humbly believed that their own sins must be greater than they knew since God threatened to withdraw his gift of Ivan from them.

But the princes and boyars were not so prayerful. They had grown a little tired of Ivan. Perhaps the Tsar was a little too pious for them, even in that pious age. Certainly he was too democratic. He had given signs that he could rule the country without their advice. As counsellors he had raised men of common birth on to an equal footing with them, or had even preferred such. The leading spirit in the tacit opposition to the Tsar was Vladimir Andreyevitch, the son of Prince Andrew, whom Helena had done to death. Vladimir had grown to maturity in the rough era of the Shuiskies. He was older than Ivan, less religious, more of a soldier. He had campaigned with the army at Kazan and understood himself as the real hero of the conquest of the city. As Ivan's brother Yury had remained in Moscow, Prince Vladimir was the person of highest lineage in the army after the Tsar. And in the triumphal homecoming, he had been honoured more than any other prince. But he had a secret chagrin and that was the birth of an heir to the Tsar. Had Ivan had no male issue, he saw himself as the chief claimant to the throne in the case of Ivan's death. He had precedence over Ivan's brother Yury.

This pretension and speculation may seem somewhat absurd, seeing that Ivan was destined to rule for another thirty-one years. But God hides destiny from man, and it did appear in March, 1553, that the first Tsar was on the point of death.

Ivan was morbid. Actually he was a man of tremendous vitality, though, at the age of twenty-two, he could not have entered into the fullness of physical life. The counterpart of his religious asceticism and

piety was a strong sexuality. In that sense in his early
years he may be said to have been balanced. For he was
no religious milksop. Nor was he by temperament a
recluse or hermit, unfitted for a throne. He was over-
awed by the supernatural and the power of the dead
over the living, but his body normally was a fountain
of life. His mind as arbiter between Byzantinism and
the lusts of the flesh was naturally vigorous. His intellectual difficulty was that of accommodating himself to the implacability of God's wrath. The way of
doubt or disbelief was sealed. He never doubted. An
unfaltering believer, he must see in calamity God's
punishment for sin. His prayers and prostrations he
offered as an indemnity to God for the sins of his
people. His campaign against Kazan was intended to
obtain favour with God, for himself, and for Russia. If
he had known a way to follow the example of Christ
and offer himself as a "full, perfect and sufficient sacrifice, oblation, and satisfaction" for the sins of Russia,
the young Ivan might have done so. He performed his
sacrifice according to his light. But he was unable to
stop the striking hand of God. In the year 1553 clouds
shut off the celestial light, clouds ever darkening and
blackening and changing day into night.

In his religious combat on behalf of his people Ivan
was chiefly aided by the priest Sylvester, who had interpreted the campaign against the Tartars in the spirit
of the crusades. But on this seeming deathbed of
March, 1553, he seemed to be deserted by Sylvester.
He discovered that Sylvester was worldly. Sylvester
thought about his own future. If the Tsar died and he,
Sylvester, had supported the wrong faction, he would

be likely to find himself shorn of influence. It was a question whether he would associate himself with the Tsaritsa's kindred, the Zakharins, or with the faction of the Tsar's cousin, Vladimir Andreyevitch. He judged that Prince Vladimir would be the stronger and supported him. So also did Alexey Adashef and his father Fedor.

There is little doubt that had the Tsar died Prince Vladimir would have seized the reins of government if not the throne itself. A plot developed rapidly when the Tsar fell ill. Prince Vladimir and his ambitious mother, Euphrosyne, began to canvass the boyars and to make gifts and gather supporters for a palace revolution. The Kremlin was buzzing with intrigue. It is possible that Anastasia in her anxiety for her husband might have been unaware of the conspiracy which was on foot. But her uncles, Daniel and Vasilly Zakharin, did not ignore it. Should Prince Vladimir prove successful the Tsaritsa would soon be removed from the scene, the infant Dimitry would be passed over and in some danger of being killed. Fortunately Ivan, though prostrate, was in complete possession of his faculties. He might still do something to preserve loyalty if he called the rebellious faction to his bedside and made a solemn and dramatic scene. So the Tsar's secretary, Mikhailof, made bold to tell the sick man that he ought to make a will. Ivan did not rebuke him. The suggestion was apt. He dictated a will and signed it bequeathing his Tsardom to Dimitry, naming him as his successor, the unique sovereign of Russia.

That done, he then desired that every one of his court should come in and swear an oath of allegiance to his child. Now Prince Vladimir and his friends were embarrassed by the presence of Sylvester on their side. He was privy to their plot, but he was incapable of perjury. It was impossible for him to kiss the cross in the hand of the dying Tsar and then desert the Tsarevitch after his father's death. It is possible that the others might have risked the welfare of their immortal souls. It was common enough to take a sacred oath of allegiance and then forget about it at the prompting of ambition. It would have been much safer for Prince Vladimir and his adherents to come at once and humour Ivan. After all it was not certain that the Tsar would die. There might be a miracle. God was being besieged with prayer. Ivan was nearer to the relics of the wonder-workers than anyone else in Russia. If he recovered, those who had failed to swear an oath of allegiance to his son must remain under a shadow.

The order that the princes and boyars come in to take the oath caused consternation. The conspirators turned to Alexey Adashef who had most experience in managing Ivan. Adashef felt awkwardly placed. How could he go in to the Tsar who loved him and had shown him every favour and say that in the event of his death he intended to desert his family. Instead he sent his father, who was a harmless old man, but pig-headed in his antipathy to the Zakharins.

"We would kiss the cross for thee, O Tsar, and for thy son the Tsarevitch Dimitry, but we will not kiss it for Daniel and Vasilly Zakharin," said he. "Thy son is still in swaddling clothes. That means that the Zakharins would rule over us and we know by example what that means. Think of thy own childhood!"

The Tsar was too weak to remonstrate. He lay inert, almost lifeless, listening to the hubbub of argument and angry words which almost changed to blows. Prince Vladimir Vorotinsky was the staunchest of the Tsar's adherents and gave the lie direct to Prince Vladimir Andreyevitch, so that a duel almost took place under the Tsar's bedchamber.

The first to kiss the cross in sign of allegiance to the infant Dimitry ought to have been the Prince Vladimir Andreyevitch as his lineage was highest, and the others waited his precedence. But he would not do it; so late in the evening after a day of acrimonious dispute, those willing to kiss the cross came to the Tsar's bedside and took the oath. They were Prince Ivan Mstislavsky, Prince Vladimir Vorotinsky, Ivan Sheremetief, Michael Morozof, Dimitry Paletsky, Daniel Zakharin, Vasilly Zakharin, and several clerks and other officials. It was not a very good showing. The Tsar was almost deserted. Certainly the conspirators had the majority. Possibly the terrible significance of the situation helped the Tsar to live. Opposition called into action his powerful will. He was a man who did not brook frustration. He caused a special document to be drawn up for the Prince Vladimir to sign.

The recalcitrant prince was brought in and to Ivan's face flatly refused to take the oath. Ivan told him that the sin of refusal would lie heavy on his soul. Then he told the boyars who had taken the oath that they must remain true to the same and act in accordance with their promises, should he die.

The next day Ivan warned again those who had taken the oath. He told them, in case of his death, that they must protect the Tsaritsa and escort her and the child into some foreign country where they would be safe.

"And you, Zakharins!" exclaimed he, turning to the uncles. "You've taken fright, eh? But don't think you can make your peace with the boyars! You would be the first corpses to be carried out. Show your manhood, shield my son and his mother! Do not allow my wife to be ill-treated by the traitors!"

Among the chief adherents of Prince Vladimir were Princes Peter Shchenatof, Ivan Pronsky, Semyon Rostovsky, Dimitry Nemy-Obolensky. When they heard Ivan's vigorous words to the Zakharins they became frightened. It did not seem as likely that Ivan was going to die. The bitterness and hatred in the Tsar's words showed them how dangerous their intrigue had been. After another council among themselves they came to a decision to take the oath and sneaked in one after another to kiss the cross.

Ivan, exhausted by the struggle, sank back in his bed in peace, but not to die. He had resolved, with the help of God, to live. He entered into a state of prayer which was not unlike coma, and in this state promised to go with Anastasia and Dimitry on an arduous pilgrimage to the North, to the shrine of St. Cyril near Kirilof, should he recover. Next day his temperature had gone down and he rose from his couch restored in health.

The disease from which he had suffered was called at the time the "fiery fever," but was rare and little understood. The Tsar's recovery was as sudden as the attack.

The restored Ivan, full of gentleness and love, returned good for evil. The silly old father of Alexey Adashef he promoted to be a boyar. He behaved like one, he ought to be one. Alexey Adashef and Sylvester, who "like Herods wished to destroy my little one," he seemed to forgive. Prince Vladimir Andreyevitch came forward hesitatingly to congratulate him on his recovery, and Ivan stroked his head caressingly and treated him as if there had been no trouble of any kind. Seeing the Tsar in such a pleasant and forgiving mood the other boyars fawned upon him and thanked God that his health had been given back to him. Ivan kept his counsel. He knew who had been his enemies when he was a child and who were now in reality his enemies— the boyars.

The Tsar's outlook was, however, very different, because he had in reality lost his trust in Alexey Adashef and Sylvester. Their defection was a shock. It rendered Ivan more lonely as a monarch and to that extent froze his sympathies. Such a morbid and religious character needed the mellowing influence of social intercourse. And he could not shut his eyes and deceive himself. Anastasia reminded him. Adashef and Sylvester had frightened the Tsaritsa and she no longer tolerated them as the confidants of her husband.

Still God had been merciful. He had given back the Tsar his health. Ivan must fulfil his promise and go with his family on pilgrimage. Some thought the Tsar unwise to desert Moscow and affairs of state at this point. He ought to have applied his mind to dealing with the dangerous situation at Kazan. The idea still obtained that the Tsar was weak-willed and could be diverted from his intentions. Perhaps this was because

he seemed to have leaned on various counsellors or because he had so meekly forgiven those who had opposed his will when he was ill. We have Maxim the
Greek, a picturesque religious mountebank, living in a
strong odour of sanctity in a hermit's cell at Sergey-
Troitsky. He had been banished by Ivan's father, the
Grand Duke Vasilly, but freed by Ivan himself. He
became one of the more showy ascetic figures at the
great *lavra* of St. Sergey. The real ascetics of Russia,
of whom there were thousands, reserved their speech
for God and had little converse with Tsars or men. But
monasteries must have their show pieces in living saint-
hood. Maxim in his cell was full of Byzantine lore and
vivid in converse. He was the type of man Ivan enjoyed a talk with, and before setting off on the long
pilgrimage he paid this holy man a call.

It is said that those interested got there first and put
Maxim the Greek up to the best line of argument:
"The fulfilment of unwise promises is not acceptable to
God. God would be much more pleased if, as a token of
gratitude for the miracle of thy health, thou shouldst
embark on a new campaign against the Tartar."

This was the special line of Sylvester and Adashef
who were very eager to turn the whole of the Tsar's
attention to the east.

"God is everywhere and thou couldst find Him at
Kazan as easily as at Kirilof."

But Ivan when he was dying had promised to go to
Kirilof and he had not promised to go to Kazan. He
would go to St. Cyril because his mother had gone there
before he was born and prayed for him. He had been
there before—but in the womb. He would retrace his

steps to the fountain of life. For that reason he was not persuaded in the least by the counsel he obtained from Maxim the Greek. It was decided to terrorize him, but that failed also. It is said that Alexey Adashef bore a message to the Tsar after he had left the cell of the hermit. It was a prophecy that if he persisted in making his pilgrimage to the North he would not bring the Tsarevitch Dimitry home alive.

It is probable that such a prediction was not explicitly made, but that after the event some general warning as to the danger to the health of the baby was remembered and hailed as a prophecy which had been fulfilled. Men craved signs from God. Ivan waited to keep Easter in Moscow, but at the melting of the ice set forth, accompanied by his brother Yury, his wife, and the infant Dimitry. They journeyed chiefly by boats via Uglitch due north to the confluence of the Sheksna and the upper Volga. Thence they were rowed a hundred miles up the Sheksna through bleak and desolate country to Kirilof Monastery. And on this journey the precious Tsarevitch died. It is not known how, whether it was the result of a chill or disease or accident that he died. All that is known is that it was a little dead body that was brought back to the Kremlin. An irony—the boyars made so much trouble about swearing allegiance to the child, thinking the father would die, but it was the father who lived and the child that died.

The grief, the despair of this event has not been chronicled. No one knew the extent of it but Ivan and Anastasia. It was dumbfounding. On a pilgrimage undertaken as a fulfilment of a promise to God, the Almighty had struck again, at them, Ivan and Anastasia, and at Russia. Direst calamity added itself to calamity. What then were their sins and the sins of Russia that God should visit them in this way? Sins too great ever to be expiated?

XIV.

BIRTH OF THE SECOND TSAREVITCH

THE dead body of the infant Dimitry was buried in June in the Cathedral of the Archangel Michael, at the feet of his grandfather, the Grand Duke Vasilly III. Nine months later Anastasia gave birth to a successor, the Tsarevitch Ivan.

The Tsar returning from his pilgrimage had still retained the meekness which he had shown on rising from his bed of sickness. He gave good for evil and if he felt resentment showed none. He listened patiently to the preachings of Sylvester, treated Alexey Adashef as if there had been no breach and he was most gracious and kind toward his cousin Prince Vladimir Andreyevitch. No vengeance of any kind was taken on the great princes who had been the adherents of Prince Vladimir in the previous March. Ivan's demeanour produced great uneasiness. The rebellious princes kept expecting a blow to fall on them and got into such a state of nerves that some of them, like Prince Semyon Rostovsky, planned fleeing Moscow betimes and taking refuge in a foreign country.

The rumour went round of a conversation which Ivan had had on his pilgrimage. He had met a cantankerous old monk by the name of Vassyan, once Bishop of Kolomna and a spiritual counsellor of Ivan's father, the Grand Duke Vasilly. Vassyan had been removed from his see and banished by the boyars during Ivan's minority, but he had been a good friend of

Ivan's father. For that reason Ivan had been eager to converse with him.

It is not clear who could have eavesdropped the intimate conversation between the young Tsar and the old recluse, but Prince Kurbsky, most garrulous and literary of courtiers, wrote it down as if he had the shorthand notes. Ivan was supposed to have asked the old man "How should I govern that I might keep the nobility in check?"

According to Kurbsky, Vassyan answered: "Have no counsellors wiser than thyself; keep to the rule that thou art the person to teach, but not to be taught; order and be obeyed! Then wilt thou be firm upon the throne and have all in thine own hands."

Ivan is supposed to have kissed the monk's hand and to have replied: "My own father, had he been alive, could not have given me better advice."

Ivan did not recall the old monk from banishment and give him back preferment in the Church. Vassyan on the brink of the grave asked nothing of man. Kurbsky surmised that as the boyars had wronged Vassyan he would nurse the desire for revenge and therefore would prompt Ivan to place his heel on the neck of the nobility. But in view of Ivan's conduct upon return, it might just as credibly be surmised that Vassyan gave advice which was purely Christian: "Reward evil with good; win thy people with love!"

Ivan continued to rule without violence or cruelty, as he had done since the burning of Moscow and his public "repentance" for his own and his people's sins. A change was coming, but it was not yet. When he returned from the pilgrimage he resolutely set himself to

deal with the problem which had called for action
when he had been stricken with fever, the pacification
of the region of Kazan. One punitive army had already
been beaten and its commander, Boris Soltikof, taken
prisoner by the tribes. Daniel Adashef, Alexey's
brother, had been sent to the scene of action, and,
aided by Cossacks, had done some damage to the
enemy, but he had insufficient force at his disposal.
The Tsar sent therefore a very considerable army
headed by Mikulinsky, Morozof, Sheremetief and
Kurbsky. Throughout the winter of 1553-4 the Russians smote the tribes, killing thousands and taking
captive great numbers of women and children. The
Tartar prince Yanchura was killed and one of the chief
leaders of the Cheremises, Aleka. The new Mahometan
fort on the Mesh was destroyed. Ivan was well pleased
and sent all the commanders gold medals to wear.

Ivan this time had not crusaded with his army but
remained in his capital. A messenger had arrived from
St. Nicholas Monastery, where the Dvina flows into
the White Sea, saying that a great ship, the like of
which had never been seen before, had come to anchor
there and that strange men of an unknown nation had
arrived. What was his Majesty's pleasure concerning
them?

This was Richard Chancelor on the *Bonaventure* of
160 tons from Deptford, the survivor of Sir Hugh Willoughby's party of merchant adventurers, the rest of
whom froze to death on the coast of Russian Lapland.
Chancelor came to anchor on the 24th August, 1553.

The Russians of St. Nicholas Bay had fled from
them as from spirits. Later they had prostrated them-

selves before Master Chancelor. "They, being in great feare, as men halfe dead, prostrated themselves before him, offering to kiss his feet." But he, "comforting them by signs and gestures," helped them up from the ground with his own hands. Then they became good friends, but it was evident they did not dare to trade with him without the permission of their sovereign, who the English learned was called Ivan Vasilievitch, and "the countrie was called Russia or Moscovie." The "barbarous Russes" then learned that the strange visitants to their coasts were called Englishmen.

No one knows what fantastic things were rumoured in Kholmagora, which was at that time the main port of the northern Dvina, for there were no interpreters of the language. But that the curiosity was immense was manifest, and that curiosity communicated itself to Moscow and the Tsar when the northern messenger arrived. Ivan commanded that horses and sledges be provided for the travellers at his expense, and that everything be done to bring them safely to Moscow. The messenger was much delayed in his return because he "had long erred and wandered out of his way" and Chancelor had already set off south and met him on the way. Having the Tsar's missive to aid him, the people struggled, yea fought with one another, as to who should have the honour of putting the horses to the sledge. Chancelor had little idea where he was being taken, probably little guessed that the journey was "very neere fifteen hundred miles."

Chancelor and the English merchants arrived in Moscow in December, 1553, but were allowed to wait some little while. They were not at once presented to the Tsar. Probably they were being spied upon to ascertain whether they were God-fearing men and Christians and worthy of the report which had been brought from the north. They had time to look round at the unfamiliar sights of a strange capital which they found to be as big as the "Citie of London with the suburbes thereof," but like true Englishmen they had already got bored by the place and were greatly relieved when, after about a fortnight, a messenger came to them and told them that the Tsar would receive them. The picture which is given in Hakluyt shows Ivan as he was at twenty-three years of age, in the midst of his court.

Captain Chancelor and the merchants were escorted to the palace and being

"entred within the gates of the court, there sate a very honourable companie of courtiers, to the number of one hundred, all apparelled in cloth of golde, downe to their ankles: and being conducted into the chamber of presence, our men beganne to wonder at the Majestie of the Emperour; his seate was aloft, in a very royall throne, having on his head a Diademe, or Crowne of golde, apparelled with a robe all of goldsmith's worke, and in his hand he held a sceptre garnished and beset with precious stones: and besides all other notes and appearances of honour, there was a Majestie in his countenance proportionable with the excellencie of his estate. On the one side of him stood his chief secretary [Mikhailof], on the other the great Commander of silence, both of them arrayed also in cloth of golde. And there sate the Council of one hundred and fiftie in number, all in like sort arrayed, and of great state.

"This so honourable assembly, so great a Majestie of the Emperour, and of the place might well have amazed our men and dashed them out of countenance, but Master Chancelor, nothing dismayed, saluted and did his duty to the Emperour, after the manner of England, and delivered unto him the letters of our king, Edward the Sixt."

Possibly the *dyak* Mikhailof acted as interpreter. The Tsar glanced at the letter which was duplicated in various languages, among them Greek. He then asked them a few questions and dismissed them until dinner, which was in the early afternoon and once more they were conducted into the "golden court."

"They finde the Emperour sitting upon an high and stately seate, apparelled with a robe of silver, and with another Diademe on his head, and our men being placed over against him, they sit down. On each side of the hall stood foure tables, each of them layde and covered with very clean table clothes, whereunto the company ascended by three steps or degrees. The guests were all apparelled with linen without, and with rich skins within.

"The Emperour when he takes any bread or knife in his hand, doth first of all cross himself upon his forehead. . . . Before the coming in of the meate, the Emperour doth first bestow a piece of bread upon every one of his guests, with a loud pronunciation of his name and honour: The Grand Duke of Moscovie, the Tsar of Russia, Ivan Vasilievitch doth give thee bread. Whereupon the guests rise up and by and by, sit downe againe.

"This done the Gentleman Usher comes in with a

notable company of servants, carrying the dishes, and having made reverence to the Emperour, puts a young swan in a golden platter upon the table, and immediately takes it thence again, delivering it up to the carver and seven of his fellows to be cut up and distributed to the guests with like pomp and ceremonies. In the mean time the Gentleman Usher receives his bread and tasteth to the Emperour, and afterwards, having made his reverence, he departeth.

"Touching the rest of the dishes, our men can report no certaintie, but this is true, that all the furniture of the dishes and drinking vessels which were for the use of a hundred guests was all of pure golde, and the tables were so laden with vessels of gold, that there was no room for some to stand upon them.

"We may not forget that there were 140 servitors arrayed in cloth of gold, that in the dinner time changed thrice their habit and apparell, which servitors were in like sort served with bread from the Emperour, as the rest of the guests.

"Last of all, dinner being ended, and candles brought in, for by this time night was come, the Emperour calleth all his guests and noblemen by their names, in such sort that it seems miraculous. . . ."

Ivan had changed his crown before dinner and according to Richard Chancelor's own story he changed it twice during dinner, "so that I saw three several crownes upon his head in one day."

After this gracious reception and banquet the Englishmen evidently had a very good time as everyone knew that they had been honoured by the Tsar. They were free to observe and to note anything that was of interest to them. There is no doubt they were greatly impressed and surprised by the grandeur and power of Ivan. The description given of the army as they saw it is notable:

"All his men are horsemen. He useth no foot soldiers but such as go with the ordnance or labourers. The horsemen are all archers with such bows as the Turks have, and they ride short as do the Turks. Their armour is a coat of plate with a skull on their heads. Some of their coats are covered with velvet or cloth of gold. Their desire is to be sumptuous in the field. . . . The Duke himself is richly attired above all measure. His pavilion is either covered with cloth of gold or silver, and so set with precious stones that it is wonderful to see it. I have seen the Kings Majesties of England and the French Kings pavilions, which are fayre, yet not like unto his."

Chancelor had several conversations with the boyars, visited Novgorod, Yaroslavl and other towns and towards the end of February he was permitted to depart home to London with a message from the Tsar to the King of England. The message was an offer to make a treaty whereby English merchants should have "Free marte with all free liberties, through my whole dominions, with all kind of wares, to come and go at pleasure."

In truth the Tsar made much parade before the English travellers and intended to impress them. He was a man of great imagination, in his way a precursor of Peter the Great. He had that persistent instinct of Russia, while being semi-oriental, to identify itself with the west. Influenced by the Church, by the Metropolitan, Sylvester, and Adashef, he had extended his

Tsardom eastward, but he was turning toward the west, the Baltic and world power. He had not taken the title of Tsar without coveting the counterpart of vast dominion. Mysterious England will remain on the horizon of his mind till his last days.

But the eastern adventure was still a great preoccupation. When the English were gone home preparations were made for the conquest of the lower Volga. An expedition was fitted out against the Prince of Astrakhan. The father of Suunbeka, consumed with mortal hate for Russia, must be struck again. The Khan of the Crimean Tartars had not yet reorganised his forces after his defeat by the Russians. Islam for the moment seemed devoid of fighting spirit.

Prince Yury Shemiakin was given charge of an army of Cossacks, *strieltsi*, noble youth, a very considerable force which was transported in galleys down the Volga. Mother Volga resounded with song and carouse and the measured beat of oars. It was a picnic. There was no resistance anywhere. The Tartar-Circassian garrison of Astrakhan fled at once and was pursued in all directions. Amongst the prisoners sent to Moscow were the Prince's five wives. The Russians entered into possession of the Caspian port and put a Tartar of their own choosing to rule over it, stipulating in the charter for the Russian right to fish in any part of the Volga river between Kazan and the Caspian. The inhabitants of Astrakhan should also pay a yearly tribute of 1,000 sturgeon and 40,000 altines. This was agreed to and the chosen Tartar, Derbish, became the local tsar and first taster of the best caviare in the world.

Ivan had the news on the 25th August, which was his

birthday. He was in the midst of the fête which he and
Anastasia and the court and the old Metropolitan Makary were celebrating. The splendid tidings came at the
right moment. The Tsar had grown to be twenty-four
and Russia was growing with him. The event was
epochal. The purely local and domestic fame of Ivan
grew apace. Despite the calamities that fell upon Ivan
and Russia from time to time, this was certainly an era
of victory and expansion. The Tsar adopted a new
style of beginning for edicts and letters. . . . "In this
the 21st year of our reign over Russia, the third over
Kazan and the first over Astrakhan."

Once more the sun shone on Ivan. God who had
taken had given again. He was victorious in the cause
of Christendom. Kazan was in complete subjection to
him. There was peace and prosperity in Moscow. Intrigue and faction seemed to be baffled by Ivan's mildness. He was in friendly intercourse with his cousin
Vladimir whom he seemed to have won back to loyalty.
His happy life with Anastasia continued without a
cloud. And she had given him another heir, the infant
Ivan, who seemed more sturdy than the child who had
preceded him.

The Tsar made a new will appointing Prince Vladimir Andreyevitch guardian of the Tsarevitch in case of
his death, regent, ruler of the land, recognising him as
the true successor to the throne if the Tsarevitch died.
In this we may see the fruit of Ivan's reflections on
what happened before. He felt he could trust Prince
Vladimir even if he could not trust his mother, the
Princess Euphrosyne. He had won Vladimir over.
Vladimir took an oath to be true to the interests of the

Tsarevitch and to protect the Tsaritsa. He promised not to spare his mother should she contrive anything against Anastasia and the child, to be impartial in the administration of the state and to do nothing secretly from the Tsaritsa, the Metropolitan and the Council of Boyars. He agreed to limit the number of his armed servants to 108. The Tsar's brother Yury was to be granted certain lands. Yury was simple-minded and had no pretension to the succession.

Prince Vladimir had been persuaded to desert his own adherents. Perhaps for that reason the Rostovsky family decided to pack up and go into Lithuania. If Ivan chose to punish them for their disloyal conduct of the previous year they had no protector. Prince Semyon and Prince Nikita Rostovsky were both arrested near the Lithuanian border. Prince Semyon Rostovsky, as the head of the family, was brought to trial and condemned to death for his treasonable action. But the Metropolitan Makary and Sylvester and several of the archimandrites pleaded for his life and he was banished instead to prison at Bielozersk, and the rest of the tribe was set free as "stupids." The main defence of the Prince Semyon had been mental deficiency. The Rostovskies therefore became a scoff for a season. Ivan, however, had really wished to have them executed and stated at a later date that he had been thwarted in this by Adashef and Sylvester.

XV.

RUSSIA FACES WESTWARD

TROUBLE arose with Poland and Lithuania regarding the recognition of Ivan's title of Tsar. Sigizmund Augustus, Grand Duke of Lithuania and elective King of Poland, was not sure what pretensions were involved in tsardom. He did not like new-fangled titles. Surely Ivan IV was not putting himself on a level with the Holy Roman Emperor or the Sultan! Poland at that time was a great and flourishing State and certainly did not consider itself in any way inferior to Muscovy. Although Muscovy was Christian it was barbarous. Poland knew that it was more civilised and therefore Sigizmund Augustus ignored Ivan's aggrandisement and sent his ambassadors accredited to the court of His Majesty the Grand Duke of Moscow, but not of His Majesty the Tsar of Russia. In retaliation Ivan addressed his letters to the Grand Duke of Lithuania and omitted to call Sigizmund Augustus King of Poland.

When, in 1553, Sigizmund's ambassadors arrived in Moscow their papers were handed back to them. The Tsar did not ask them to dinner. They explained that they had come to try to arrange "eternal peace." "That may be so," said the Tsar's secretary, "but you have not made a very tactful beginning."

"You must restore all the lands you have in time past annexed from the duchy of Lithuania. When you have done that we will conclude a treaty of permanent peace. Then we will discuss the question of the title of Tsar which would also have to be recognised by the Emperor and the Pope," said the ambassadors.

Ivan did not feel the necessity of concluding a pact of this kind and so the ambassadors returned to Poland. A state of war now technically existed between the two countries, but as the Tartar and Mahometan danger in the east and the south was not entirely liquidated, the Tsar instructed his emissaries to obtain a temporary peace with Poland. Actually Sigizmund Augustus had no intention of going to war with Muscovy, but Ivan, though dissuaded by the Metropolitan, Sylvester, and Adashef, did entertain the notion of fighting Poland and Lithuania at some time and freeing Kief from Polish rule. He kept the question of his unrecognised title alive. A reasoned statement of his claim to the title was sent to Sigizmund.

Besides the historical validity of the title Ivan had now conquered Kazan. The princes of Kazan were called tsars and the conqueror of a tsardom must be entitled to be considered a tsar. When Astrakhan was conquered he informed Sigizmund Augustus of still another reason why he should have his title recognised. Sigizmund congratulated Ivan on his victory over the infidel, but would not call him tsar. The Polish king was obstinate. He would not recognise the title, but he would treat for everlasting peace. He sent Ivan another emissary, this time one of the nobility, Pan Tishkovitch. This gentleman was not received by the Tsar. But it was arranged that the Metropolitan should grant him a state reception with full honours.

Tishkovitch could afford no satisfaction on the sub-

Sᴍᴀʟʟ ᴄᴀᴘs Sɪɢɪᴢᴍᴜɴᴅ Aᴜɢᴜsᴛᴜs, Kɪɴɢ ᴏꜰ Pᴏʟᴀɴᴅ

ject of the title, but still prated of the need for a treaty of permanent peace. Ivan had quite sufficient cause for war, but the hour for a reckoning with Poland had again to be postponed. Ivan had touched an exposed nerve in the north and was at war with Sweden.

Russians and Poles would rather fight than not, but their hostility was founded more on mutual antipathy than on economic or vital necessity. But a war for the possession of ice-free ports on the Baltic was in the chart of destiny of Russia, and what Ivan would begin Peter the Great was to consummate. With a sort of blind instinct sixteenth-century Russia turned toward the conquest and destruction of Livonia.

When the next batch of English merchants arrived in Moscow they found Ivan so much occupied with projects for new wars that he had not much time to give them. Actually, Chancelor arrived in Moscow for the second time on the 4th October, 1555. The Tsar had lately returned from another Eastern battlefield. All the preceding summer the Khan of the Crimean Tartars had been on the warpath. The Khan had been put to flight and 60,000 horses had been captured, most of these Steppe ponies, but 200 being thoroughbred chargers fit for nobles to ride. There had been some bloody fighting and serious casualties on both sides. Ivan Shermetief was wounded and the brave voivode Sidorof was killed. The southern Tartars were beaten off for another winter. Ivan mechanically turned his attention to the west, to Poland, Lithuania, Livonia, Sweden.

Livonia, which has long ceased to exist as a geographical entity, was a territory made up of what is now part of East Prussia, part of Latvia and Esthonia. It had a fairly rich trading community concentrated in Riga, Reval, and Dorpat. Its people were Finns, Letts, and Germans, but the Russians indiscriminately called them Germans. It was ruled by a chivalric order, the Teutonic Knights and their Grand Master, mediaeval and in a state of decay. Politically and militarily it was weakly held. Its unprotected wealth was a temptation to its rapacious neighbours. Alexey Adashef had the task of making known the Tsar's grievances.

"Why is it that Dorpat is so backward in paying tribute?" asked he.

The Livonians were astonished. They had no sense of humour.

"What tribute?" they asked. "We have never heard, nor have we read in any documents of our people having paid tribute to the Grand Duke of Moscow."

"Oh, I'm surprised," replied Adashef. "Do you not know that your forefathers invaded Livonia from beyond the sea and broke into the territories of the grand dukes of Moscow, who, not wishing to shed Christian blood, permitted them to stay there on condition that they paid tribute? The people did not pay, but now it will be necessary for us to collect the arrears."

There had been a tribute imposed, not in coin but in honey. Adashef proposed that it be commuted for gold and the Livonians, who did not dare to refuse, asked for three years' grace when they promised to pay all. In three years' time they might find allies in Swedes or Lithuanians, to support themselves against the Russians. Both Swedes and Lithuanians were rapacious, but possibly not so dangerous as the Russians.

Gustavus of Sweden made war on Ivan IV because of encroachments upon his territory bordering the Gulf of Finland. His information regarding Russia as a fighting force was out of date and it was clear from the first that he had under-estimated the strength of his enemy. Russia laid siege to Wiborg and ravaged the territory round about, taking so many prisoners that the price of Swedish girls was a shilling each.

The rumour that Russia was entering into a trading relationship with England was being spread abroad. The Livonian merchants were annoyed: there was a boycott of Russian goods in Riga. The Swedish merchants were annoyed and Sweden addressed a rather foolish remonstrance to England. The Flemish merchants were annoyed. When Chancelor and his friends were looking over the goods in the bazaar of Novgorod, the Flemings got them gaoled for an infringement of their monopoly, but Ivan had them speedily liberated. Polish and German traders were also apprehensive and jealous. This first Anglo-Russian commercial understanding certainly brought Russia enemies.

In February, 1555, Queen Mary granted a charter to the Russia Company. On the 4th October, Richard Chancelor appeared in Moscow for the second time. With him were George Killingworth, the Russia Company's first agent, Henry Lane and others. The letter which they presented to Ivan contained a surprise. Edward the Sixth was dead. This letter was jointly from Philip and Mary, "King and Queen of England, France, Naples, Jerusalem and Ireland, Princes of Spaine and Sicilie, Archdukes of Austria, Dukes of Milan and Brabant." The vast extent of their joint power must have impressed Ivan. The union no doubt remained in his mind as a precedent when in later years he conceived the possibility of marrying Queen Elizabeth.

The English were again well entertained. Ivan signed a commercial treaty. The English merchants were granted great privileges and found it advantageous to have a house built at Kholmagora on the Dvina, a little above the site of Archangel, and another house at Vologda. They stayed all the winter in Russia, for they had brought a rich cargo of broadcloth and also it appeals from the meagre reports extant, some quantity of sugar. They spent nine months taking the first pickings of the curious and the valuable in Russia. It was a double commerce: they sold what they had brought with them from England and they bought what they could sell or show upon their return. The Russians were friendly: there were no "incidents." Ivan appointed his first ambassador to England, Joseph Nepeia of Vologda, accompanied by two guests Phophan Makarof and Michael Grigorief, and they carried rich presents of cloth of gold and sables for Queen Mary.

The frozen company of Sir Hugh Willoughby and his mariners had been discovered in the far north and Ivan ordered that all that could be transported of their possessions should be put on Chancelor's ships to be taken to London.

The Russian argosy sailed out from the harbour of Kholmagora on the 23rd July, the *Bonaventure* of which Chancelor was captain and "grand pilot," the *Bona Speranza*, the *Bona Confidentia* and the *Philip* *and Mary.** But dire calamity visited them. A storm separated the ships. They lost sight of one another. The *Speranza*, and the *Confidentia* were lost with all hands. The *Bonaventure* was blown on to the Scottish rocks. Chancelor was drowned as were Makarof and Grigorief. Nepeia and a few sailors alone saved themselves. The Scots salvaged the best part of the cargo, but, as was natural, kept it for themselves. It was months before the Tsar's ambassador presented himself in London, but he had a marvellous reception. The whole court, the whole city, turned out to do him honour.

* The *Philip and Mary* went aground at Dronton in Norway, was refloated, and proceeded on her way months later, arriving in London in April, 1557.

XVI.

ALARMS, EXCURSIONS

TURKS and Tartars were still a recurring menace because every spring the Khan decided to be revenged for the loss of Kazan and Astrakhan. Every spring the military caravans, the laden camels, innumerable ponies, the Janissaries, the Tartar princes with hawk on wrist, the Turkish mounted archers and swordsmen, rolled northward over the plains, threatening the valley of the Oka, threatening Tula and Kolomna and Moscow. The Sultan of Turkey was behind these invasions, enraged by the wrongs of Islam. Eventually, at a much later date in Ivan's reign, the Tartars were to succeed, burn Moscow and destroy its population. The danger was real. There was sometimes an almost irresistible fury in these attacks.

In 1556 the moving Horde was taken in the flank by the Cossacks, who gained a notable victory between the Dnieper and the Don. That probably averted the danger for that year. This diversion of hostilities in the south-west attracted a Lithuanian noble of renown, Prince Vishnevetsky, who led out from his own country a large band of horsemen and entered the fray, greatly to the disgust of King Sigizmund Augustus, who would rather that the Russians weakened themselves in fighting the Moslem unaided.

Sigizmund was annoyed for many reasons. He had counted on Sweden to check Russia's ambition in the Baltic region, but the peaceable Gustavus had called off his unsuccessful army and made a treaty advantageous to the Russians. Ivan's aggressive behaviour toward the Livonians also displeased him. And now already in state papers the Tsar called himself among other things "Lord of the Livonian lands." It is not clear that that should have constituted a grievance, since Sigizmund Augustus in his state papers called himself "Grand Duke of Russia."

In February, 1557, Livonian delegates again appeared at Moscow, but as it was at once seen that they had not brought the tribute with them they were sent back to Livonia. Ivan said: "If you do not bring the tribute speedily according to your promise, we shall find a means to come and take it."

Prince Shastunof was sent to besiege the fortress at the mouth of the Narova river, opposite Narva. Shastunof did not encounter great opposition. He set off in April; in July he was in possession of the fortress which was renamed Ivangorod. Thus early Ivan penetrated to the Baltic and obtained a trading station for communication with the towns of the Hanseatic League. Not that it was entirely secure, for Narva, opposite Ivangorod, was strongly held by the Livonians. Ivan prepared for an extensive invasion of Livonia, for it seemed to him and the boyars easy of conquest. The whole summer was one of military activity. Consequent upon the fall of Astrakhan the Circassian princes from the lower Volga region and the northern Caucasian steppes had come north with great bands of horsemen to serve the Moscow Tsar. By the extension of her territory the army of Russia was almost doubled.

The production of artillery kept pace with the increase in the forces. "They have faire ordinance of brasse of all sortes, bases, faulcons, minions, sakers, culverings, cannons double and royall, basiliskes long and large, they have six great pieces whose shot is a yard of height, which shot a man may easily discern as they flee: they have also a great many of morter pieces or popguns, out of which pieces they shoot wild fire."*

Ivan had in part abolished the feudal obligation to serve in the army without pay. A tax had been imposed on trade on land and was collected into the Tsar's treasury by the *dyaks*. The possession of landed estate still entailed the service in the field of master and retainers, but the pay-value of a man in arms in lieu of taxes was determined. Large estates which could not put their just quota of men in the field were reduced or their owners had to pay a yearly indemnity—that is, the balance of the gross assessment of tax. A survey of lands was made and the hypothetical figure of the army was deduced. And all who served were paid. This accounts for the great increase in the forces at the disposal of Ivan.

In the midst of the great military preparations for the extension of the war in Livonia, one of the most intrepid merchant-explorers arrived in Moscow, Anthony Jenkinson, on his way with English goods for the mart of Bokhara. Mirth has been provoked by the travellers' tales which bemused the English people in the sixteenth century, but Anthony Jenkinson gave one of the most remarkable and valuable accounts of Rus-

* Hakluyt, Vol. II: *Nepeia's Return Home.*

sia extant either in the Russian or any other language, and he did not tell of "men whose heads did grow beneath their shoulders."

Jenkinson was bidden to dinner. "At the upper end of one table were set the Emperour, his majestie, his brother [Yury] and the emperour of Kazan, which is prisoner [Ediger]. About two yards lower sate the Emperour of Kazan, his sonne, being a child of five yeeres of age, and beneath him sate the most part of the Emperour's noblemen. And at another table neere unto the Emperour's table, there was set a Monke all alone, which was in all points as well served as the Emperour [the Metropolitan]. At another table sate another kind of people called Chirkasses [Circassians], which the Emperour entertaineth for men of war."

This dinner in a splendour of gold plates and cups lasted about the space of five hours and while the guests ate and drank six singers faced the Tsar and sang to him.

The English doctor Standish, whom Jenkinson had brought with him for service at the Russian court, was accepted by Ivan and together with other English craftsmen given a salary. They all received presents of furred gowns of velvet and gold or else red damask. The doctor's gown was furred with sables, and the rest were furred with ermine or grey squirrel, and all faced and edged round about with black beaver.

Soon, with the coming of the snow, they had their sledges like Russian gentry, sitting on carpets or white bears' skins, their horses decked with foxes' or wolves' tails at the neck.

They were greatly entertained and it is clear that the

English were very welcome visitors at Ivan's court. One of the greatest dinners to which they were invited was upon Christmas Day when there dined in the Emperor's presence "above 500 strangers and two hundred Russes, and all they were served in vessels of gold, and that as much as they could stand one by another upon the tables." Jenkinson observed that there were twelve huge wine barrels of silver each of which had six hoops of fine gold. This dinner continued about six hours.

Twelve days after Christmas, at Epiphany, the whole court went out to the blessing of the waters, and the English visitors were spectators of the ceremony. For this a large square hole was made in the ice of the Moskva river.

"First and foremost there go certain young men with wax tapers burning, and one carrying a great lantern; then follow certain banners, then the Cross, then the ikons of our Lady, of St. Nicholas [the Wonder-Worker], and of other saints, which men carry upon their shoulders. After follow certain priests to the number of 100 or more; after them the Metropolitan, who is led between two priests, and after the Metropolitan came the Emperour with his crown upon his head and after his Majestie all his noblemen. Thus they followed the procession unto the water, and when they came to the hole which had been made, the priests set themselves in order round about it. At one side of the same pool there was a scaffold of boards made, upon which the Metropolitan was set. But the Emperour's Majestie stood upon the ice. After this the priests began to sing, to bless and to cense, and did their service, and so by the time they had done, the water was holy. Which being sanctified the Metropolitan took a little thereof and cast it on the Emperour, likewise upon certain of the dukes [nobles] . . . there came above 5,000 pots to be filled of that water: for the Muscovite which hathe no part of that water thinks himself unhappy. And very many went naked into the water, both men and women and children."

Among other notable descriptions by Jenkinson is that of Palm Sunday in Moscow:—"There is a horse covered with white linen cloth down to the ground, his ears being made long with the same cloth like an ass's ears. Upon this horse the Metropolitan sitteth sidelong like a woman. In his lap lieth a fair booke, with a crucifix of goldsmith's work upon the cover, which he holdeth fast with his left hand, and in his right hand he hath a cross of gold, with which cross he ceaseth not to bless the people as he rideth. . . . There are to the number of thirty men which spread abroad their garments before the horse, and as soon as the horse is past over, they take them up again and run before and spread them again, so that the horse do always go on some of them. . . . One of the Emperour's noblemen leadeth the horse by the head, but the Emperour himself, going on foot, leadeth the horse by the end of the rein of his bridle with one of his hands, and in the other he had a branch of a palm tree."

This tableau was followed by crowds of gentry and populace. They went from cathedral to cathedral within the Kremlin. "Which being done, the Emperour's Majestie and certain of his noblemen went to the

Metropolitan his house to dinner, where of delicate fishes and good drinks there was no lacke."

At Easter Anthony Jenkinson obtained permission to continue his journey to Bokhara. On the 23rd April, 1558, he set out by Riazan and the river Oka to Nizhny Novgorod, thence by the Volga to Kazan and Astrakhan, across the Caspian Sea to the deserts of Turkestan, and he was the first Englishman in Bokhara, which he reached on the 23rd of December.

XVII.

WAR WITH LIVONIA

THE Livonian ambassadors returned with gifts
for Ivan, but without the tribute and the Tsar
would not accept the gifts. It is true he regaled
them with dinner, but he played a practical joke upon
them. There was the usual superb banquet, but the ambassadors were served fast dishes only. The mirth at
their expense must have been considerable. Shig Ali
waited on the Livonian frontier with 40,000 men,
most of them Circassians and Cheremises, recruited
from the south-east, a force even more inclined to rapine and murder than a Russian army. With Shig Ali
were such intrepid commanders as Ivan Sheremetief,
Daniel Adashef, and Serebranny. Andrew Kurbsky and
Michael Vasilievitch Glinski also had commands. The
unsuccessful ambassadors returned home, and the Tsar
gave the signal for invasion.

The Teutonic Knights, living in fine castles, had become effeminate, a comic opera order of chivalry, now
more skilful in tilting against ladies than against men.
On this the historiographers of both sides agree. They
were not capable of offering much resistance to the
Russians. Shig Ali went in and did great slaughter and
brought away rich booty. Livonia was a fat land to
plunder. The invasion began on the 22nd January,
1558. The knights did not pay much attention. They
were celebrating the wedding of a distinguished citizen
of Reval. The Tsar's army laid waste the country south

and west of Dorpat on a radius of 150 miles, burning the farms and the villages, slaying the males and taking into bondage the women and children. Rape and hideous brutality are said to have marked this campaign. Many girls were outraged; many were destroyed by the barbarous tribesmen. It could not be called war, there was little or no armed resistance. It was a punitive expedition having as its object to spread terror far and wide and convince the knights, the merchants, the Grand Master, and the Bishop of Dorpat that it would be more prudent to come to terms and pay the tribute.

The Russian army did not attempt to storm fortified towns such as Dorpat, but they reduced to ashes such substantial settlements as Marienburg, Altenthorn, Neihaus. There was a sally of German forces from Dorpat, but the Russians repulsed it with great loss. Part of the army then pushed north to the Baltic shore and, beginning with Wesenberg, ravished the coastal villages all the way to within thirty miles of Riga. Towards the end of February, encumbered with spoils, they returned from this foray, passing Narva which, however, they did not attack and going to Ivangorod, which was now a Russian base.

The treatment of the Livonians was approved by the Tsar and the campaign must have been popular because it was so profitable. Shig Ali and the princes did well. Glinski so far forgot himself as to lead some bands into Russian territory and commit the same outrages as had been so commendable in Livonia. Ivan reprimanded him severely and ordered him to make restitution for the farms he burned and the plunder he took.

Then wailing Livonia wished peace. Shig Ali said to them: "You know on what terms." The Grand Master prepared to send new ambassadors to Moscow. Ivan proclaimed an armistice, beginning with Lent to last till Easter. But the knights in Narva broke faith and trained their guns on Ivangorod. Ivan sent Prince Temkin to destroy a dozen Livonian villages as his express comment on the shots fired from Narva. But that did not hurt the knights who, against the will of the burgomaster and the merchants of the town, continued to fire into Ivangorod. The inhabitants of Narva were terrified that the same fate would be theirs as had overtaken the villagers of Livonia. At night they sent out representatives to speak for them in Ivangorod, and they declared that they wished no better than to become the faithful and peaceful subjects of the Tsar. Delegates were sent to Moscow to state this case. But Ivan's terms were the surrender of the keys of the city and of the person of the commander of the knights, Schnellenberg.

Whether they would have been able to arrange that surrender is doubtful, but in their absence the warfare had intensified. Reinforcements were expected from the Grand Master. The Russians were enraged beyond measure and ready to take advantage of any opportunity to be revenged. Fire broke out in Narva. Legend says that drunken Germans broke into the house of a Russian merchant in the city and seeing an ikon of the Blessed Virgin in pride of place snatched it from its little throne and threw it on the kitchen fire. The ikon, face downward in the embers would not burn, but a fire broke from it. Part of the city was seen to be in flames and the Russian army seized the moment to storm the walls. The army moved without the orders of its commanders. Some got into boats on the Narova river, some broke the doors from the houses in Ivangorod and navigated these across the stream, others made rafts of logs. When the princes saw this spontaneous attack they could not withhold their support from the glorious exploit and gave orders to that part of the army which had not yet moved, to follow up behind the others. Daniel Adashef, Alexey Basmanof and Ivan Buturlin distinguished themselves. The defenders were in a state of the utmost confusion and could not repel the attack. Narva was taken as by miracle.

Soon the knights asked peace and they were allowed to ride away with their wives. The Russian flag waved over Narva. The ikon of the Blessed Virgin was found in the ashes and at the Virgin's recovery of honour the fires in the city died down. The Russians captured 230 cannons and the wealth which the knights had left behind. It was recognised that the inhabitants were for the most part on the side of the Russians, and they were spared. Most of them willingly took an oath of allegiance to the Tsar.

Ivan was enchanted by the news. There was public thanksgiving in the cathedrals and feasting in the halls. The Metropolitan also was pleased and orders were given that Narva be purified from Latin and Lutheran taint, that a cathedral be built and that the little wonder-working ikon of the Blessed Virgin be placed in it.

The Grand Master was now willing to pay a huge indemnity and sent delegates to offer it in exchange for peace. But Ivan said he had conquered Narva and in-

tended to keep it. Peace could be obtained by the
Grand Master becoming the Tsar's vassal. Otherwise
Russia would capture and take over the whole of
Livonia.

Those terms were unacceptable, and so the war continued, its feature now being not so much spoliation as
the reduction of lesser fortresses and the enrolment of
the people as Russian subjects. The unfortunate Letts
and Germans were only too glad to take an oath of
allegiance and obtain personal safety. The Grand Master Furstenberg resigned in favour of an ambitious
young knight, Ketler, who sought assistance in every
country round about and obtained much sympathy and
little help.

Sigizmund Augustus was the most annoyed by the
Tsar's success. It was not either easy or prudent for
him to make war, but we can judge his sentiments by
the words he wrote in a letter to Queen Elizabeth:

"The Muscovite, puffed up in pride with those
things which he hath brought to the Narve, and made
more perfect in warlike affaires, with engines of warre
and shippes, will make asault this way on Christendome, to slay and make bound all that shall withstand
him: which God defend."*

The Emperor Charles, who might have given aid to
Ketler, had just made his great renunciation and gone
into retirement from the world. The Knights of the
Golden Fleece would not come to the aid of the Teu-
tonic Knights. No one came to help them. On the 18th
July, 1558, the great city of Dorpat surrendered to

* Hakluyt: *Navigations*, Vol. II.

Prince Peter Shuisky and his army. Eastern Livonia, almost the whole of what is now known as Esthonia, passed into Russian hands. The war went west through the autumn and through the winter of 1558–9, to the borders of Prussia, to the gates of Riga, with fire and sword and havoc indescribable.

In February, 1559, somewhat exaggerating, Prince Serebranny sent a message to the Tsar to say that Livonia was destroyed. The King of Denmark interceded on behalf of Livonia, and Ivan, menaced once again by the Khan of the Crimea, granted an armistice. The Tartars had entered Russian territory and Polish-Lithuanian land as well. There was some ground for an understanding between Sigizmund and Ivan. The positions were reversed. Whereas a few years previously Sigizmund had sought to make a treaty of permanent peace with Russia, now Russia sought a similar treaty with Poland. But Sigizmund said, "Give us back the city of Smolensk and we will make a treaty and go to fight the Moslem together."

Far from giving back Smolensk which the Russians had wrested from Poland in the previous century, Ivan thought still of winning Kief, Podolia, the Ukraine, traditionally Russian territory, languishing under the sovereignty of the Polish kings. The restitution of Smolensk was not a basis of argument. On the 16th September, 1559, Sigizmund Augustus entered the Livonian war by undertaking to protect the Teutonic Order and its possessions from Russia. He then, with great presumption, notified Ivan that he must evacuate Livonian territory and undertake no fresh invasion, as Livonia was under his protection.

Daniel Adashef had been sent against the Crimean Khan and, aided by Prince Vishnevetsky, obtained a series of resounding victories in the summer of 1559. But the campaign afforded Livonia a breathing space. The Russian army was much occupied. If not met and crushed, the Tartar Horde might still break through and sack Moscow. Tartars were, in any case, a greater menace than Poles or Livonians. The latter could never threaten the capital.

Ketler, however, believing that the Poles would mobilise against Russia, laid siege to Dorpat and other fortresses now in Russian hands. This brought the main Russian forces back with vengeful sword upon Livonia. Andrew Kurbsky and Daniel Adashef throughout the summer of 1560 chased the Teutonic Knights from castle to castle, laid waste the country, trampled the power of Livonia underfoot. Sigizmund Augustus did nothing to help the country he was supposed to be protecting. The sun shone on Russian arms. All went well. But then in July, the unanticipated happened. Fate struck a frightful blow at Ivan, a blow greater than any imaginable defeat in the field. The Tsaritsa Anastasia fell sick and died. This was a blow at his heart, at his faith, possibly a blow at his mind.

XVIII.

THE DEATH OF ANASTASIA

IVAN, after the conquest of Kazan, had shown himself less warlike. He let others do the fighting and did not expose himself personally to danger. It is true that the army had gained much self-confidence and did not need the inspiration of his presence. But it is rather surprising that the young monarch did not display a growing appetite for military glory. But then the campaign in Livonia was not holy war. There was not so much scope for a prince who fought by prayer. Christians were fighting Christians. The war was secular and selfish. It was merely a war for the extension of the temporal power and empire of Russia. It may be surmised that the Tsar who did not pretend to generalship would not have shone in Livonia. But in the various campaigns against the oncoming Tartar, Ivan had also remained passive. He had ridden out once or twice, as if to put himself at the head of his army, but he had never come in contact with the enemy. Intellectually and spiritually, he had been active. His was the will and inspiration behind Adashef, Sheremetief and the rest of his commanders. But for eight years he had lived a sheltered life.

The first reason is that Ivan was no soldier. The Tsar who did not much care for hunting, did not care for camp and the life of the field. No hot blood urged him to the fray. The second reason was caution. He was

protecting the future of the Tsaritsa and his heir. Since
the disillusionment during his illness in 1553 the Tsar
had been haunted by the fear that in the event of his
death, the boyars would set aside his son the Tsarevitch
Ivan and that Anastasia would be imprisoned in some
distant convent. It is true that he had bound his cousin
Vladimir Andreyevitch by an oath to support the Tsarevitch, but nevertheless it was not uncommon for man
to risk his eternal salvation for a throne. He trusted his
cousin, but if he died would not pressure be brought to
bear on him by the boyars that he should break his vow
and take the throne? Although the Tsar employed and
indeed honoured Alexey Adashef, he never forgot the
fact of his disaffection at the critical moment in 1553.
He still listened to the spiritual advice of the priest
Sylvester but he never forgot that he was no friend of
Anastasia. He could count on the devotion of the Metropolitan, but Makary was old and frail. Even with the
full authority of the Church the Metropolitan was no
guarantee for the future of wife and heir. The only
guarantee lay in the preservation of his own life and
person as a shield until the Tsarevitch Ivan reached
maturity.

It had been possible to make an end of all who had
shown themselves opposed to his line. But Anastasia
was opposed to violence and bloodshed at court. "Let
us fight the enemies of Russia, but not one another."
Ivan's forbearance, which shines like wisdom, was
largely due to her influence. Her pleasure lay in the relief of suffering and after every great victory in the
field she obtained the release of many prisoners as an
act of grace to God. For this the English traveller in

1558 could say of Ivan "I think no prince in Christendome is better beloved."

Ivan lived in grandeur in the Kremlin, never being seen but in magnificence of cloth of gold and gems, or flaming scarlet and sables. He behaved with immense dignity. He was not merely a piece of living tapestry. He received petitions from all and sundry and for the first time in Russian history the poorest man in the country could have access of some kind to the sovereign. He was vigorous in the Council of the Boyars. There was freedom in that Council to have a point of view other than his own. Upon occasion he was openly thwarted by Adashef but his anger was not kindled against him. Often he was guided by the wisdom of Adashef and took his advice, but in some instances, such as that of the war in Livonia, he insisted on his own judgment and Adashef bowed to it. He did not strike off heads like Henry the Eighth, nor burn people at the stake like Mary. Yet he was obeyed as none other, and if a man was told to go anywhere he ran. Men let their hair grow when they had incurred his displeasure and did not employ a barber until he smiled on them again.

Anthony Jenkinson, when he returned from his bold expedition to Bokhara, bringing him a present of "a white Cowes taile of Cathay," was used in the same style and dignity as when he had arrived.

In his religious exercises the Tsar showed the piety of an Edward the Confessor. And he was notably loyal to the Church and to the Metropolitan Makary. His reforms had not taken the form of spoliation which they threatened. His chief regard was that monks should be monks and pray, but not farmers and traders, out of which commercial and worldly interest had arisen much corruption of morals. He encouraged the silent witness of extreme asceticism. As for himself none was more rigorous in observing the many fasts. He gave alms abundantly and spent much on the building of churches. The cathedral which he had commanded to be built in the Great Square as a thank-offering and memorial for his victory over Kazan, rose in magnificence before his eyes. It was called the Cathedral of the Intercession of the Blessed Virgin. In six years from the digging of its foundations it was finished. No Vasilly Blazhenny, Vasilly the Fool, had yet come to revile him for his sins and steal the name of the cathedral for himself. There was nothing in Ivan's life with which either he or others could reproach him.

Moreover the wrath of God seemed to have been appeased. In 1553 the plague in Novgorod and Pskof was exorcised by prayer. God had taken the Tsarevitch Dimitry, but he had made restitution in the following year by granting the Tsarevitch Ivan. God had shown his mercy in repeatedly protecting Moscow from the invasion of the heathen. God had blessed the line of Ivan's succession by even granting him another son, Fedor, whom Anastasia bore him in 1558. Now if one son died yet the other might live. The fanatical desire that the succession might go to his children was perhaps derived from his fervent, almost superstitious, love and veneration for his dead father and mother. Like a reserved sacrament the self-pity of the orphan remained exalted in his being, with never failing votive lamps. God also had smiled on Ivan's doubtful war in the west, and by the intervention of the Blessed Virgin, Narva had been delivered into his hands.

But the war with Livonia was undertaken by the Tsar's will. Adashef, Sylvester, Kurbsky and many others were against it, and they never failed to suggest, if the Tsar caught a cold, or the Tsaritsa or the children were unwell, that it was God's punishment for an unholy enterprise. In November, 1559, Ivan and Anastasia went to the monastery at Mozhaisk to pray, but when they were about to return to Moscow the Tsaritsa became ill and Sylvester, who was with them, instead of turning to prayer, had the temerity to see again a sign of the displeasure of the Almighty. Adashef, who was in part responsible for the travelling arrangements of the Tsar, had, for once, lacked forethought. There was no medicine to hand and what was worse, there was no sleigh suitable for conveying a sick woman back to Moscow. What exactly was the matter with Anastasia no one knows. The suggestion that poison had been placed in her wine was an afterthought. But the Tsaritsa's condition was no mere indisposition. Anastasia was seriously ill and in need of immediate medical advice, warmth, care, the things that could not be had at the rigorous monastery at Mozhaisk in the midst of winter. The Tsar was terribly anxious, and also enraged. To the lack of care at the time when she fell ill was ascribed the progression of the malady from which, in the following year, she died.

It is curious that no details of the Tsaritsa's illness have come down to us, the more especially as, in after years, Kurbsky gave credence to the rumour that she had been poisoned. Doubtless the English doctor,

Standish, was brought in to consult—but of that nothing. The Tsar did not believe she had been poisoned. In November, 1559, she had the first attack. She made a partial recovery but in July, 1560, she had another and more severe attack of the same disease. Her condition was greatly aggravated by terror. A fire had broken out on the Arbat and, driven by a strong wind, spread with fury, threatening to devastate the whole city as in her wedding year. Smoke penetrated into the chamber where she lay. She could hear the roar of the fire, and the red glare of the conflagration came through her windows. She was in a hysterical state, past care of priest or physician. The Tsar did the best he could. He hurriedly removed her from danger, escorting her litter to his villa in the village of Kolemenskoe, near Moscow. Then he returned and worked with all his court for the extinction of the flames. In this he was successful, though not until after enormous havoc had been made.

He returned to the bedside of Anastasia, but he did not find her calmed. Possibly she was delirious and still imagined herself in the burning city. Neither priests nor doctors could mend her, nor, as we may imagine, the passionate and dreadful agony of prayer of her husband. On the 7th of August, at five in the morning, the Tsaritsa died.

The people of Moscow cried. The Tsar, without his crown, walked in the funeral procession, and groaned.

XIX.

THE FALL OF ADASHEF AND SYLVESTER

THE Tsar's character seemed to undergo a change after the death of Anastasia. Possibly it reverted to what it had been before his repentance and conversion in 1547. For thirteen years he had lived a godly and righteous life, the friend of the poor, the wisest ruler Russia had known. We left the "Terrible" setting fire to the vodka-soaked beards of the men of Pskof, and there has been a long interregnum of an angel. The devils of violence and lust were expelled from his soul, and Anastasia closed the door. Now the door was down and the devils rushed back, hungry and revengeful.

It is rightly judged in the Orthodox Church, that giving way to despair is one of the most baleful of sins. It is one of the most dangerous, a doubting of God's providence, a negation of faith, a rebellion against God's will. Of course, in a cynic, despair is only a great self-dissatisfaction and has not these implications. But Ivan was an implicit believer. He lived with God. He interpreted every event in the light of God's dealings with him. We do not know what the Tsar said in his despair. There is no chronicle of that. Did he revile an unjust God? Did he, like Job, curse the light of his life: "Let the day perish wherein I was born, and the night on which was said, there is a man-child conceived"?

We only know that at the burial, lest he do violence

to himself, he was supported by his brother Yury and his cousin Vladimir. And the Metropolitan reminded him that a Christian ought not to meet calamity with despair. The chief commentary on his state of mind is provided by the fact that after the funeral the Tsar gave way to drunken debauch and within a week held a mistress in his arms. "After the Tsaritsa's death, the Tsar began to be wild and very adulterous," wrote a scribe of the time.*

At first, of course, the court was all tears, condolence, gloom, long faces. But when the Tsar's new mood was realised the boyars put aside a grief which they little felt. Anastasia had been the friend of the common people of Moscow and they were sincerely moved by her end, but she was too pure and virtuous to please the court. And her family, the Zakharins, were upstarts in the eyes of princes of nobler birth. The Tsar remained angry with Adashef and Sylvester. The one he called a dog, the other a hypocrite. It was not difficult to whisper to Ivan in his drunken state, "They must have used sorcery to be able to inflict themselves on your Majesty for so many years."

During the illness of the Tsaritsa, the Tsar must have broken with Sylvester. The priest gave the Tsar his blessing and retired to a wilderness monastery some hundred miles from Moscow, near enough to be easily recalled when pardoned. Did he pray there for Anastasia's recovery? He had good need. If he prized the hold he had on the Tsar's conscience and will, it was certainly important that she recover. That he had once wished her ill, that he had favoured the setting aside of

* *Synodal Manuscripts* No. 364.

the first Tsarevitch in favour of Prince Vladimir Andreyevitch had not been forgotten by the Tsar. And
Sylvester had put himself in a trap by knowing too
much about God's wrath. If the Tsaritsa died, Sylvester had pre-certified it as God's punishment on the Tsar
for making war on Livonia. Anastasia did die, and the
priest was shorn and sent to the most distant and desolate of monasteries of the time, Solovetsk on the White
Sea, where meditating on his Master, he had leisure to
forget. Completely dead to the world, Sylvester's life
ceased to affect history, and the manner of his death is
unknown.

Ivan's profound mortification with Sylvester is expressed in one of his letters in which he says that he has
no desire to judge Sylvester *here*. The judgment will
be *there*, when their souls arrive together before the
"Divine Lamb."

Touching Alexey Adashef, the "dog," the man whom
he had raised from nothing to be in effect his Grand
Vizier, the chief administrator of Russia, the man who
drew up the new penal code, the man who made the
commercial treaty with England, the Tsar had less
scruple. There was a trial at which Adashef was not allowed to be present to defend himself. In the Council
of Boyars he proved to have few friends. The Metropolitan interceded for him as he had done for Sylvester,
but he was overruled. Ivan found he could dispense
with the wisdom and the authority of the Church.
Alexey Adashef was imprisoned in Dorpat. Two
months later he died, some say of a fever, others say he
was killed, again others say he took poison, in that way
indicating his guilt, his conscience would not let him

live. But it needed a robust constitution to survive for long in a sixteenth-century prison.

There is little doubt but that Alexey Adashef was a good-hearted and wise Russian. The greatness of monarchs is often due to their ability to find men of probity and genius to undertake the administration. The Tsar went back on his own youthful judgment when he attacked the career of Adashef with virulence. The success of his reign up to this point owes more to his sagacious use of Adashef than to any other circumstance. The anomaly in the favourite's career was his failure to stand by the Tsar in 1553 when he thought that Ivan was dying. He rose in the realm much as Wolsey in England rose under Henry VIII. And the psychological reason for his downfall had something in common with that of Wolsey. There was something more than good Latin in that phrase of Wolsey's *Ego et meus rex;* he had the temerity to own an allegiance other than to the sovereign who had raised him. Adashef thought it wiser to support Vladimir Andreyevitch. But that wisdom had o'erleaped gratitude and simple loyalty. It was a grievous wrong. It is not recorded that he ever asked pardon for it. Ivan waited and watched and used him, but the personal bond between them was broken.

For the rest, it is said that Adashef himself was kind and distributed a great alms. He kept ten lepers in his house and washed them with his own hands.

Having disposed of Adashef and Sylvester the Tsar thought it as well to exact a fresh oath of allegiance from all his nobles. The latter, rejoicing in the fall of the upstarts, probably did not fathom the Tsar's character, nor understand that he was merely beginning to carry out a long postponed revenge. He would be revenged on all those who had ranged themselves against the Tsaritsa in 1553, and on the representatives of those who had incurred the wrongs of his childhood.

The Tsar's rage fell first on the intimate circle of Alexey Adashef. His brother Daniel, hero of several fields, an intrepid soldier, was arrested and forthwith put to death. There was no reason, no charge. Probably the word "treason" was not even spoken. The Tsar's will did not require a reason. Daniel Adashef was killed and with him his little boy, aged twelve. It is not even recorded how they were murdered. The ferocity of the act is in greater contrast because of the mildness of Ivan during the previous thirteen years. Suddenly the pious Tsar, submissive to advice, temperate in government, committed a revolting violent crime. And he knew it was a crime, or to put it in his language "foul sin." As it were to make revenge on God, he went into grievous sin with his eyes wide open. Ivan was more intelligent than the head of the Church, Makary. Makary believed in witchcraft, sorcery, black magic and had the power, which he doubtless exercised, to send sorcerers to the stake. But Ivan did not at that time believe much in sorcery. He was well aware that Alexey Adashef had had no power over his mind except the power of his intelligence and spirituality. When he played chess with him Adashef raised no knights from the dead and contrived no spell to place his king in jeopardy. Also when Moscow was burned to the ground in 1547, he would not accept the Metropolitan's version that the fire was the work of sorcerers. Instead he

saw in it God's punishment for sin. It must be thought
that now, when he was under the influence of potent
meads, he merely allowed it to be said that certain
people were sorcerers. He gave the order for people to
be destroyed as an indemnity exacted from God for the
blow which had been struck at him.

One of the worst of his new "sins," was the murder
of Maria Magdalena and her five sons. Maria Magdalena was a widow, who upon the death of her husband
had renounced the flesh and entered upon a career of
self-imposed asceticism and holiness. She had loaded
her body with chains which had entered into her flesh.
By years of fasting and meditation and prayer, the old
lady had attained a degree of sanctity which had struck
the popular imagination, so that she was thought to
have miraculous healing power. She was naturally a
friend of the poor and the suffering, and that had appealed to Alexey Adashef. Perhaps under her influence,
he washed the lepers whom he kept in his house. She
was a well-known religious intimate of Adashef. So it
was whispered in the Tsar's ears that it was through her
dark arts that Alexey had obtained a power over his
mind. So he had her murdered, and her children too.

Ivan had begun to kill in families rather than in-
dividually. He dealt with the Adashef cousins and
brothers-in-law as Macbeth did with the family of
Macduff. But it was not a precaution lest surviving
children might be revenged for their parents' death; it
was motiveless ferocity. But when he killed a family
he took all their goods.

The dignified Tsar of the golden court, seen by
Chancelor, Jenkinson and the other English discover-

ers, had now changed to a strange burlesque figure who wore his great crown somewhat askew. He reeled about the palace after dinner, with new favourites of a new kind. There was no independent and sagacious Adashef, no dignified Sylvester raising his hand in the name of God. The new intimates of the Tsar whispered to him of desirable women, of getting married again. In an irresponsible vein Ivan declared that he would wed one of the sisters of his enemy, the King of Poland. The drunken whim became a set purpose. In his vanity, it seemed to him he had but to ask Sigizmund Augustus for the best of his sisters and the lady would be sent to him. He instructed his envoys to go and spy on the girls and see which was best worth having. There were two sisters, Anna and Catherine; the envoys should pick the plumper of the two. If either was over twenty-five years of age, that disqualified her. She must not be dried up, she must be healthy and be devoid of vices.

A strong lust possessed the Tsar, even invading his religious life. Now he omitted or forgot the fasts, and forgetting his own past rigour in this respect, he began to call the correctly pious boyars hypocrites. The honour of Russia seemed compromised by his behaviour. One night the guests were romping in the palace with masks on their faces. The Tsar, tipsy with mead, also had a mask on his face and he tried to put one on the face of the unwilling Prince Repnin. Repnin tore it from the Tsar's hands, threw it on the floor, stamped on it. "The sovereign can play the buffoon, but I at least as a boyar and a member of the Council, will not play the fool." Ivan in rage drove him from the palace. A few days later Repnin was murdered by the Tsar's orders. Kurbsky says that he was killed as he knelt in prayer at church. Kurbsky put most things in the worst possible light. In a letter the Tsar said that Repnin did not perish in church, but in any case he was killed for his remonstrance with the Tsar.

It may be said in extenuation that it was at this time the Tsar's intention to make another and a final repentance, to renounce his throne, be shorn as a monk and end his days at that stern Monastery of St. Cyril of Bielozersk, to which he banished so many of his subjects. The drunken justification which he made to himself was: "They killed my Anastasia," or, as he put it in a letter to Kurbsky: "Had they not separated me from my darling* there had not been so many victims." It is interesting that though changing in so much, he did not deny the happiness of his union with Anastasia. Though he intended to have a new bride at the earliest possible moment, the memory of the dead Tsaritsa was still hallowed in his soul. Though he dropped many of his prayers, the prayers for the soul of Anastasia were not forgotten, and he lavished a great alms in her name.

But the envoys had gone forth to spy upon the Polish sisters and it did not occur to Ivan that his presumption was impossible, that in fact it almost amounted to an insult. Sigizmund had hated and thwarted him ever since he took the title of Tsar. In effect, at this moment he was at war with Russia, since he had declared himself protector of Livonia and given the Russians notice to evacuate the Livonian lands. It is true that he had sent no troops to carry out his treaty with the Teu-

* *Yunitsa:* heifer.

tonic Knights. There had as yet been no clash between his forces and those of the Tsar, though it might occur at any moment on the Lithuanian border.

Doubtless King Sigizmund was astonished. But he did not say at once that such a union was unthinkable. Poles are never blunt in their refusals. Envoys came from Moscow to Warsaw to look at the king's sisters and choose. They chose Catherine who had in any case the bigger dowry. Sigizmund said he was not in principle opposed to the match, though he had rather that they had chosen Anna. Subject to the approval of the Emperor and to his sister remaining within the Roman Catholic communion, he granted his consent, or appeared to do so. Actually he intended nothing of the kind. He had decided to put the price of Catherine and peace too high. Marshal Simkovic was sent to Moscow bearing the king's terms for the union. The Tsar should relinquish to the crown of Poland and Lithuania the cities of Novgorod, Pskof, and Smolensk, and the territory bordering on Livonia.

Simkovic arrived in Moscow on the 6th February, 1561. He had a sheaf of proposals, one more annoying than the other. There was a story current, that Sigizmund instead of a bride sent Ivan a white mare. As Simkovic remained twelve days in Moscow it is not likely that his behaviour was in the least disrespectful. But the terms he offered involved a slight which Ivan did not pardon. Ivan dismissed the idea of a matrimonial alliance with Poland and decided upon war instead.

The Tsar appeared to be deeply chagrined. Although he had not seen Catherine, he had set his mind on

marrying her. His will did not brook being thwarted.
It is said he wrote to Sigizmund telling him that a
hole had been dug in the earth for his severed head.
Whether that be true or not, one can well imagine his
craving bloodshed to wipe out his humiliation. But the
court made light of the affair. Just as it had said "Anastasia was delightful, but there are others," so now it
pointed out that this Catherine was far from being
unique. The Poles made good wives, but there were in
his own dominions even better types, promising greater
delight in matrimony. The Circassian princes claimed
that their women were the most beautiful in the world
and the charms of the daughter of a rich Circassian
were canvassed with the Tsar. This young Mahometan
was brought to court and she lifted her veil that Ivan
might see what were her charms. It seems the Circassian
princes had not exaggerated the beauty of the daughter
of Temgryuk. The Tsar, for the ease of his conscience
and the comfort of his body, must have her in marriage. It was never without a sense of sin that he in-
dulged in unconsecrated fornication. His repentance
moods were violent, and despite his morbid resolve to
renounce the throne and become a monk, the difficulty
of asceticism in the matter of sexual indulgence was
great. It must have been for that reason that the Metropolitan, so soon after the death of Anastasia, had recommended him to take another spouse. But for the
Church, and the sense of sin, it would have been more
normal to have taken the Circassian as a concubine. For
she was a woman of no importance in the realm. As a
preparation for marriage, she was forthwith baptised,
but she brought no shade of Christian feeling or tradi-

tion to conjugal life. She was not fitted to be the step-mother of Ivan's children. She was illiterate and Asiatic and tribal and knew nothing of Russia. But the training and instinct of the women of polygamous tribes is to please men upon the marriage couch and they are, as it were, "raised for the table." The daughter of Tem-gryuk was primitive and passionate, and legend, which may do her wrong, says that she was very loose in her morals after she was wed. She was baptised into the Christian faith with the name of Maria and the wedding took place on the 21st August, 1561, four days before Ivan's thirty-first birthday.

Anthony Jenkinson, on his second expedition which he purposed into Persia, arrived at Moscow on the day before the marriage ceremony. To his surprise he received no honourable attention and the treatment of distinguished foreign visitors was very different from that he had experienced in 1557.

"His Highnesse having great affaires, and being at that present ready to be married unto a Ladie of Chir-cassi, of the Mahometicall law, commanded that no stranger, Ambassador, nor other, should come before him for a time, with further straight charge, that during the space of three dayes that the same solemn feast was celebrating, the gates of the citie should be shut, and that no person, stranger or native, certain of his household reserved, should come out of their houses during the said triumph, the cause thereof unto this day not being knowen."

So Jenkinson was not bidden to the marriage feast, nor was he called to the birthday rejoicings on the 25th of August. August passed without any attention.

Alexey Adashef was no longer in Moscow, taking charge of foreigners in his capable way. The atmosphere had changed. There was a new set of underlings, for all Adashef's friends and assistants had either been destroyed or banished. On the 6th September, Jenkinson received a general invitation to a state banquet, but a functionary of the court came to him and demanded from him the Queen's letters. He said he would deliver them personally into the hands of the Tsar. The official said he must have the letters, otherwise he would not be allowed to come to the banquet. Jenkinson was characteristically English. "In that case," said he, "I shall remain at my lodging." The banquet took place but Jenkinson was not there.

One of the boyars remarked to the Tsar that the Englishman had been bidden to the feast but had not come and Ivan must have been surprised. Next day Jenkinson caused a petition to be presented to the Tsar and he had his way, for he was commanded to appear and was thus able to deliver his letters personally. There is no doubt the Tsar thought highly of him for his refusal to be intimidated by an intermediary. Ivan had a profound respect for kings and queens as such, by God appointed, and believed that their personal envoys were entitled to behave with the greatest dignity. And Queen Elizabeth's letter was not only flattering to the Tsar, but showed the high esteem in which Jenkinson was held at court.

Since Jenkinson's first visit to Moscow, Queen Mary had died. The Virgin Queen was on the throne of England. It was perhaps surprising that she sent no presents to Ivan. Being of an economical disposition, Elizabeth had allowed the Russia Company to make up a chest of gifts for the Tsar and the Tsarevitch Ivan: "Either wine, cloth of golde, scarlet or plate." The company's gifts were at Jenkinson's discretion. It is possible that the gifts were presented in the Queen's name. Ivan was well pleased with them. It may be imagined, though it is not recorded, that the Tsar asked the English traveller many questions about Elizabeth, and especially regarding her matrimonial intentions. It could not be supposed that the Queen of England would long remain unmarried. It crossed the restless mind of the Tsar that he had missed a good opportunity. He might have married the Queen of England, as her predecessor had married the King of Spain. But it was not too late. Having surfeited himself with the Circassian he began to look round and make other plans. The heathen Tsaritsa had been commanded to be baptised. Constraint had been put upon her. She had been bribed by the prospect of royal marriage. There ought not to be difficulty in setting her aside. The matter would bear thinking over.

Jenkinson was kept in Moscow all the autumn and winter and was not allowed to depart on his mission into Persia. The Tsar was preoccupied and the underlings were successful in preventing Jenkinson being brought before his Majesty again. In despair of being granted passports, he decided to return to England. But it was far from Ivan's policy that he should return to the Queen and say that her recommendations had been ill-received. Ivan saw that he would have to allow him to proceed on his adventure into Persia. Therefore he called him to his presence and was most gracious,

IVAN THE TERRIBLE

From a painting by Vasnetsof.

asking him to dine with him in the presence of the ambassador of Persia. He received a cup of wine at the Tsar's own hands.

Ivan not only gave him strong letters of commendation but entrusted into his hands certain business of his own, for the most part the purchase of gems and silks. In using him thus personally, it is possible that he was testing the Englishman to see what measure of reliability he would have as his personal envoy touching another matter of greater delicacy.

In June, 1562, Jenkinson set off for Persia in the company of the ambassador of that country and made a perfectly successful journey. He established a foundation for English trading and he also accomplished the Tsar's errands. He returned to Moscow on the 20th August of the following year, and the Tsar was greatly pleased with him.

"I came before the Emperour's Majestie and presented unto him the apparel given unto me by the Sophie, whose highnesse conferred with me touching the prince's affairs, which he had committed to my charge; and my proceedings therein it pleased him so to accept, that they were much to his contentation, saying unto me, 'I have perceived your good service, for the which I do thank you, and will recompence you for the same,' wishing that I would travel again in such his other affairs, wherein he was minded to employ me."

When Anthony Jenkinson was ready to depart for London, he committed to him "our trustie and secret message, to be declared unto the Queene's Majestie herselfe, thy Mistresse, at thy coming home."

The Tsar of Russia had proposed himself to be the

husband of the Queen of England. Jenkinson profited by the occasion to ask for broader privileges for the Russia Company. In this, perhaps, he was a little unwise, staking the future of the company upon a favourable reply from Queen Elizabeth. When time passed and no answer came, the merchants and agents of the company felt the Tsar's displeasure.

XX.

THE TSAR BECOMES MORE MARTIAL

IN the summer of 1560 a large army, 60,000 horse and foot, with forty siege guns and fifty smaller cannon, was in the field. Fellin, a place of much strength, was taken and the ex-Grand Master, Fursten-berg, was taken prisoner and sent captive to Ivan. The Tsar extended to him the clemency he reserved for fallen monarchs, gave him an estate in Kostroma and allowed him to end his days in peace.

In 1561, when the project of a marriage between Ivan and Catherine fell to the ground, Sigizmund Augustus did, in a half-hearted fashion, send troops to the defence of Livonia. As the Teutonic Knights had been worsted everywhere, it may be presumed that his real intention was to snatch a slice of the territory of a moribund power. Sweden by consent had taken Reval. The Grand Master Ketler had made public renuncia-tion of his office. The partition of Livonia among neighbouring powers became certain. On the 28th No-vember, 1561, Sigizmund Augustus had himself pro-claimed sovereign of Livonia and Ketler agreed to be-come his vassal. To complete the answer to the Tsar's proposal of marriage, Sigizmund Augustus arranged a matrimonial alliance with Sweden. Catherine was af-fianced to John, Duke of Finland and heir to the Swed-ish throne, and, in 1562, they were married. Poland through the centuries has always wished to be a mari-time power, and this dynastic splice with Sweden did seem to assure an outlet to the Baltic. But such pretensions required the guarantee of physical force. Ivan waited no longer. He notified his commanders that he was at war with Lithuania. The war was with Lithuania rather than with Poland. It was a war with the Grand Duke of Lithuania, not with the King of Poland, though they were the same person.

Ivan resolved to be revenged in person for the affront done him by Sigizmund Augustus in making a union with his sister Catherine impossible. That Lithuanian troops had entered Livonia and taken over territory in the name of the new sovereign did not mean so much to Ivan as the personal affront. He mobilised one of the largest armies he ever put into the field. It was estimated at 280,000 men, though the figure must have been exaggerated by the inclusion of a large number of camp followers.

Ivan had got rid of some of his best generals. Daniel Adashef was dead. Prince Michael Vorotinsky had been banished with his family to Bielozersk. Prince Dimitry Kurliatev and his family had been destroyed. All these had been removed because of their intimacy with Alexey Adashef. They were a serious loss to the state and to the army. Apart from his cousin, Vladimir Andreyevitch, whom he had as yet spared, the staff of the new army was largely Asiatic. As if under the influence of his new wife, Ivan was attended in great honour by exalted Tartars and Circassians, converted and unconverted, Shig Ali, Ibak, Tokhtamish, Bekbulat, Kaibula, but he had the aid and advice of Princes Ivan Mstislavsky and Peter Shuisky, who had been in command of the army in Livonia for some years. Ivan

Sheremetief had not yet been thrown into prison; Kurbsky had not yet fled, and these also were to be found serving under Ivan in this great army.

With his immense host, half of which was Eastern, he moved forward upon Lithuania, like one of the great khans. Sigizmund Augustus had never imagined that the Tsar with such an army would take the field, and, indeed, did not believe that the force was so great. He ordered his kinsman Radziwill to go forward with 40,000 men mobilised at Minsk, but Radziwill took fright when he came in view of the Russian horde. The Lithuanians in terrorised mobs fled before Ivan. On the 31st January, 1563, the army reached the walls of the great trading city of Polotsk. On the 7th February, it stormed the outer forts. On the 15th it took the city. Ivan added another title to his name and called himself Grand Duke of Polotsk.

The Lithuanians had made but a feeble defence of their city. The Russians had not become sufficiently enraged to put the inhabitants to the sword. But they looted the place as they had in years past looted Kazan. The plunder was immense. The Tsar confiscated the treasury and also the goods of the richest citizens. Large quantities of silver and gold were sent to Moscow. There was a large Jewish population which gave more trouble to marauders than the Tartar merchants had done in Kazan. The Tsar ordered them all to be forcibly christened, and those who resisted were to be drowned in the river. The Latin churches were rased to the ground or re-consecrated. Orthodox shrines were set up. The Tartar soldiers murdered several of the Roman Catholic monks.

The Tsar sent his brother-in-law, Michael Tem-gryuk, who had evidently been converted along with his sister, as a personal courier, bringing tidings of victory to the Tsaritsa and carrying a jewelled cross to the Metropolitan. Ivan was well pleased with himself. What he had achieved at Kazan in 1552 he had repeated eleven years later at Polotsk. And it must be thought he had less resort to prayer. Under Mahometan influence he was striking more and praying rather less. Still, he must be fighting God's battles even when proceeding against his fellow Christians. Hence probably the onslaught on the Jews. But it must have been difficult to disguise the fact that this was a most unholy war. It was a war of personal revenge, a war of aggression and spite. Polotsk was a place of great strength; if he could take Polotsk he could presumably conquer the whole of Lithuania. He was pleased because he had demonstrated to Sigizmund Augustus that he was a greater and more powerful monarch than he. Now Sigizmund could have peace upon condition of the cession of the whole of Livonia and of the body of Catherine. "But Catherine is married to the Duke of Finland." "That is nothing to us." The Tsar would hold her as a hostage, but with complete respect to her person.

The army of Polotsk, encountering feeble opposition, overran the country, threatening the cities of Vilna and Mstislavl, destroying the farms and the villages and collecting an enormous booty. Sigizmund Augustus, though he has the reputation of being one of the best of Poland's kings, was not warlike. He did not head an army and go to make a personal reckoning with the vainglorious Tsar. He had heard that a sumptuous coffin had been made for him in Moscow and brought to Polotsk if he liked to come and inhabit it. He decided to keep his distance from the inside of a coffin. He was greatly frightened, and sent to the Crimean Khan asking him to take the opportunity to lead his Tartars upon undefended Moscow. For a Christian king to make such a proposal to the heathen was a strange development. The Khan promised, but it was difficult to lead his wild horsemen over the snowy steppes and he did not move. Fortunately for Sigizmund and Lithuania the Tsar was restless. His martial mood passed. The capture of Polotsk had satisfied him. Instead of seizing the opportunity of annexing the greater part of Lithuania he decided to return to the comfort and carouse of Moscow. He ordered the inhabitants of Polotsk to be revised and the dangerous people to be driven out, the remainder to be disarmed. He ordered up-to-date fortifications to be built with all speed. He left a garrison in the city under the control of Peter Shuisky, Vasilly and Peter Serebranny and then granted Sigizmund Augustus an armistice while terms of peace might be discussed. That was a great relief to the Polish king, who promised to send envoys to Moscow to treat and at the same time kept urging the Tartars to move. The Tsar then set his face towards Moscow to receive the acclamations of his people for the victory and to obtain the customary blessing of the Church. He returned to drink and to go a degree more mad and cruel.

XXI.

THE TURN TO GREATER VIOLENCE

THE unreasonableness of the Tsar's behaviour suggests some mental disease, possibly some syphilitic infection of the brain. It must have been difficult to foresee where he would strike. We have decided that he had determined to be revenged on the faction which, in 1553, had refused to take the oath of allegiance to the late Tsarevitch Dimitry, but in fact his behaviour after the death of Anastasia was not so logical. He took his cousin, Vladimir Andreye-vitch, with him to the war in Lithuania, holding him in high honour. Upon victory, he even sent a special message to Prince Vladimir's mother, the ambitious Princess Euphrosyne. She was living on her estate at Staritsa and must have felt she might return to favour when her son, with a large retinue, was allowed to go to her to celebrate the return from victory. But it was not long afterwards that the Tsar forced her to become a nun and she was banished to Bielozersk and then by his orders drowned in the lake there.

Ivan enjoyed a popular triumph in the streets of Moscow. He must have wished to have repeated the theatrical moment of his return from the conquest of Kazan. The Circassian Tsaritsa, as if in imitation of Anastasia, had given birth to a son in his absence. But the return had not the grandeur of the return from Kazan. For the capture of Polotsk was not a victory for Christendom; it was only a victory for Russia. But there was a greater orgy of feasting and merrymaking.

One of the most cruel and unreasonable acts of the Tsar was the arrest of Prince Ivan Sheremetief, a hero in battle and a good friend of Ivan's, having stood by him in 1553, a religious man, of virtuous life. He was thrown into a foul dungeon and tortured, though without any expressed charge that has come down to us. Later, he was banished to Kirilof. An order went forth to seize his wealth, but nothing could be found, because he had already given it to the poor. The Tsar himself, in a cold-blooded and shameless way, had himself admitted to the cell where Sheremetief was chained. Was it to show the soldier prince that the Tsar was everything and he was nothing? All that we know of the conversation is the question: "Where hast thou hidden thy wealth?"

The year 1563 was one of death. Towards the end of April the new baby, the Tsarevitch Vasilly died, having lived only five weeks. This year the Metropolitan Makary also passed away, and another link with the past was broken. For some time Makary had wished to take refuge from the court which he saw going wrong. He felt he was too old to reprove the Tsar for his sins. Some younger, more vigorous Metropolitan was needed to curb the vices of the time. He wished to go to the wilderness and live his last years as a rigorous ascetic, but always he had been persuaded to remain, and now at last he was called from the scene where he had been such a notable figure. There is no doubt that in his time the Metropolitan had been wise and had exerted a very beneficial influence upon Ivan, but for several years he had been senile and incapable of much action beyond the repetition of prayer.

This year also, the Tsar's younger brother Yury fell sick and died. There was a state funeral in the Kremlin and Ivan seemed much moved. Yury had been an affectionate brother. He had not stood in Ivan's way, being neither ambitious nor intelligent, and he had been a close and loyal friend of the Tsaritsa Anastasia. And his wife Ulyana was a very good woman, by repute, another Anastasia. She voluntarily entered a convent after her husband's death, but the Tsar had her cell filled with luxury, as if to deny her the sacrifice of the things of this world. The simple sister of mercy shall have a court and retinue even though she inhabit a cell in a convent. Ulyana had the mild stubbornness of a *religieuse*, but in opposing the Tsar's lavishness of affection, she aroused his rage, which had become instant and ungovernable. Ivan killed her.

Prince Vladimir Andreyevitch was charged with "unrighteous." The word *nepravda* was used; perhaps it could be construed "falseness." In this charge was included his mother Euphrosyne. On the intercession of a great number of people Prince Vladimir was pardoned. But he was forced to live on his estates at Staritsa and the personnel of his retinue was changed so that Ivan might have trustworthy information regarding his doings and intentions. With queer inconsistency the Tsar treated him with affection, even while he was having him watched and even rode out to Staritsa to carouse with him upon occasion.

Ivan at this time carried about with him a long

wooden staff with a steel point. It was a stout wand about four feet long, a heavy spear the top of whose shaft was a carved handle. The Tsar developed a habit of striking people with this staff, sometimes killing them. No one could calculate in advance his favour or his rage. He began to be possessed by murderous whims. In the year 1563 began the great dread of him which earned for him the name of "Terrible." For neither the new marriage, nor victory in the field had mellowed him. As he had begun after the death of Anastasia, so, it was clear, he would continue, getting possibly worse. Men fled from his service. The cause of Christendom was sullied by him and therefore the crusading Vishnevetsky returned to his own country and made his submission to Sigizmund Augustus. The King of Poland was ready to pardon him, but he must now serve in the army of Lithuania and fight against the Russians, erstwhile his friends in arms. Being a man of honour he could not do that. And Sigizmund of Poland, not being a man of honour, had him sent, a prisoner, to the Sultan of Turkey, who had him cruelly put to death.

The Cherkassky princes, Alexey and Gabriel, fled into enemy country. It is evident that a number of Russians deserted Russia to enter the service of Poland. The greatest of the refugees was Prince Andrew Kurbsky, who had been an intimate friend of the Tsar from childhood days. He went to Volmar and joined the Polish army. From a place of safety he wrote a letter to the Tsar. It is said that Ivan, receiving the message, leaned with his staff upon the messenger's foot and transfixed it to the earth as he stood before him. Then

he ordered the messenger to read the letter to him. It
ran:

"To a once serene majesty, made famous by God,
but now darkened by your sins, by the infernal hate in
your heart, diseased in conscience. To the tyrant, unex-
ampled among the most unfaithful Lords of the world,
heed these words! In the confusion of grief in which I
am now, I can say little, but it will be true. Why dost
thou bring torment upon the strong men of Israel, the
glorious leaders of war given thee by the Almighty,
shedding their holy, victory-bringing blood in the
Churches of God? Did they not burn with ardour for
their Tsar and fatherland? By slanderous invention
thou hast found the loyal to be traitorous, Christians to
be sorcerers, light to be darkness and sweetness bitter.
Was it not by these men that the yoke of the Tartars
was broken? Was it not they who took the German
fortresses to the honour of thy name? And our reward
is destruction. Dost think that thou art immortal? Is
there not a God and a court of judgment of the Highest upon a tsar? In my confusion of heart I cannot say
all the wrong thou hast done me. I will say but one
thing: thou hast deprived me of holy Russia. My
wounds suffered for thy sake cry out to God. He sees
the heart. I have examined my conscience, my actions,
my secret thoughts and I do not discover that I have
transgressed against thee. I have led thy regiments and
never shown my back to the enemy. My glory has been
thine. It is not for a mere twelvemonth or two years
that I have served thee, but for many years, in hardship
and bold enterprise, not seeing my mother, deprived of
my wife, far from my dear country. Count the battles,
count my wounds! I don't boast; God knows all about
it. To him I commend myself in the hope of the inter-

cession of the Saints and of my ancestor, Prince Fedor Yaroslavsky.

"We have parted from thee for ever and thou wilt not see my face again until the Dreadful Judgment. But the tears of the innocent are preparing execution for the torturer. Beware of the dead, those killed by thee; for they stand around the throne of the Almighty demanding revenge. Thy army cannot save thee, nor can the words of flatterers render thee immortal. The unworthy boyars, those who are now the companions of thy effeminacy and debauch, who bring thee their children for thy lust, cannot save thee.

"Let this letter, wet with my tears, be buried with thee, that thou mayest appear with it at the judgment of God. Amen. Written at Volmar in the domain of King Sigizmund, *my* sovereign, from whom, by God's help, I hope to obtain pardon and consolation in my misfortunes."

The Tsar, having heard the letter read, coldly ordered the messenger to be taken away and tortured, that he might give further information.

The servant proved staunch and the Tsar's anger fled. He found the letter interesting. It was as if Kurbsky had developed an extremely aggressive and unexpected attack in a game of chess. Ivan gave the opening considerable thought before he replied. He was in his way deeper than Kurbsky. Despite all that Kurbsky wrote to the Tsar and about the Tsar, he never understood his springs of action, the psychology behind the history. His writings have become a sacred museum piece, the greatest source for the study of Ivan's reign. And yet, following him implicitly, the historian may go wrong. Ivan replied:

"Unfortunate one, why dost thou damn thy soul by treason? Why save thy perishable body by flight? If thou art true and virtuous, why wish to avoid death at my hands and a martyr's crown? What is life, wealth or the glory of this world? Vanity and vexation of spirit when death brings the soul's salvation. Take lesson from thy messenger who would not betray his master under torture, even at the gates of death, and be ashamed, seeing that thou hast fled at one angry word from me, burdening thy soul and the souls of thy ancestors with treason. For they took an oath of allegiance to my grandfather, not only for themselves but for their descendants."

Ivan's reply was long because he went over the military career of Prince Kurbsky and pointed out to him in detail that it had not been so glorious as he seemed to be imagining. Kurbsky was feasting when the Khan was turned to flight and let him get safely away. With an army of 15,000 at a later date he failed to beat a mere 4,000 Lithuanians. In the taking of Astrakhan he had no part. . . . "Your grace never saw the city. . . . When God gave Kazan into our hands, what did you do? You robbed. . . . You malingered at Pskof . . . but for the refractoriness of you and Alexey Adashef, the whole of Livonia would now be in our hands. . . . You say you shed blood; well, we shed sweat and tears because of your insubordination."

As for his cruelties, the Tsar denied them flatly. The sovereigns of Russia had never been called to account, whether they pardoned or executed their subjects. . . .

"So it was, so it will be. I am no longer a child. My spiritual needs are supplied by God's grace, the Im-

maculate Virgin Mary and the Holy Interceders. Instruction from men I do not ask. Thanks to the All-
Highest, Russia is prosperous. My boyars live in peace
and love. Alone thy friends intrigue and make mis-
chief. Thou threatenest me with Christ's judgment on
high, but is not God's power manifested on earth?
That is the Manichean heresy! You think God is only
to be found in heaven and the devil in hell. No, no,
God's sovereignty is everywhere, in this life as in the
life to come. You wish to surround the heavenly throne
with my victims . . . another heresy. As the apostle
hath said, 'No man hath seen God.' When thou askest
me to bury thy letter with my body, I inquire, hast
thou lost the last spark of Christianity? For a Christian should die in love and charity to his neighbours
and not in spite.

"Finally as a crowning treason thou callest the town
of Volmar a domain of King Sigizmund, hoping for
favour from him and renouncing the sovereign given
thee by God. Thou has chosen a better sovereign! Thy
great sovereign is a slave of slaves: is it surprising that
slaves praise him? But I say no more. Solomon tells us
not to waste words on fools and certainly thou art one."

Kurbsky became at once an active adviser of Sigizmund Augustus and was rewarded with an estate at
Kovel in Poland. To betray one's country even when it
is governed by a tyrant is hard of defence. One must
suppose that Kurbsky hoped the Tsar would soon be
removed by some revengeful hand, in which event he
might be able to return. But in aiding and abetting an
inroad of the Tartars he was not only untrue to his
sovereign but to his Church and the traditions of his
religion. The Khan moved at last and laid siege to

Riazan, but the city was stoutly defended and he retired discomfited. Kurbsky and the other Russian deserters were enrolled in the Polish-Lithuanian army and moved under Radziwill to recapture Polotsk, but they also failed. The Tsar's armies fought well despite the barbarity of their ruler. It was clear that the flight of Kurbsky had not shaken the throne. Ivan had the chance, could he have taken it, to start afresh, wiser, more balanced and more mature, but he could not arrest his mental and moral deterioration.

Ivan's distrustful nature brooded on the disaffection of Kurbsky. His uneasiness was not allayed by victories in the field. He bit his lip as he looked over the boyars, his golden court ranged in front of him in the palace at dinner. He listened to conversations. He received tale bringers and encouraged them with rewards. He chose to believe that there was a widespread conspiracy against him and could not obtain enough information about it because there was no conspiracy. Many were arrested and tortured, but put to the question they gave nothing away, because they knew nothing. Since Kurbsky's reproof, Ivan seemed to crave more blood, as it were, to send him a better answer than that in which he cited Holy Writ. The new Metropolitan Afanasy, brought from the Chudof Monastery, was spiritless. Or perhaps in the Kremlin atmosphere he was out of his depth. He had no more initiative than a court chaplain and was far from rebuking the Tsar. Ivan's new favourites, Alexey Basmanof, Michael Saltikof, Afanasy Viazemsky, Ivan Chibotovy, were toadies who applauded vice and encouraged cruelty and lust.

In December, 1564, the Tsar decided upon an extraordinary action which in a way prefigures the strangeness of the latter part of his reign. He quit the city and went wandering off into the unknown, without fixed destination, leaving his route to the "guidance of God." Early in the morning of the 3rd December a great number of sleighs with horses and drivers assembled on the snow of the Kremlin square. There was a farewell service in the Cathedral of the Assumption. Those boyars who were up and out looked on in astonishment, for they had heard nothing in advance. The Metropolitan Afanasy gave his blessing, but he also was ignorant of the Tsar's intention. Workmen were busy removing the gold and silver and precious stones from the palace to waiting sledges. That must have been the most surprising feature. The Tsar and the Tsaritsa and the two sons got into sleighs. The court favourites got into their sleighs. The Tsar's secretariat got into sleighs and with them a number of other functionaries. And then they drove off leaving no address.

Merchants and princes had kissed the Tsar's hand as he left, but as they watched the cavalry escort and the sleigh horses gallop away they were filled with misgiving. The strange departure seemed to bode ill for the future, for Moscow and for them. But mere misgiving changed to panic when the city received the first messages from the Tsar upon his journey. "Unable to brook the treachery by which I was surrounded, I have forsaken the state and taken my way whither God shall direct."

It was not that the people of Moscow apprehended punishment; the Tsar said nothing of that, but merely that he was tired of them and had left them, like a rebellious husband who flees from wife and home. God's anointed had taken his blessing, such as it was, away from them. "What shall we do now that our lord and master has abandoned us?" cried the common people. Trade for a time was paralysed; shops did not open; houses remained shuttered. The common people invaded the Kremlin, asking for victims as they had done after the great fire. Let them but know which of the boyars had incurred the Tsar's displeasure, they would make short work of him.

Some such consternation must take place in a hive of bees when the sovereign is lost. The people swarmed out of their houses breathing danger and alarm.

The Metropolitan Afanasy consulted with the boyars. Something must be done. At first it was mooted that the Metropolitan himself should pilgrimage to the Tsar and beseech him to return. But Afanasy, by himself, had neither the strength of character nor the necessary moral authority to make much impression on the sovereign's will. Instead the bishops constituted themselves a delegation in the city's name. They set off to humble themselves in the snow before the Tsar, and there followed them Princes Ivan Dimitrievitch Bielsky and Ivan Mstislavsky, all the boyars, courtiers, lesser nobles and court officials. No one dare remain behind.

Meanwhile the Tsar had finally set up house in a little town north-west of Vladimir, a hundred miles from Moscow, Alexandrof, generally called the Alexandrovskaya Sloboda, certainly the most curious place

for God to have indicated to him as a refuge. On the
5th of January, 1565, the column of repentance and
sorrow reached him there. And all implored him to
come back, appealing chiefly to his known piety. He
could abandon the court, but how could he abandon
the sacred temples of the capital, the relics of the
saints. "Remember!" said the bishops, "thou art not
only the guardian of the state but of the Church. In
thy absence who will preserve our faith in truth and
purity? Who will save millions of souls from eternal
destruction?"

The pinning of men's salvation upon a tsar as if he
were the Christ was certainly slavish, but it was calcu-
lated flattery. All knelt: the Tsar alone stood. He enjoyed the dangerous tableau of absolute power. They
had not only implored him to take back the material
power over their bodies and estates but had implied
jurisdiction over their souls, even to damnation. Ivan
harangued them at length, showing himself as erudite
as the young Henry the Eighth when he earned the
title of Defender of the Faith. But that harangue was
but a verbose preamble to the declaration of his real
purpose.

"Nevertheless," said he, "for the sake of Father
Afanasy, for your sakes, pilgrim archbishops and bishops, I do agree to take back the throne, but on the following conditions: I shall be free to execute which
traitors I desire, free to visit with my displeasure, be it
by death, arrest, the confiscation of estate, without in-
curring any anathema or demur on the part of the
clergy."

The petitioners welcomed this with joyful tears. "Do anything with us, but come back!" was the tenor of their reply. Ivan admired their humble spirit and, smiling, begged that most of them would remain and celebrate Epiphany with him at Alexandrof.

XXII.

THE STUDY OF REVENGE

If this part, gentles, do like you well,
The second part shall greater murders tell.

ON the 2nd of February, 1565, the Tsar re-en-
tered the capital which he had abandoned two
months before, while thousands of people on
their knees in the snow wept for joy that he had been
vouchsafed to them again. And yet, stealing a glance
at the divine face, they saw there strange disorder. The
stately young Tsar, as yet only thirty-four years of age,
was grey-faced, dishevelled and bent. In plucking the
hairs from his beard in his rages he had given himself a
look of mania. What was left of his beard was un-
combed and awry. And much of the hair from his head
seemed also to have fallen out. His gaze was fixed in a
deliberate squint; he seemed to see no one of all those
who welcomed him back. In his furrowed brow brooded
the pent-up unsatisfied resolve of murderous revenge.
Ill-kempt, uncared for, distraction in his aspect, his distrustful mouth twisted as in pain or nervous determination to be revenged, he made his strange entry into the
city, with all the church bells ringing as the sleighs in
slow procession moved over the frozen snow.

Upon arriving at the Kremlin the Tsar made several
announcements. First he would not live any longer in
the Kremlin and a new fortified house should be built
for him with all speed in the midst of the city, among
the townsmen's dwellings, between the Arbat and Ni-

kitskaya. He re-enumerated the faults of the boyars and obtained confirmation from the Church of immunity from criticism in the measures he intended to take against those who had incurred his displeasure. Then he signified his intention of selecting a thousand of the gentry to be his personal bodyguard. This band would be called the *Opritchina*, a name which he had himself coined. It had not been heard before in Russia and certainly was intended to express something new. Certain streets in Moscow were designated as the dwelling places of the *Opritchina* and the inhabitants of these streets would have to move elsewhere. At the same time the Tsar's secretaries produced an elaborate scheme of disinheritance and redistribution of estates, wealth, and revenue.

This scheme was a development of the Tsar's earlier ideas expressed through Alexey Adashef in the new penal code of 1550. In effect it was intended to replace the great barons and the appanaged princes by the *Opritchina*. It envisaged an autocracy supported by paid servants instead of an autocracy encumbered by the independence of a wealthy and powerful nobility. The *Opritchina*, like a depraved Jesuitry, guaranteed in advance by the Church of God's pardon for all crimes committed in the Tsar's name, should place their conscience at the disposal of Ivan, being otherwise paid a salary for their services.

The boyars who were not included in the *Opritchina* were to be called the *Zemschina*. The duties of the first related personally to the Tsar; the duties of the second were civil and administrative and may be said to relate more particularly to the State as apart from the court.

One of the first actions was for the Tsar to take 100,-
000 roubles from the treasury of the *Zemschina* for
the expenses at Alexandrof. Together with the Tsar's
growth of cruelty there was an increase in his avarice,
which, owing to the ferocity of the former, is sometimes overlooked. The confiscation of personal effects
gave an added pleasure to execution.

He had arrived on the 2nd February; on the 4th the
executions commenced. Kurbsky's wife and family
were destroyed. The famous general of the Kazan
campaign, Prince Alexander Gorbatof-Shuisky was
executed. With him to execution went his son Peter,
aged seventeen. There was a pitiful scene in the Red
Square. The son was to be beheaded first, but the father
could not bear the anguish of seeing his son die. He was
permitted to go first to the block. Then when the head
rolled off the son picked it up and kissed the dead face
before submitting himself to the executioners.

Several other boyars died the same day and Prince
Dimitry Sheviref met a dreadful end, impaled on a
stake in his rectum. The wretched man, all day a-dy-
ing, fervently prayed to his Redeemer till the end. One
of those who was beheaded was Prince Peter Gorensky,
caught on horseback leaving the city. The only reason
vouchsafed for these executions was that the victims
had been sympathisers with Kurbsky, but of some that
could not in justice be said. Few of those who perished
had been intimately associated with the fugitive prince
or dreamed of following his example and fleeing the
country.

The general punishment of this bloody day was not
confined to executions. Many who escaped the block

were banished to distant parts. Bail amounting in some cases to as much as 25,000 roubles was taken from others as a guarantee that they would not flee the country.

There were, however, some pardons. The heroic soldier, Prince Michael Vorotinsky, who had been banished to Bielozersk, was brought back to Moscow. Yakovlief, a near relative of the late Tsaritsa Anastasia, had been condemned, but at the last moment, on the appeal of the clergy, was reprieved.

In this way a great reign of terror was inaugurated. The next deed was the enrolment of the *Opritchina*. Seated with his favourites, Basmanof, Viazemsky, Skuratof, the Tsar developed his scheme. For preference the wilder and younger of the children of the boyars were chosen for the new bodyguard. A special oath was contrived for them. They should know neither father nor mother, only their Tsar. They should keep themselves to themselves and not frequent the houses of the *Zemschina*, not even those of the merchants. Actually the Tsar enrolled not 1,000 but 6,000. And they were given fixed places of residence, free of rent or price, and to each there was a small revenue attached. Some 12,000 people were rendered homeless to make room for them. These new guards of the *Opritchina*, being for the most part younger sons, had been poor, but at a stroke of the pen now became comparatively rich. And seeing the power vested in them, they at once began to oppress their neighbours to embellish their houses and estates. For they were outside the law and could not be called to account for any of their actions. They had power to inflict fines for misdemeanours and flog a man publicly till he paid what they demanded of him.

The Tsar's imperial guard of 6,000 bandits thereupon set forth to terrorise the country. They were the hounds of the Tsar and the rest of his subjects were their prey, in sign whereof some of them wore upon occasion dog's-head masks. One cannot quite believe that the whole 6,000 habitually went about in dogs' heads and carried a broom at their saddle bows, though that is indicated by some historians.

Ivan having forged this fearsome instrument of destruction, plunged once more into repentance and prayer. But it is characteristic of his religiosity that he did not undo the evil which he had done. He let the evil thing go on, like an inquisitor who repents while his victim is burning alive but will not move away the fire. The period of debauch following upon the death of Anastasia was now followed by a period of fanatical gloom. The piety of Ivan's earlier years under the influence of Sylvester had been brighter. Now his reason was darkened by the shadow of a demon across it. He writhed in an agony of repentance and prayer, but must go on torturing God.

Distrust also had grown. In Moscow he was possessed by a frenzy of fear, the only escape from which was in violent action. He heard the death watch in the Kremlin. A meteor flaming across the sky suddenly seared all hope in his being. No man has ever been more nervous about comets. He became possessed of a hypochondriac restlessness. The new house in Moscow, strongly fortified and guarded as it was, gave him no sense of security. Behind every wall of the capital lurked an assassin. At least he fancied so and it is surprising if no one was thinking of removing him. But the Russians, passive to Fate, have ever proved pitifully incapable of assassinating those who oppressed them. The belligerent, cruel, vigorous Ivan was safer than an idealist would have been. For slaves and Slavs require a tyrant to rule over them.

One of the anomalies of Ivan's character was that he had both boldness and panic fear. He lurked about his palace, craven, walking on tiptoe, but he could break forth at the head of an army or the *Opritchina* to slay thousands. His political measures, the establishment of the *Opritchina* itself, show a bold spirit. What exactly he was up to in Alexandrof when he pulled the hair out of his head and beard in handfuls no one knows. One must surmise a battlefield of Good and Evil, where Evil triumphed and the good in him was dreadfully murdered. In Moscow he would not sleep near the revered bones of his ancestors because his soul had become unclean. Hence the house in the city. But he could not find rest there either. He must hie him back to the battlefield of Alexandrof where his soul was lost, to see if he could find it again.

In the Church of the Mother of God in Alexandrof he had a cross made on every brick. He adorned its altar with gold and rubies. About his house there he had a fosse dug across which demons could not spring, and a steep slippery rampart up which they could not climb. He called the place his Freedom and the military post outside the town where all visitors were challenged was called Unfreedom. Certain streets in the town were devoted entirely to the bodyguard and houses of stone were built there. New churches and shrines sprang into being. The obscure little settlement, surrounded by dense forests, put on unwonted grandeur and swarmed with armed men. It was like some fairy-tale city which wanderers find after being lost in track-less woods. And it was ruled over by prince stranger than folklore e'er invented. In fantastic piety the Tsar decided to make his palace there into a monastery and the members of the *Opritchina* into monks. He himself would be the abbot of this strange monastery. There were three hundred men of the *Opritchina* and they all became monks wearing black cassocks over sable neck-lets and cloth of gold.

The Tsaritsa?—the fact that the abbot had a wife and was living in sin was ignored. And yet the monastic life was not make-believe. The Tsar himself drew up the monastic rules for the new order and was an ex-ample himself in keeping them. At four in the morning, with the Tsarevitch Ivan and his younger son, he went himself to ring the bell to call the brethren to early matins. Woe betide the sluggard or the late-comer! The service lasted to six or seven and the Tsar pros-trated himself so repeatedly and with such fervour that sometimes his brow would be marked with blood from beating the floor so many times. From eight till ten came matins proper and then the brotherhood would sit down to breakfast. But in that meal Ivan did not take part; as if conscious of being more sinful than the rest, he remained standing in the presence of the soldier-monks, reading aloud a religious homily. What was left over from this meal was taken out and given to the beggars. After that the Tsar would partake of luncheon alone. In the afternoons, he would, it is said, visit some dungeon and torture a prisoner, which put him in good spirit for the rest of the day.

At eight all gathered together again for vespers. At ten Ivan would go to his bedroom where three blind men took it in turn to tell him fairy tales and legends until he fell asleep. But he seldom slept within this space of time, because at midnight he must again repair to church to begin the day with prayer.

The story of these strange doings must have got abroad and Sigizmund Augustus thought that he might profit by the situation. Ivan received ambassadors of foreign powers at Alexandrof; it was impossible to disguise the fact that he was abnormal. To what extent he was mad, it was of course difficult to assess. Sigizmund asked the Russian ambassador in Warsaw: "What is the *Opritchina?*" But he replied: "There is no such thing." Nevertheless the King of Poland believed that there was, because fugitives from the tyranny of the *Opritchina* constantly crossed his frontiers to put themselves under his protection. When he learned that Ivan spent most of the time in Alexandrof saying prayers, it seemed an excellent moment for the disaffected boyars to seize the power of Government in Moscow, and, through a Russian intermediary, he started a treasonable correspondence with the leading nobles of the *Zemschina.*

The active government of the country fell into abeyance. The *Opritchina* had all the law. No case could be brought into court and won against them. The boyars saw themselves attacked and plundered on their estates. They grew poorer. The *Opritchina* grew richer.

Their new houses filled with the spoil of other men's houses. Yet there was a strange inability to rebel. The terror of the Tsar's power for revenge seemed to paralyse all action. Trade left Moscow; the merchants groaned, but they dared not present a petition. The Tsar's practice of receiving petitions from his subjects lapsed. Some member of his bodyguard inevitably seized any petition intended for the Tsar's hands and answered it as he thought fit, that answer being commonly rapine or murder. The Church also was passive, as if it were the will of God and Russia had been delivered to the devil to destroy.

The Metropolitan Afanasy must have bitterly repented his weakness and the weakness of his bishops in agreeing to condone all actions of the Tsar. It was far from the tradition of the Church to behave thus supinely toward the actions of the monarch. From earliest times the Church had used its power of intercession for mercy and had dared to denounce the cruel and the vicious no matter how mighty they might be. In treating the Tsar as divine the Church was untrue to the Gospel which clearly distinguishes between the things which are Caesar's and those which are God's. But Afanasy was weak. Not only did he allow innocent men and women to be tortured and killed, but he had not the moral courage to denounce the mockery of the Tsar's monastery at Alexandrof.

Then the irresponsible nature of the Tsar's religious behaviour entered another phase. He entertained numerous German prisoners from Livonia and began an intellectual flirtation with Protestantism. He admired Germans and was inclined to be lenient toward them.

They had the distinction of being educated people.
The gentry were good conversationalists; the lower
orders were skilled craftsmen. He had long shown a
tendency to employ Germans and let the country profit
by their scientific knowledge and craftsmanship. But it
is, nevertheless, surprising to find Eberveld almost successful in converting Ivan to the Augsburg Confession. The Tsar even permitted the Lutherans to have
churches in Moscow. It was all too much for the Metropolitan Afanasy who, falling sick in May, 1566, decided to retire to a monastery cell.

It is possible that Ivan was preparing himself for
marriage with the great Protestant queen. He awaited
the return of Anthony Jenkinson from England. If
Jenkinson brought a statement of the terms on which
Elizabeth would marry him, it is possible that Ivan
would have, by a stroke of the pen, endeavoured to
make Russia a Protestant country. He was capable
of it.

Jenkinson had had a long and personal conversation
with Elizabeth. What he told her and what she replied
has not been handed down in history. The English
traveller, so profuse in commercial information, proved
unfortunately to be a good messenger and extremely
discreet. But one thing is clear from his correspondence
and that of his fellow travellers. England was interested in business in Russia and in business alone. The
discovery of Russia, Bokhara and the marts of the
East had no element of glory in them. The interest was
money-making rather than discovery; trade was more
than life or honour. Queen Elizabeth was the head of
a trading community. It might even be said that she

was a good business woman. That is one of the reasons why she was so popular. The sovereign did not batten on the country but helped it to greater prosperity. Therefore, as far as Russia was concerned, the Queen put the affairs of the Russia Company in absolutely the first place. She could call the Tsar brother and give him all his titles, and even blush with pleasure at a proposal of marriage. It was "rather delicious" that a great potentate of the east, someone in the nature of the Great Mogul, should ask her hand. But the serious consideration was trade. Jenkinson had obtained wider privileges for the English merchants in Russia. Merchants of other powers were jealous of the progress the Russia Company had made. Elizabeth could jeopardise all this good business by a firm refusal of Ivan's offer. She could easily have been very rude. For Ivan had a wife living and the proposal was not unlike asking her to enter his harem. Instead of that she flirted and played for time. She had no intention of getting married to anyone else. So she had plenty of scope for flirtation. The discussion of possible terms of union could be protracted and during the time, still further privileges could be obtained for her merchants.

Jenkinson arrived in August or September, 1566, and remained a long while, being held in high honour. He must have witnessed the *Opritchina* in action, must also have been entertained at Alexandrof, but concerning what he saw and of his conversations with the Tsar he seems to have left nothing in writing. What we have as an explicit result of his conversations is the granting to the Russia Company of a trading monopoly in the whole northern region of Russia, the goods of other na-

tions to be confiscate, their ships and people, if found
in the north, "Confiscate and forfeited to us the Emperour and Great Duke." And the English merchants
should have free access to Dorpat, Narva and other
regions lately conquered by Russia. In short, Ivan
granted a very flattering treaty of commerce. What
Ivan asked in exchange is not set down in words. Nor
have we the secret message which Jenkinson conveyed,
nor the contents of the Queen's letter. But this time
Her Majesty did vouchsafe to send the Tsar a present
and the envoy did not have to procure something suitable from the chests of the Russia Company. We can
believe that Elizabeth asked the Tsar some questions
which were difficult of answer and made some demands
other than the granting of trading privileges. Time was
on the side of Mr. Anthony Jenkinson, Queen Elizabeth and English business. Ultimately, however, Jenkinson had to return to the Queen's Majesty, promising
to obtain an explicit answer to the Tsar's proposal, and
to return with it quickly to him.

XXIII.

THE METROPOLITAN PHILIP

THE Church was about to choose Herman, Archbishop of Kazan, to occupy the place of the Metropolitan Afanasy, but the Tsar interfered. Herman was sent back to Kazan and an invitation was sent to one of the most devout ascetics of Russia, to Philip, the abbot of the Monastery of Solovetsk on the White Sea. It was to this forlorn Arctic retreat that Sylvester had been banished. Sylvester had been received there as a holy man rather than as one in disgrace. He had recounted to the abbot all that had befallen him as the spiritual guide of the young Tsar. How unexpected was the call that came to the abbot, Philip! But it was like a sign of grace. The Tsar had sent for Sylvester's abbot. Might that not mean that he was looking for a spiritual successor to Sylvester?

Philip was of noble birth, but in adolescence had set himself against the vanity of a boyar's life. Rather than attend at court he had chosen to save his soul in the wilderness. His progress in self-dedication had not passed unnoticed by the Tsar who corresponded with him and sent him gifts for his altars and material for building. He knew that Philip in his limited sphere was a fine administrator. He combined holiness and good sense and that was rare. The angels could count his prayers but he had drained the tundra and raised a reindeer farm. He had cleared the forest and made roads. He had started a salt factory; he had made a fleet of fishing vessels. He had repaired the monastery buildings and trimmed the wick of the lamp of God burning in the farthest north.

One cannot accept Kurbsky's story that the Tsar rejected Herman of Kazan because he called upon him to repent and bethink himself how he would appear at the Last Judgment when the Almighty bade him justify his behaviour as Tsar. Herman was a virtuous archbishop but he lived in the comfortable see of Kazan and could not be the shining witness that Philip was. Ivan was not a reasonable monarch but he would not forgo Herman for Philip in the hope of finding someone more subservient to his tyranny. He deliberately invited a man of tremendous moral authority to be his spiritual *vis à vis*, his partner and equal in the dual control, by Church and State, of Russia.

There is a curious entry in the log book of Southam and Sparke, English sailors seeking a waterway from the mouth of the Northern Dvina to Novgorod: "We arrived at a monastery named Solovky. . . . At our being at the monastery, there was no Abbot for the place as then chosen. For 15 dayes before our arrival, the Abbot was sent for by the Emperour, and made Metropolitaine of the realme, as he now is. The number of the monks belonging to the monastery are at least 200."

Outside the city of Novgorod, on his way south, Philip was met by a delegation from that city begging him to intercede for them and avert the Tsar's anger with which they were threatened. Even then, three years before it happened, the dreadful punishment of Novgorod by the Tsar, was apprehended.

Philip, a world-forsaker, returned to the world, and as he approached Moscow, the clamour of a distraught Russia grew increasingly upon his ears. In his humility he felt that the task was too great and that he had neither the strength nor the wisdom to be the chief authority of the Church over this turbulent, suffering, and sinful people. In his first conversation with the Tsar he deplored what was going on and he refused the responsibility of the Church for the sins of the court. He would not be Metropolitan: he was too small a vessel for the cargo the Tsar wished to place upon it. He could not give his blessing to the affliction of Russia, the *Opritchina*. The vicious side of the Tsar was angry but the repentant side felt that it had found a great support. Instead of driving Philip from his presence Ivan felt even more convinced that he had found the man he needed.

The Tsar could not order him to be Metropolitan. He might persuade the servile bishops to elect him, but he had not the authority to make the appointment if a man of God refused to take it. On what terms he persuaded Philip we do not know, but it could only have been for the good of Russia and the salvation of the people. The abbot tried to make terms in advance. He wished the *Opritchina* disbanded, the redistribution of estates annulled and the patrimonies restored to the original owners. Ivan did not accept these terms and yet Philip became Metropolitan. And he undertook not to abandon the see at any time as a protest against the Tsar's conduct of state affairs. It was nevertheless surprising that Ivan should choose such a strong opponent of the *Opritchina* to be the visible head of the Church.

On 11th August the ceremony of consecration was performed in the presence of the Tsar, his two sons, and Prince Vladimir Andreyevitch, the bishops and archbishops.

In his address to the throne Philip recommended the Tsar to become once more the father of his people and turn away his eyes from the flatterers who pressed around him and observe justice in dealing with his subjects, telling him that the victories of love were more glorious than those of war. Ivan, as if resolved to turn over a new leaf, listened to him with profound attention and for some months afterwards was a different man, cherishing the new Metropolitan with marked affection and checking the tyranny of his retainers.

Philip, blessed by the people, enjoyed halcyon days and he started building churches in Moscow in the name of the patron saints of Solovetsky Monastery, St. Zosima and St. Sabaty. But the happy interlude came to a rude end through the development of Sigizmund Augustus's conspiracy with the *Zemschina*. The spies of the Polish king had informed him fully of the doings of the *Opritchina*. He had realised that Russia was divided against herself and that the number of disaffected nobles was large enough to start a civil war. The passive *Zemschina*, if roused to action, could destroy the *Opritchina* and dethrone the Tsar. The king's emissaries had been going to and fro between Poland and Moscow for some time. It is not surprising that one of them at last was intercepted. It was a great opportunity for the Tsar's favourites to restart the reign of terror and enkindle again all the Tsar's frantic suspicions.

It is probable that some of the boyars entertained Sigizmund's proposals. A certain Russian settled in Lithuania, a courier, acted as the king's chief agent in the conspiracy. This man, Kozlof, brought letters to Mstislavsky, Bielsky, the lately pardoned Michael Vorotinsky and others. But the letters were intercepted or the scared princes brought the treasonable missives personally to Ivan. At first the Tsar was amused and he wrote answers in his boyars' names. "Let King Sigizmund give them the whole of Lithuania, White Russia, Galicia, Podolsk, and his domains in Prussia and they would start a civil war." The old Prince Federof, the Tsar's equerry, was made to reply "How can you think that I with one foot in the grave would endanger my immortal soul by an abominable treason?"

At first Ivan dealt with the conspiracy in great good humour. There was some gleam of geniality in his forged reply, some suggestion of urbanity and greatness. But the Tsar's morbid afterthoughts were more powerful than his bright intellect. Distrust surged back on him and with it doubt even of the loyalty of the new Metropolitan. He looked around him and believed that everyone was secretly in league against him. His change of mood began with the mockery and murder of old Prince Federof.

"After all," he reflected, "Federof must have been thinking of going over to Sigizmund." In the presence of the whole court he made Federof put on his own mantle and crown. He took him by the hand and led him to the throne. Then bowing low he hailed him as Tsar of Russia and wished him long life. Some of the other boyars laughed and thought it an excellent jest.

Ivan greatly enjoyed play-acting and theatrical poses.
At the same time surrendering the crown to another was
a recurring thought in his mind. His behaviour was incalculable because he did not know himself what he
would do next. He received his cue from his subcon-
scious mind. He might have enforced the Tsardom on
old Federof for months as he did on a later occasion
upon Prince Simeon. But he did not. He killed him instead. "As I had power to make thee Tsar," said he, "so
surely I have power to bring thee down again." And he
raised his knife and stabbed him to the heart. Federof
fell, tumbling backward from the dais.

The body was hacked to pieces in the palace yard.
Federof's "holy" wife, childless and consecrated to
Christ, was killed also; as wanton a murder as the first.

Now the *Opritchina*, held in check for some months
by Ivan under the influence of Philip, broke loose once
more. The three most important generals, Mstislavsky,
Bielsky, and Michael Vorotinsky escaped vengeance,
but for the rest the word went forth to destroy all those
who might have joined in King Sigizmund's conspiracy. The three leading princes of the Rostovsky family
were despatched. The Rostovskies had once been on
the point of fleeing to Lithuania, so it might well be
thought that they would make the attempt again. The
pardon which they had obtained in 1554, through the
intercession of Alexey Adashef and Makary had not
been freely given by Ivan. He had regretted it ever
since and brooded over it. Thirty men set off for
Nizhny Novgorod, where one of the Rostovskies was
in command of an army and they brought his head and
put it at Ivan's feet and he kicked it from him. Ac-

cording to Kurbsky, Prince Peter Shchenatof was slowly burned to death in a baking pan over a fire in a monastery cell. Ivan Pronsky was drowned. State Treasurer Tiutin, with wife and family, was cut to pieces by the Tsaritsa's brother and a band of ruffians. Many other prominent men were executed or murdered together with their wives and families. The *Opritchina* plundered their houses and their villages. They destroyed their cattle and the fish in their streams and lakes, destroyed even their dogs and cats. Great numbers of common people were killed and sometimes even babies in their cradles were not spared. A story is told of two men who were sent to destroy a family, but their hearts melted when they faced a certain baby boy who was smiling in his crib. They brought the child to Ivan who kissed it and then hurled it through a window and it was given to the bears. The executioners who had shown pity were ordered to be sliced to death with swords.

Terror once more reigned in Moscow and in Russia as a whole. Masked men with long knives went from street to street robbing and killing. The dead lay unburied in the roads, no one daring to associate himself with the victims of the Tsar's wrath lest the same fate befall him. A feature of the murders was the stripping naked of the victims. This was to avoid soiling garments with blood. Clothes were often a valuable part of the plunder. The stripping of the women naked was also common, brutal violation preceding murder.

These dreadful happenings took place in the winter, spring and summer of 1568. The Metropolitan met the resurgence of Ivan's violence by prayer, but that was not enough. At first he was able to reason with the Tsar and was bold enough to denounce his sin to his face. But then Ivan avoided him. One day, however, Ivan brought a great number of the *Opritchina* with him into the Cathedral of the Assumption, all in high hoods and black cloaks. The Tsar himself was dressed as the abbot of his fantastic brotherhood. Some of the party were tipsy and it is probable that Ivan himself was under the influence of mead. Divine service continued as if there had been no interruption. Three times the Tsar approached the Metropolitan, as it were to receive his blessing, but Philip paid not the least attention. Then some of the *Opritchina* began to murmur.

"Holy father!" said one of them. "The Tsar Ivan Vasillievitch is asking blessing."

Then the Metropolitan bent his gaze upon the black-cowled Tsar. "Who art thou imitating?" he asked. "Falsifying thy goodness behind a calico mask. . . . Since the sun began to shine in the heavens no honourable sovereign has offended his people thus. O Tsar, while we raise the Holy Sacrifice at the altar thou sheddest innocent Christian blood in the churches of God. Even in the most pagan countries there is law and justice and mercy, but in Russia none of these things. Robberies and murders are committed everywhere in thy name. But high as thou art on the throne, there is yet another, our Judge and thine. How, thinkest thou, thou wilt stand at His tribunal in the deafening chorus of the cries of the tormented, in the welter of the blood of the innocent? As the shepherd of souls, I bid thee beware of the One God."

Ivan in rage struck his steel-pointed staff on the

stone floor of the cathedral. "Monk, be it as thou hast spoken. Up to now I have spared you rebels more than was necessary," he cried in a strange voice, "Henceforth I shall act according to the character thou hast given me." And he strode out of the cathedral.

That day a great number of clerics were arrested and put to the torture. More of the boyars belonging to the *Zemschina* were seized and killed, among them Prince Vasilly Pronsky. The Tsar had promised a worse tyranny, but worse could hardly be unless he laid hands on the Metropolitan. But that also was to come. There was another scene in church on the 28th of July, 1568. The Metropolitan objected to the attire of one of the *Opritchina* who had entered. This trifling incident caused an outburst from the Tsar who roundly accused the Metropolitan of hypocrisy, evildoing, and sedition. It was difficult for him to deal with the Metropolitan. Philip had by now a reputation for holiness and was regarded by the masses of the people as a living saint. Either this reputation or the authority of the Church was too great to allow a public murder. Ivan with his favourites set to work to collect evidence wherewith to blacken the prelate's good name. Emissaries were sent to Solovetsky Monastery to gather what gossip they could find. Most of the monks there were staunch in upholding Philip as a model of piety but the abbot Paisy perjured himself in the hope of obtaining preferment.

Enough was invented to form an indictment. The Metropolitan was arraigned before a court in Moscow and the abbot Paisy was brought forward as the chief accuser. Philip met persecution with great firmness, saying that he would rather die a martyr's death than see the Tsar's crimes continued unchecked. "You are to be judged: you are not the judge," said the Tsar, but he did not at once arrest him or deprive him of his see. Philip continued the Divine services, expecting the blow to fall daily, hourly.

It was on the festival of the Archangel Michael, on the 8th November, that Basmanof and others burst into the Cathedral of the Assumption and assaulted the Metropolitan as he stood at the altar clad in all the pomp of his office. A band of the *Opritchina* with brooms in their hands set upon the Metropolitan and tore his vestments from his body, put a white garment on him, perhaps a sheet, and hurried him away to a cell in the Monastery of the Annunciation. There was a great hush in the cathedral but the masses of the people followed the rude sledge on which the Metropolitan had been thrown, crying and shouting. And the crowds about the monastery remained waiting, expecting a miracle.

Next day Philip was convicted of practising sorcery and condemned to life imprisonment. Then he forgave his enemies and once more appealed to Ivan to repent and to remember the traditions of his forefathers. That had not the least effect. Philip was taken to a dungeon and loaded with irons. But wherever he was sent crowds gathered to be near a living saint who was giving his life for his faith. He had to be moved. Ivan knew he was a holy man, relented somewhat and might conceivably have recalled him to Moscow. But he sent one of his favourites, Skuratof, to obtain the old man's blessing. He was a monastery prisoner at Tver and the

Tsar was on his way to his dreadful vengeance on Novgorod. Philip refused a blessing, saying: "I bless the good undertaking to do good. Thee I cannot bless." Skuratof jumped on him and strangled him. So fell one of the greatest pastors of the Russian Church. Cyril, Archimandrite of Troitsky Monastery, became Metropolitan in his place.

XXIV.

DEATH OF SECOND TSARITSA

THE Tsar expected the return of Anthony Jenkinson with an answer from Queen Elizabeth, and appears to have been somewhat annoyed when the Queen sent Thomas Randolfe to him instead of her previous emissary. Or the Tsar in black mood after the unfrocking of the Metropolitan, overlooked the arrival of the English ambassador. Randolfe was not received warmly and was kept over four months waiting in Moscow before Ivan expressed a wish to see him. He arrived in Moscow at the end of September, 1568, but was not received at court until the 20th February, 1569. During that time Randolfe was virtually a prisoner in the house provided for him. For guards were placed upon it to see that he never went out of it and that he received no visitors. Food and drink were delivered at the house daily, but no messages or letters were delivered. All supplications and requests for liberty were refused.

Although there is no evidence to that effect, it may be surmised that Randolfe had submitted his papers to an intermediary and had not followed the example of Jenkinson of insisting on doing what business he had personally with the Tsar. He bore no definite answer from Queen Elizabeth to the Tsar's proposal of marriage, he had merely come in quest of further commercial privileges. Had he arrived with a magnificently worded refusal he must have been received with honour and dignity. But to answer a proposal of marriage by asking for more facilities for trading was an affront.

It must also have been known to Ivan that Randolfe bore him a very shabby present from the Queen, which was a silver cup with some quaint verse graven on it. Such a gift might have been more suitable to a Lord Mayor than to an imperial suitor. Ivan may have pondered whether it would not be more politic to have Randolfe murdered and then send an elaborate apology. The English ambassador was well aware of the sort of outrage being perpetrated daily in Moscow and "Had no small cause to doubt that some evil had been intended."

Randolfe's account of Russia in 1568–9 is by no means as rosy as the accounts given by earlier English visitors to Russia. The provincials were drunken, their vices abominable. When at last he was presented, Randolfe was not impressed with the court. He felt that its magnificence had merely been staged that day to impress him, "by my estimation, 300 persons, all in rich attire, taken out of the Emperor's wardrobe for that day, upon three ranks of benches, set round about the place, rather to present a majestie, than that they were either of quality or honor."

When he bowed to the boyars and they paid not the least attention he decided to keep his hat on in the presence of the Tsar which, however, passed uncensored. Tartars and infidels were allowed to keep their hats on. The Tsar gave him his hand and entered into converse with him. The English envoy experienced a remarkable change of treatment. After his first short parley two noblemen were deputed to escort him back

to his lodging and within an hour of his arriving there
. . . "comes a duke richly apparelled, accompanied
with fifty persons, each of them carrying a silver dish
with meat, and covered with silver. The duke first delivered twenty loaves of bread of the Emperor's own
eating, having tasted the same, and delivered every
dish into my hands, and tasted of every kind of drink
that he brought."

These precautions against poison seem rather curious
seeing that the ambassador and his attendants had
lived there several months on unsampled rations. But it
is possible that the Tsar was preoccupied at the time
with thoughts of poison. It was the great poisoning era
in Europe, the heyday of Catherine de' Medici. Ivan in
any case showed a desire to make up to Randolfe for
past privation. He intimated that he would have private discourse with him. Hope of winning the hand of
Elizabeth must have again entered the Tsar's mind.
One night Randolfe was bidden to the palace on the
Sparrow Hills outside Moscow, and he talked to Ivan
there for three hours alone.

Concerning the matter of their conversation Master
Thomas Randolfe proved unfortunately discreet. We
are assured by Anthony Jenkinson that the Queen did
instruct Randolfe and that he had power to treat with
Ivan concerning his "princely and secret affairs." But
we can only surmise that Randolfe misled the Tsar,
thinking it better to win his favour and obtain some
more trading privileges than to endanger everything by
telling the blunt truth. Jenkinson declared afterwards
that he did not believe that Randolfe could have compromised the Queen's favour in order to extend com-

merce, but it rather looks as if he did. There was always one clear good reason why Elizabeth should not consent to marry Ivan and that was that the Tsar was married already. A monarch who proposed to get rid of his consort in order to marry another could be played with and put off by words. Ivan was pleased with what Randolfe said to him and resolved to wait for the return of Anthony Jenkinson with an explicit answer. And possibly things might be made more easy for Elizabeth if the Tsaritsa died that year, preferably a natural death. . . .

With his mind more at ease concerning his princely and secret affairs, Ivan willingly heard Randolfe's plea for extended privileges and signed a new treaty with him safeguarding the overland trade routes to Persia and Bokhara, giving licence to build more warehouses, releasing certain English prisoners, regulating traffic in Livonia. He did not do all this for the Russia Company without some ulterior hope. Ivan signed the new treaty. He granted all facilities to Randolfe to return to London and sent along with him his ambassador, Andrew Savin, and he sent rich presents to the Queen. It is not surprising that in the outcome, when nothing came of his proposal, and the Queen did not take the trouble to say him yea or nay, he vented his displeasure upon the English trading community and treated their privileges as void. But when in July, 1569, Randolfe sailed away, the Tsar still hoped for a good issue. On the 1st September of the same year the Tsaritsa died, it was said of poison.

If the Tsaritsa was poisoned it is more likely that the Tsar himself committed the deed than anyone else. She had no political significance and Ivan had long since been indifferent to her charms. The mourning was almost a mockery. The Tsar himself declared that the Tsaritsa had been poisoned and no one gainsaid him. The question was whom would he accuse of having poisoned her.

The death took place in Moscow, but very soon after the funeral the Tsar repaired to Alexandrof in a diabolic humour and there he decided he would make an end of his cousin, Prince Vladimir Andreyevitch and his family. That revenge he had been storing for many years; it is surprising that his cousin had survived so long. But he did not tack on to him the accusation of having poisoned the Tsaritsa. The charge was that he had given poison to one of the palace cooks and suborned him to place it in the Tsar's food. Prince Vladimir and his wife were summoned to Alexandrof and, according to one report, were given each a goblet of poison and forced to drink it in the Tsar's presence.

By other accounts they were beheaded or shot or drowned. Actually, in Russian annals there is no narrative of this crime. It was left to foreign visitors to Russia to record it. But in whatever way they were done to death, they disappeared from the pages of history in the autumn of 1569. And two sons disappeared also. It is said that the people of Russia were not afraid to show their grief and go into mourning for Prince Vladimir. The Tsar calmly announced that there had been a conspiracy against his life and he intended to be merciless toward all those privy to it.

XXV.

VENGEANCE ON NOVGOROD

THE Tsar in his megalomaniac mood swept on to greater murders. He had been concerned as to the loyalty of his subjects in Novgorod and Pskof and in the spring of the year had taken hostages for the good behaviour of the cities, 500 families brought from Pskof to Moscow, 150 families from Novgorod. There was no real disaffection, but the citizens of these cities nursed the tradition of their independence. Of the two, Novgorod was greater and prouder, but Pskof had been the last of the independent duchies to be merged in the unity of Muscovy. The old families in Novgorod remembered that the city had been a state in itself, capable of entering into separate treaties with foreign powers. It was Novgorod *the Great*. The city had its own history and legend. It regarded Moscow as a parvenu city, much as in later centuries, Moscow regarded St. Petersburg, or to bring it nearer home, somewhat as Edinburgh regards Glasgow. There is nothing seditious in these reservations of local pride.

Both Novgorod and Pskof had grievances, especially since the inauguration of the *Opritchina*, but they were nevertheless abjectly servile to the Tsar's will, like the whole of the rest of Russia. The rumour that they were about to ask the protection of King Sigizmund Augustus was even absurd, because Sigizmund had shown himself incapable of protecting foreign cities. The Russian garrisons in the cities of Livonia bore constant witness to that fact. More absurd still was the alleged plot of the Archbishop of Novgorod to have Novgorod incorporated in Lithuania, a voluntary entering of Orthodoxy into a *mêlée* of Protestantism and Romanism. But someone was found to forge the documents of this alleged plot.

Certainly the removal of the families to Moscow caused a smouldering ill-will during all the summer and autumn of 1569. They grieved in Pskof and Novgorod for the loss of cousins while the said cousins languished in exile in Moscow, not a few finding their way to prison or torture chamber. Torturing commoners was a sport, not merely the Tsar's hobby but the custom of the gentry and the allowed amusement of their children. The Tsar's favourites, Basmanof, Skuratof, Viazemsky were brutal torturers. The Tsar's eldest son Ivan, aged fifteen, had part and lot in his father's brutality. The social history of the time is defectively chronicled because the wrongs of common men were not wrongs. A human victim for an enraged bear was merely a show and the victim's alleged crime a matter of small account. It was greatly the exception for power of any kind not to be used tyrannously. The barbarity of Ivan the Terrible stands out in relief in history, but it was encouraged by the example of his subjects. Or it can be put another way: when the Tsar was cruel he was imitated by everyone who had power down to the "petty pelting officer." The angry ape ravished the land. The actual background of terror in which Russia lived in 1569 was monstrous.

The Tsar required a pretext for punishing the people

of Novgorod and the charge of treachery was fastened
on them through the instrumentality of a tramp who
brought to Moscow the story of a plot. Some of the
Tsar's favourites must have been using this tramp, who
had for himself merely some petty grievance against
Novgorod. The story in which he was primed was that
the archbishop and leading people of Novgorod had
written a joint letter to Sigizmund Augustus offering to
desert the allegiance of the Tsar. That letter had not
actually been sent but reposed behind an ikon of the
Virgin in the church of St. Sophia in Novgorod. Ivan,
hearing this, at once despatched an agent to Novgorod
and the criminal letter was discovered in the place
which had been indicated. The fact that the archbishop's signature had been very carefully copied showed
that someone of more erudition than Peter the tramp
was responsible for it. On the strength of a cock-and-
bull story and this forged letter Ivan decided upon the
chastisement of Novgorod. He was at Alexandrof. He
had disposed of his cousin, Prince Vladimir Andreyevitch. He meditated murder on a much larger scale.

In December, 1569, accompanied by a large band of
the *Opritchina*, his son Ivan, and many nobles, the Tsar
set off from Alexandrof on a punitive expedition. It
was a sheer blood quest. On their way to Novgorod the
Tsar's band massacred the inhabitants of the town
of Klin and there was no question of their having written a letter to King Sigizmund, either forged or un-
forged. Here was let loose arson, rape, murder, robbery.
The streets filled with the bodies of the dead, among
the corpses being many women and children. Butchery
spread from the town to the surrounding villages.

The Tsar's bands rode everywhere, brandishing naked swords which dripped blood. And so to the city of Tver where Skuratof strangled the ex-Metropolitan Philip.

At Tver Ivan had a spell of torturing God; that is, he prayed five days in a monastery while his executioners wandered from house to house and street to street murdering whom they wished. And Philip was buried behind the high altar of the cathedral, with a martyr's crown.

And all the way from Tver to Novgorod raged the ferocity of the Tsar and his bodyguard; every little town was ravaged by fire and sword. And people the bands met in the open country were slain because "the campaign was secret" and they must not live to tell of it.

On the 2nd January, 1570, the Tsar and the *Opritchina* arrived on the confines of Novgorod. In effect the Tsar with a large army had arrived. With devilish coolness the Tsar made his plans for the murder of the city. First of all precaution was taken that none of the population should flee; a high timber rampart was built around the city. All the churches of the city were locked so that no victims should take refuge at the altars. The monks were evacuated from the monasteries and the doors of these institutions were sealed so that no victims might hide themselves in obscure cells or escape by underground passages. The houses of all the rich merchants and leading citizens were padlocked with their inhabitants inside them. All officials and the lesser clergy were arrested and bound. The market and the shops were closed. No church bells rang: there was just before the execution the most dreadful calm of apprehension.

The Tsar's pavilion had been set up outside the rampart which he caused to be built. He now demanded and obtained a stricter discipline from the armed bands. He did not at once deliver the city to death and until he gave the signal, no executions were commenced. The Tsar had certain plans. The army which he had brought with him had to be paid. There were many expenses in connection with the expedition. As the Church in the person of the archbishop had conceived the alleged horrid treason, it was fitting that it should be called upon to defray the cost of punishment. There were several thousand priests and monks in the city; Ivan therefore decreed that each of them should be called upon to pay a fine of twenty roubles. How poor monks who had forsaken the world and its vanities should be able to raise such a sum he did not enquire. Those who failed to pay were stripped naked, tied to posts in the streets and the squares and flogged till they said where they thought the money could be obtained. The order was to go on flogging them from morning till night till the money was found or they were dead. Thus the first hundreds met their cruel end, and their bodies were taken to the monasteries for burial. It had been simpler for Ivan to seize the gold plate and the treasures of the churches, but that would have been open robbery of God and as an opening act Ivan pretended to have scruples. But he did not raise much money by the impost on the clergy; it was not long before he sanctioned the robbery of the churches themselves.

On the 8th January, the Tsar, accompanied by the Tsarevitch and a large detachment of troops, entered the city. The Archbishop Pimen followed by a number of clergy bearing crosses and ikons came forth to meet him. There was a strange scene on the large bridge in the middle of the city where the Tsar refused to accept the Archbishop's blessing. Instead Ivan denounced Pimen to his face as a traitor and told him that the cross he bore was not life-giving but an instrument of murder.

"I know your purpose and that of your revolting flock," shouted the Tsar. "You were preparing to go over to Sigizmund Augustus. You are no pastor but a rapacious wolf, an enemy of the Church, a hater of my crown."

But then he ordered the Archbishop and the religious procession to march on to the church of St. Sophia, where, in strange contradiction of himself, he listened patiently and devoutly to Divine Service and, as usual, prostrated himself and prayed with great fervour. After this he proceeded to the Archbishop's palace and seated himself at table with a very large company. He began to dine and all seemed to be going well.

But the Tsar's brain functioned strangely as if some revolving film kept passing over the light of his intelligence. Suddenly his eyes blazed with a sort of meteoric light. He ceased eating; he turned to the princes and boyars at table and gave vent to a howl of inarticulate rage. This yell was recognised as a signal by his bodyguard who at once seized the old Archbishop, bound him, and put him in a dungeon. The spoliators rushed off to sack the palace and remove everything of value. The Tsar continued his dinner.

Next day his plans for punishment were declared.

Each day there would be mustered some thousand of the inhabitants to be tortured to death in the presence of himself and his son. There was much variety in cruelty. Loving husbands and wives were tortured in one another's presence. Mothers saw the babes from their breasts ill-treated before their eyes, before they themselves were flogged to death or roasted over slow fires. Holes were made in the ice of the river and whole families were pushed under. Ivan was educating his son and heir, whom, however, he was destined to murder.

It is recorded that these mass tortures and executions lasted five weeks. They were accompanied by the looting of all the property of the citizens. The Tsar then rode out of the town to kill the neighbouring farmers and destroy their horses and cattle and he visited the monasteries in all the country round about, seizing what gold could be found and putting the clergy to the sword. All scruples about sacking churches had by now disappeared and there was not much left of value in any shrine of Novgorod. However on the 12th February the Tsar called together what was left of the population to tell them they were pardoned and to beg that they would pray for him when he had gone.

With ashen face in the dawn light, the Tsar stood in a street in Novgorod and hardly looked at the stragglers who had been rounded up to hear his proclamation. His eyes, it is said, were dull, the rage in them burned out. "People of Novgorod, still living," said he in a low voice. "Pray God to bless our rule as Tsar; pray for the Christ-loving army that it may conquer all its enemies both seen and unseen. May God judge that traitor to me, your Archbishop Pimen and his evil advisors. Theirs is the responsibility for the blood which has been shed. May the wailing and crying cease in the city! Forget your wrongs! Live and prosper! I leave with you my new governor, Prince Peter Danielovitch Pronsky. Go now in peace to your homes!"

Thus ended the chastisement of Novgorod the Great, making a page in history which has not its like in the annals of Europe as a whole. Some say that 60,000 perished. Kurbsky wrote that the Tsar killed 15,000 in one day alone. Taube and Kruze, two Germans at court, estimate 27,000. But suffering and death cannot be added up to make an intelligible total. No one counted, but the horror of the Tsar's act remains through the centuries.

Ivan the Terrible seemed to be tired when he left Novgorod, but he actually set forth to repeat in Pskof what he had done in the sister city. The army with him had not sickened of butchery and plunder. When the Tsar arrived with his armed bands outside the city, the inhabitants were almost paralysed with fear. But Ivan was tired or sated. He spent the night in the monastery of St. Nicholas outside Pskof. The people of the city did not sleep, but prayed all night. And at midnight all the bells of the city began to toll. The Tsar was awakened. He turned in bed and listened. "They are all praying to be saved from the Tsar's wrath," he murmured, and the thought flattered him. He was touched: he decided they should be spared. The next morning the whole population of Pskof received the Tsar kneeling.

XXVI.

FALL OF THE FAVOURITES

THE crazy holy men chatter-jabbered against Ivan, Nikola in Pskof, silly Vasilly in Moscow, and doubtless many others. "Were human voices silent the stones themselves would cry out against thee, Ivashka! Here is a piece of raw meat, eat it though it is Lent. That will be nothing to thee, living on human flesh and blood. God's anger followeth thee. For every torment thou puttest on innocent men here on earth, ten times that torture will be inflicted on thee in hell. As a sign I prophesy that when thou tryest to bring down the bell of the Holy Trinity thy horse will fall down dead. God's lightning has been sent to seek thee and will find thee!"

It is said that Ivan was browbeaten by an emaciated saint of Pskof, that going to this crazy ascetic for blessing, he fled aghast from his presence. He dare lay his hand on an archbishop or allow a metropolitan to be strangled by one of his servants but he dared not punish a fool in Christ flaring with the knowledge of God's anger. But the evidence that Ivan was really frightened by the anathemas of Nikola of Pskof is slight. Certainly his best horse fell dead while his men were taking down the cathedral bell. But that did not prevent him from taking it. And he filled many waggons with the treasures of the churches and the monasteries. Ivan had plunged into sacrilege and robbery of God and was not dismayed. He did not release the

Archbishop Pimen, but had him sent bound to Alexandrof, together with a number of leading citizens and clerics of Novgorod, to have another field of torture and death at his leisure. And although actually the people of Pskof were spared, the *Opritchina*, unchecked, scoured all the country round about, murdering landowners and their tenants and plundering estates.

For the time being Ivan the Terrible was sated. He returned to Alexandrof and began a post-mortem inquiry into the guilt of Novgorod. He had, it must be thought, convinced himself that a conspiracy had taken place. Now he had second thoughts on the subject. He was convinced that Pimen had not planned to hand Novgorod over to Sigizmund Augustus without some connivance in Moscow. He now believed that his deceased cousin Prince Vladimir had been privy to the conspiracy. But Vladimir could not be raised from the dead to be tortured again. And Ivan craved further action upon the living. So the prisoners of Novgorod were put to the question. They were made to say all they knew and then under the strain of torture to invent accusations against others. Probably they were guided by the inquisitors as to whom they should incriminate.

It should not be forgotten that the Tsar's wrath had been pending for some years. The discovery of the alleged conspiracy only brought it to a head. In the summer of 1566, when Philip was on his way from Solovetsky Monastery to Moscow, he was met by a deputation of Novgorodians who had asked him to intercede with the Tsar that the cloud of his displeasure might be lifted. There was therefore a true story of apprehension which could be recounted in the torture chamber. And then to the question—Why were they apprehensive? many vaguely incriminating answers might be made. "From whom had they received intelligence that they were under the Tsar's displeasure?" Novgorodians had kinsmen and friends at court. One by one, these were seized and tortured so as to enlarge the amount of information. For five months the Tsar and his agents tortured and collected evidence.

The investigation took a surprising turn. The inquisitors showed a clear desire to have the Tsar's favourites incriminated. A certain Fedor Lovchikof testified that Prince Viazemsky had forewarned certain Novgorodians to flee the Tsar's wrath. This proved sufficient to taint the most intimate of the Tsar's favourites with treason. Ivan decided to destroy him and in characteristic fashion sent for him and had a long confidential conversation with him on state affairs, not hinting his suspicion or his intention. Viazemsky was dismissed from the Tsar's presence with apparent warmth of affection and trust. But when the prince got home he found the greater part of his household had been murdered in his absence. Viazemsky shrugged his shoulders. He was a cruel and heartless prince who had aided and abetted Ivan in all his butcheries. The murder of his best servants he could bear with equanimity. His coolness under the blow would, he thought, be evidence, if that were needed, of his unwavering loyalty to his master. He was mistaken: that evening he was arrested and marked for a dreadful end.

A like fate overtook Alexey Basmanof and his son Theodore, drinking companions of the Tsar, bullies, cads. A number of the more bloodthirsty of the *Oprit-china* suddenly found themselves the victims of the cruel lust they had furthered. They were tortured but not killed out of hand. The Tsar was collecting and saving his victims for a *grand finale* of his vengeance on Novgorod. But along with his disgraced favourites were many innocent men such as Ivan Viskovaty, a member of the Council of Boyars, Semyon Yakovlief, Nikita Funikof, the *dyaks*, Vasilief and Stepanof. Some 300 people were made ready for a mass execution in Moscow.

It seems strange that this monstrous Ivan should have been waiting all this summer of 1570 for an answer from Queen Elizabeth, would the Queen marry him or no. He was a discontented widower, but took no new consort to fill up the time. His ambassador Savin was worrying Cecil to have Anthony Jenkinson sent back to Russia and also that the Queen's answer "be written in Russ, as his master understood no other language."*

The Queen did actually write on 18th May, but her letter contained no reference to matrimony. No, her Majesty has taken as serious the alleged plots against Ivan and the contingency that he may be in danger of losing his throne. In which case the Queen assures him of free ingress and egress to and from England and will appoint a fit place where he may remain as long as he likes *at his own charges.*†

Ivan was not pleased. He withdrew his favour from the Russia Company, seized the goods of some of the

---

* *State Papers* (foreign), Nos. 894-5-6.
† *State Papers*, No. 935.

merchants, seized some of them personally. He soon discovered that some of the English traders had been consorting with traitors. It must have been difficult to find Russians wholly safe from the accusation of treason. For the Tsar's favourites of one day were his felons of the next.

However, on the great day of execution, July 25th, 1570, there were no English led out to die. The Tsar was probably thinking but little of foreign affairs, being wholly engrossed and obsessed by his hobby of cruelty. Cruelty had fed on itself and developed a monstrous growth. In the Tsar's preoccupation there was no speck of human sympathy or mercy. In the various torture chambers and dungeons the three hundred were being twisted and lacerated and burned and mutilated, but kept alive. In the square among the booths of the Kitai-Gorod many infernal contrivances were put up. An enormous cauldron of water was suspended over a stack of faggots, huge frying pans, tight moving ropes for fraying bodies asunder, pens with angry bears, gallows.

At the sight of these engines of torment the shopkeepers of the Kitai-Gorod slunk off to hiding places, leaving their goods unguarded and their tills full of money behind their counters. And the people of Moscow hid in their cellars and would not come out. It seemed as if the doings at Novgorod were to be repeated on the inhabitants of the capital. On this strange summer day all the streets of the great city were empty and a dreadful awe reigned everywhere. Alone, crippled Vasilly, the fool in Christ, squirmed in the roadway and reviled the Tsar as he passed, the people's saint, after whom the great cathedral in the Red Square will be called instead of the Interceding Virgin as Ivan had had it consecrated.

The three hundred prisoners were led out, barely able to walk. The executioners were in their places, likewise a detachment of the *Opritchina*. Ivan was there on horseback, but there did not seem to be a single spectator. Moscow had boycotted the spectacle and the Tsar was annoyed. He was providing his subjects with a great sight but they would not come out of their houses. But he must have onlookers. He stayed the executions while a number of the bodyguard went from street to street and routed up the people. And he himself pranced into the town on his horse, crying: "Come, good people! There is nothing to be afraid of. No harm shall overtake you."

In this way the theatre of death was packed with trembling men and women and every vantage ground was filled with unwilling witnesses, even the roofs of the houses. As a preface the Tsar asked the crowds whether he was not justified in destroying traitors and they cried "Long live your Majesty!"

Actually the proceedings started with a number of reprieves, the chief of which was that of Pimen, Archbishop of Novgorod, who was banished to a distant monastery. The reprieves were mostly for the Novgorodian prisoners, not for the new state prisoners inculpated by the tortured. Of these, however, several failed to appear on the square. Viazemsky had died in agony at the hands of the inquisitors. The elder Basmanof had also died in prison. It is said that Ivan made Theodore Basmanof kill his father, so as to tack eternal damna-

FOOLS IN CHRIST, VASILLY AND ARTEMY

The naked figure is that of Vasilly Blazhenny, in whose name the great cathedral dedicated to the Virgin by Ivan the Terrible in thanks for his victory over Kazan came to be known.

tion on to the destiny of the young roisterer. But Theodore Basmanof, one time monk of the Tsar's mock
brotherhood at Alexandrof, comrade of Ivan in alco-
holic and sexual debauch, came out bound like the rest,
and there was no premature death or last minute pardon for him.

The chief prisoner was Prince Ivan Viskovaty who
was hung head downward and sliced to death. The
orgy of torment and execution lasted four hours. The
Tsar accompanied by his admiring son had a great day.
He dispatched one of the prisoners with his steel-
pointed staff. After the show, father and son went to
the home of the executed Ivan Viskovaty and they demanded all the treasure in the house and Ivan assaulted
sexually the grief-stricken widow while the young Ivan
ravished the eldest daughter. This was the domestic aspect of the executions. The Tsar and his heir went to
the home of the chief prisoner and ravished the women,
and the women of the lesser prisoners were maltreated
by the *Opritchina*. Sexual brutality was far from the
natural simplicity of rape. Rape is a euphemism for
what was done to many women. As a fitting ending to
the sexual debauch some eighty widows were drowned
in the Moskva river. But whatever we may write of all
this it should be remembered that the actual happenings were much worse.

After a few days Ivan continued the executions.
The wretched rags of mutilated bodies lay about unburied, decaying rapidly in the July heat. The *Opritchina* were ordered to go about with their long knives
and chop the corpses up small so that they might be
more easily disposed of. The dogs of Moscow fought

one another for Christian flesh. There were gnawn ends of human beings in the roadways and the indifferent Muscovites kicked them as they walked to and from their shops.

But the bells were beginning to toll for the Scourge of God and a graver terror. The bells were beginning to sound the oncoming Plague.

XXVII.

MOSCOW DESTROYED BY THE TARTARS

NEXT month was the Tsar's birthday and he was forty years of age. And he made merry with new favourites. There were sounds of revelry by night in the new palace. Clowns, buffoons and jesters amused the monarch now. It was a time of heavy drinking, of overeating, of sexual excess. Ivan had become a glutton. In looks he had begun rapidly to deteriorate. He was still unbowed and had a presence and bearing which struck instant fear, but he was rougher in his aspect, fatter. His wild face marked by ungoverned lusts and limitless distrust was prematurely old and he had already much grey hair. Cruelty breeds cowardice and there was a widening yellow streak in Ivan's character which made him in his latter years incompetent as a soldier. Many of his victims had shown by their fortitude that pain can be overcome by the strength of the spirit. Men had died in fearful torments saying all the while they suffered: "God save the Tsar!" But the hobby of inflicting pain had not taught the tyrant the truth about pain. He was utterly lacking in sympathy, but he exaggerated the idea of pain in his own mind. He grew less capable of facing the danger of pain to himself and was ready to flee instantly from any danger threatening to himself. When in the spring of the following year the Khan of the Crimean Tartars, assisted by refugees from Ivan's court, put Moscow in jeopardy, the Tsar fled incontinently from the field and sacrificed the capital to save his own person. The Ivan of faith who took Kazan had disappeared; so had the fiery Ivan who took Polotsk.

The mere catalogue of the Tsar's murders becomes wearisome. One must assume that these murders were nevertheless still diverting to those who contrived them or looked on. There was the murder of Ivan Vorontsof, son of the friend of Ivan's childhood. The nameless were more numerous than the named, but among the latter were famous military leaders, heroes of the army, wealthy lords and men of great family connection. Most of the murders had their own feature of barbarity or finesse in cruelty which provided interest for a connoisseur. Voivode Golokhvastov, knowing he was in danger, hid himself in a monastery on the Oka. "He is seeking God," said Ivan. "Let us help him to get to heaven more quickly," and he had him blown up in a cask of powder.

Another day Ivan had a few wild bears let loose in a crowd of people in a Moscow market place—to see how they would tear and maul their victims, and to witness the terror of the scene.

One day at dinner the Tsar poured hot soup over one of his jester princes. The prince cried out with pain and would have torn himself away from the monarch's presence, but then Ivan stuck a knife in him and killed him where he stood. At another gathering to dine, a courtier named Mitkof had the temerity to tell Ivan that the mead he drank was mixed with the blood of his subjects. The Tsar lifted his steel-pointed staff and struck him dead. On another occasion a Lithuanian noble, a prisoner about to be killed, struck at Ivan, but the Tsarevitch intercepted the blow and knifed him. Bravo, little prince! You are as cruel as your father. They will not kill him to make you Tsar! Naturally, much less of the life of the Tsarevitch is recorded than of the Tsar, but it is clear that father and son had become comrades in murder and debauch, equally ruthless and shameless. There was no enmity between them. This was probably because their tastes were similar and because the Tsar in his deliberate wickedness was not thwarted in corrupting his child. They were grossly united and in later years, it is said, took it turn about to sleep with one another's wives.

This autumn of 1570 was a tragic one for Russia, followed by a winter and spring and summer progressively more tragic. Owing to the destructive raids of the *Opritchina* on the estates of all who did not belong to their number a great area of land fell out of cultivation. There was so much indiscriminate robbery and no legal redress, and so much tax-collecting in kind for the upkeep of the *Opritchina*, the army and the Tsar's servants, that farmers were inclined to limit their tillage to the amount required to feed themselves. This coincided with a failure of crops. The summer of 1570 was very wet. In the autumn there was already a shortage of wheat and rye. In the winter there was famine. The peasants ate the bark from the trees. Cannibalism broke out in some districts and families began to eat the smaller children. There were manifest signs of the wrath of God which now came upon Russia like the plagues of Egypt. Coincident with famine was a raging pestilence and following plague and famine came the fire and sword of the Tartar. The Horde broke north once more destroying all on its way, farmhouse, village, city, even to Moscow itself.

An agent of the Russia Company thus reported what he found:

"We understand very heavy news. The Moscow is burnt, every stick, by the Crimme, the 24th day of May last, and an innumerable number of people. And of the English house, was smothered Thomas Southam, Tofield, Waverley, Greene's wife and children, two children of Rafe, and more to the number of 25 persons were stifled in our beer cellar: and yet in the same cellar was Rafe, his wife, John Browne, and John Clarke preserved, which was wonderful. And there went into that cellar master Glover and master Rowley also, but because the heat was so great, they came forth again with much peril, so that a boy at their heels was taken with the fire, yet they escaped blindfold into another cellar, and there as God's will was they were preserved. The Emperor fled out of the field, and many of his people were carried away by the Crimme Tartar. . . . What with the Crimme Tartar on the one side and with his cruelty on the other he hath but few people left. . . ."*

And Jenkinson writing to Lord Burleigh tells of a great plague cutting across all roads. By the Tsar's command no one is allowed to go from one region to another without special permit and if a traveller is caught he is at once burned to death with all his effects. Some 300,000 have already died of the plague. The Tartars have burned and consumed all the country . . . "a just punishment for such a wicked nation." It

* Hakluyt: *Letter of Richard Uscombe.*

would seem that the Englishman did not think that the Russian nation was more worthy of God's mercy than the tyrant who governed it.

Ivan was negligent. But he was not so sunk in his vices that he let the reins of government fall out of his hands. He remained extremely active in affairs of state. He had no manifest despair. He made many decisions of all kinds every day; the Tsardom did not in any way lapse. Thus, failing to obtain a satisfactory answer from Queen Elizabeth, he withdrew at a stroke of the pen almost all the privileges of the Russia Company and granted them instead to the merchants of other nations. His personal ambition as Tsar was not dimmed. Now Sigizmund Augustus had one foot in the grave and was visibly failing. Ivan hoped to add to his titles and power and become in a few years King of Poland and Grand Duke of Lithuania. He concluded a three years' armistice with him, as it were allowing the decrepit king just that amount of time to live. Despite Ivan's debauches he never seemed to have a "morning after"; he might behave eccentrically but his mind was clear. He received ambassadors; he discussed affairs of state; he played chess, moving pieces as large as tankards on an ivory board; he continued to play his greater game of international chess. This correspondence game with annotations would fill a fair-sized book. There was the frustrate manoeuvring of his knights Taube and Kruze in and about Reval. There was the Danish development, whereby Magnus, brother of the King of Denmark, was drawn into Ivan's northern intrigue. Magnus was betrothed to a daughter of the murdered Prince Vladimir Andreyevitch. This would have made

him a close kinsman of the Tsar. Ivan promised him
five barrels of gold, gave him a bodyguard made up of
released Livonian prisoners and gave him an army with
which to chase the Swedes out of Esthonia. Taube and
Kruze were won over by the Swedes. There were many
complications and difficulties. Euphemia, the daughter
of Vladimir Andreyevitch, died before the marriage
with Magnus could be solemnised. Ivan must keep the
Dane at all costs. He offered him Euphemia's young
sister, Maria, a child who had not reached puberty.
The five barrels of gold became her dowry and Magnus
accepted. Ivan was merely using the Dane as an advanced pawn, intending for himself the conquest of the
Baltic littoral and the chastisement of its peoples.
There lay his intellectual preoccupation which caused
him to be negligent in the protection of his realm from
the Tartar.

It is true that Ivan had a presentiment of danger,
for towards the end of 1570 he sent flattering messages
to the Sultan of Turkey and tried to ensure that while
he was advancing the strength of his army against the
Swedes and rebellious Livonians he should not be taken
in the rear by a horde of belligerent Mahometans. But
the Tsar's ambassadors were not successful. It had perhaps been wiser to hurl defiance at the Sultan. In Constantinople were many Russians, refugees from the
brutality of the *Opritchina*. These Russians gave the
Sultan to believe that the greater part of Russia was
disaffected by the Tsar's cruelties, that Ivan, sunk in
debauch and vice, had lost control. At the same time
Islam was at the zenith of self-conscious power. Half
Europe was quaking because of the menace of the

Crescent. The suavity and flattery of the Tsar's ambassadors only confirmed the idea that the hour had come in which the Tartars might take revenge for all the defeats and humiliations of Ivan's reign. The Sultan demanded the return of Kazan and Astrakhan or that Ivan should pay him a yearly heavy tribute.

Ivan certainly overlooked the marvellous rapidity with which the Tartars could mobilize in the spring. Innumerable horsemen swarmed to the leadership of the Khan as if summoned by an enchanter. There were no preparations, no gathering of supplies. An almost irresistible force piled up and advanced from the south like a tornado cloud. There was consternation in Moscow. The Tsar had not time to call his forces from the north-west. The regiments on the Oka represented a mere handful of men. Twice Ivan broke away from his orgies in Moscow and joined this little army endeavouring in vain to augment it. The insults of the Khan travelled ahead of the oncoming horde. Devlet Hirei challenged the Tsar to personal combat. He would cut off the ears of the malevolent tyrant and send them to the Sultan. He never doubted but that he would sweep everything before him. Ivan was neither fool nor hero; he saw he could not withstand the raging advance of a hundred thousand Tartars aided by a large contingent of Russian refugees.

The Khan turned the flank of the army of Bielsky and Mstislavsky and swept forward upon Serpukhof where the Tsar and Tsarevitch were encamped with the greater part of the *Opritchina*. Ivan would not die in battle nor risk the chance of being handed over to a merciless foe. He fled the field, fled to Alexandrof.

That did not seem safe. He decided to make for the safety of his armies of the north-west and pushed on rapidly to Yaroslavl.

Meanwhile the Khan destroyed all before him and rapidly approached Moscow. The great revenge took place. Driving thousands of panic-stricken refugees before them into the city, the Tartars were able to profit by an enormous confusion. The Russian army had retired into the city and took up positions for street fighting. There was little fighting: the victory was won by fire and smoke. A wind was blowing over wooden Moscow and the Khan having reached the outer suburbs gave orders that they should be fired. So there rose a column of fire driving forward upon the Russians more terribly than any army. Behind this slowly the Tartars advanced, but those who tried to push the advantage and start looting the city perished with the Russians. The Khan was not entirely wise. It would have suited his purpose better to be content with a smaller fire, but he allowed his followers to spread the conflagration in the outskirts and they kindled a flame wide enough to destroy the whole city so that the greater part of the plunder was destroyed. But merely as revenge his triumph was stupendous. It could not have been more terrible for Moscow. The dense smoke through which the roaring fire burst and leapt drove from district to district, suffocating and consuming. The number who died was very great. One can tell how great the danger was to life by the number of English who perished. For in a great emergency of danger English can always be counted upon to be more cool than Russians. Those Russians whom the Tartars captured were those who were lucky enough to get ahead of the fire and take refuge in the northern suburbs. The vast wooden city was utterly destroyed. Only the few stone walls and the stone churches remained standing. The Kremlin walls withstood the heat and the flame, but the gates were shut, probably by the order of the Metropolitan Cyril, who solemnly saved himself while his flock perished. In the course of three hours upwards of half a million people were destroyed. The most terrible feature was that of the struggling crowds in the roadways, trapped by themselves, wedged in, trampling on one another, unable to go forward or back or out, their bleared panic-stricken faces in the smoke, the fall of glowing embers on them, the insufferable heat cooking them *en masse*, the sudden billowing volumes of flame searing and shrivelling them like flies.

"The city and suburbs," wrote Horsey, "thirty miles compass, built most of fir and oak timber, was set on fire and burnt within six hours space, with infinite thousands men, women and children, burnt, smothered to death by the fiery ire, and likewise in the stone churches, monasteries, vaults and cellars; very few escaping both without and within the three walled castles. The river and ditches about Moscow stopped and filled with the multitude of people laden with gold, silver, jewels, chains, earrings, bracelets and treasure, that went for succour even to save their heads above water."

The spectacle of the fire was so terrifying that the Khan of the Tartars withdrew. There was no looting amid the hot ash, no despoiling of corpses. The Kremlin was not besieged nor did the archers draw their bows upon the palaces and cathedrals within. The terror of the holocaust infected the Horde. The rumour spread that Magnus was hastening from Livonia with a great army, and the victorious Tartars turned about and started homeward at the same speed at which they had advanced. Couriers informed the Tsar who had moved from Yaroslavl to Rostof the Great and he ordered Michael Vorotinsky to the pursuit. But the Khan was too strong to be harried by rearguard actions. He punished as he withdrew and cut another broad swath of destruction from north to south. The booty of his followers was enormous and it included some 100,000 virgins to be sold to the common people in the bazaars or entered in the harems of his princes, some of the choicer Russian beauties being sent to the Sultan himself. But these spoils and the actual revenge of the burning of Moscow were the chief fruits of victory. Ivan ignominiously sued for peace but when it came to the parley he bluffed and procrastinated and mobilised and organised. The Khan soon realised that he could not repeat his attack. He wished the return to the Moslem of Kazan and Astrakhan but he was powerless to obtain it.

The Tsar at Alexandrof ordered the clearing of the _débris_ of his capital. Provincials surged in to build a new city and as by miracle another wooden Moscow was soon seen rising from the charred foundations. Ivan was not moved by the calamity as he had been by the previous great fire. He made no grand repentance, but when the emissary of the Khan vaunted his master's prowess he reproved him sternly. "It was the hand of God," he said, "punishing me for my sins. The Khan was only an instrument of God's anger!"*

* See also Appendix: "The Burning of Moscow by the Tartars."

XXVIII.

THE TSAR'S THIRD MARRIAGE

AGAIN invitations went forth to the families of
Russia to send their marriageable daughters
that Ivan might look them over and choose a
bride. He had but to give the word: no one dared keep
a virgin at home. The invitation was very widely sent,
to nobles, merchants, commoners. Thousands of girls
were chaperoned to the palace at Alexandrof. The Tsar
and the Tsarevitch made the inspection. The ashes of
his capital are scarcely cold and for a new marriage he
will make carouse. The Tsar was not in the slightest
oppressed by fate. Picking a bride was an amusement
for father and son. It was decided that the Tsarevitch
also should have the choice of a wife from the assembly
of young ladies. Each of the girls had a personal interview with the Tsar. The choosing lasted for days. First
the choice was narrowed down to twenty-four and then
to twelve. The last dozen were submitted to doctors
and wise women that their physical perfection might be
certified. The Tsar and his son and their favourites discussed the merits of each of the twelve. In this they
were guided by no political considerations. The only
criterion was sexual desirability. The Tsar in this matter believed himself to be a very capable judge and a
capable adviser for his adolescent heir.

Finally the choice was made. The Tsar chose for
himself Martha Sobakin, the daughter of a Novgorod
merchant, and for the Tsarevitch, Yevdokia Saburof,
also the daughter of a commoner. The fathers of the

brides were at once raised to the rank of boyars. The Tsar was married to Martha on the 28th October; the Tsarevitch to Yevdokia on the 3rd November.

In the week preceding the ceremony there were a number of executions, chief of which was the impalement of the villainous brother of the late Tsaritsa, Prince Michael Temgryuk. The chief charge against the new victims of the Tsar's ferocity was lack of fidelity in resistance to the Khan. But there was another element in Ivan's displeasure and that was the assumed enmity of certain of the boyars against the parvenu families of Sobakin and Saburof. The Tsar's young bride became unwell. Sorcerers must be at work destroying her. According to Ivan, Martha was ill when he married her and it was impossible to consummate the union. That, of course, may have been true, or it may have been an afterthought on Ivan's part. Considering the medical precaution and advice taken it seems unlikely that the Tsar would have married a dying girl. Within a fortnight of the solemnisation of matrimony Martha died. Ivan declared at once that like Anastasia and the Circassian Maria she had been poisoned. He said he nursed her through the time and that she died a virgin. But Ivan had become a brutal sexual pervert and another suspicion is possible. We do not know what Ivan was up to in that fortnight of married life which ended in the death of his consort.

According to the laws of the Orthodox Church a man might not marry a fourth time. If the laws were observed, Ivan, after the death of Martha, must have remained celibate for the rest of his life. It was for that reason that he declared that Martha had died a virgin.

He had no intention of remaining celibate but at the same time he did not wish to quarrel with the Church over something so fundamental and traditional as the law against a fourth wife. Instead he strove to substantiate a claim that an unconsummated marriage was no marriage, in that way overriding the eternal validity of its sacrament, assuming a carnal rather than a spiritual bond. Considerable trouble was in store for him and for the Church in the disposal of his argument. But the Metropolitan Cyril died. The authority of the Tsar was greater than that of the bishops. He soon had his way and next year he was married for the fourth time.

The Tsarevitch was more fortunate in his wife Yevdokia, but he imitated his father in lasciviousness, and in a few years had her made a nun and shut in a convent in Suzdal. And he took himself another consort and in turn made her a nun and sent her to Bielozersk and took a third wife.

XXIX.

JENKINSON'S RETURN

IN 1571 Ivan the Terrible was deeply displeased with Queen Elizabeth. Andrew Savin, his ambassador, had been shabbily received in London. The English said afterwards that he had been treated well, but the man who wears the shoe knows whether it pinches. Had Savin been flattered and nobly entertained he would probably have exaggerated Elizabeth's bounty when reporting to his master. He had had difficulty in presenting personally Ivan's letter to the Queen, and when he had done so Elizabeth had roughly broken open the letter in a preoccupied way without first kissing the cross on the seal. Possibly Savin was not a very capable ambassador but he was shrewd enough to judge that Russia was treated as a second-class power. There was some petty concern to keep him in a good humour because of trade; but that was all. Thomas Randolfe had scored a diplomatic success in Russia, but it was not forgotten that Ivan had kept him a prisoner in his house in Moscow. Possibly Randolfe did not make it clear to the Queen on what terms he had won Ivan's consent to an extension of commercial privileges. Nor was it clear in London that Russia was almost indifferent to the material advantages of trade with England. The English monopoly had not been paid for and it was seen when this monopoly was abolished that other nations were eager to take up what England was dropping and Russia would lose nothing.

It is also probable that the reports of Ivan's cruelties and debauch had alienated English sympathy. Ivan had himself hinted that he was not very secure on his throne and he was taken at his word. A sovereign who behaved as he did must be in danger of assassination or civil war. Cecil's judgment was at fault. The Tsar had other reasons for pretending to insecurity. The first was that he might seem justified in the stern measures he took against traitors and those he suspected of treason. The second was the recurring whim that he would renounce his throne and seek spiritual peace in a monastic cell. He still believed that the moment would come when he would emulate the example of his contemporary Charles V and at the height of his power retire from the world. As a monarch Ivan stood somewhat discredited in London. The Queen evidently regarded his personal pretensions as ridiculous and Ivan's proposal for an alliance, defensive and offensive, did not seem to have much practical significance. Russia could not help England to fight Spain; England would not lightly be drawn into a conflict with Sweden or Denmark to help Russia. What was at stake was trade and the mutual interest could, it seemed, be only commercial. There was the trouble. Ivan was not commercially minded. He did much for the commerce of his country but he put his "private and secret affairs" far above trade. Through personal contact with the first English travellers he had become strangely Anglophile. Russians have been and are fascinated by the English and that fascination obtained then. But he had discovered that their courtly manners and admirable self-conceit masked a petty materialism. And the Queen herself was

capable of flirting with him and fooling him for the
sake of some sordid advantage to her merchants. Such
low behaviour shocked and angered him. He lifted one
finger and the trading profits of the English vanished.

England was wounded in the moneybags. Russian
affairs became suddenly much discussed. A remedy
must be sought and quickly applied. A letter had come
from Ivan couched in peremptory language. If she
wished to retain his friendship she must send an ambassador betimes. Someone must be sent who could
mollify the Tsar, assure him of the Queen's continued
affection and personal interest, explain, flatter, coax.
Randolfe was consulted, but it is probable he had no
wish to return to Russia. There was one man and only
one who might save the situation and that was old Anthony Jenkinson, tireless servant of the Russia Company at a wage of forty pounds a year, by no means
a gentleman of birth or worthy emissary, had Ivan
known. But the Tsar admired this intrepid and dignified commercial traveller and had imparted to him se-
crets to be breathed into the ears of her Majesty the
Queen alone. The strict honour with which Jenkinson
kept the Tsar's secret has become history's loss. Jenkinson was a man of honour. That at least the Tsar had
understood. He desired that Jenkinson should be allowed to return to Moscow as he had promised. The
fact that he did not return he regarded as an affront.
But if Jenkinson did at last return Ivan intended to
call him to account. He must know what he said to
Queen Elizabeth and what the Queen replied.

Jenkinson was sent. He had thought to retire to
spend the last of his years in peace at home, but the

Queen desired that he should set off on the delicate and hazardous mission of winning back the Tsar to friendship and commercial good will. He embarked in the *Swallow* in the spring of 1571 and arrived at the mouth of the Dvina in the following July. During the period of his voyage Moscow had been destroyed by the Tartars. Upon arrival he at once sent a messenger to inform the Tsar of his arrival, but his mission must have seemed to him much more problematical. His messenger did not return. The Tsar knew in August that he had come but he ignored him and sent no welcoming message of any kind. Jenkinson spent the rest of the summer, the autumn and a great part of the winter waiting in the north. While he was there the Tsar got married to Martha Sobakina, but he did not call the Englishman to the wedding. The only explanation was that the country between Kholmagora and Alexandrof was visited by plague and none were allowed to pass through. "Thus was I kept without answer or order from his Majesty, and remained at the said Colmogro, until the 18th of January following, neither having a gentleman to safeguard me, nor lodging appointed me, nor allowance of victuals . . . which argued his serious displeasure towards our nation. And the people of the country perceiving the same used toward me and my company some discourtesies."

But at last he was informed that the plague had ceased and an order came for him to go to "a city called Peraslave near to the court." He arrived at Pereslavl on the 3rd February, and was shown a house where he must live, but he was "straitly kept" and was, in effect, kept over five weeks a prisoner in this house. On the

14th March he was sent for and set off with a gentleman escort to be presented to the Tsar, but on his way a message came ordering him back to his house at Pereslavl to remain until his Majesty's further pleasure. . . . "wherewith I was much dismayed and marvelled what that sudden change meant."

Jenkinson's desperate state of mind may be imagined. He was a free-born Englishman, a bold and intrepid traveller; he had been treated on his previous visits to Russia with princely condescension and rare kindness. Such treatment as he was now receiving seemed to bode ill for him personally and for English trade.

But on the 20th March he was sent for again and on the 23rd he had audience of the Tsar. And he was graciously received. "The Emperor sitting in royal state, stood up and said: 'How doth Queen Elizabeth, my sister; is she in health?' To whom I answered: 'God doth bless her Majesty with health and peace, and doth wish the like unto thee, Lord, her loving brother.' Then his Majesty sitting down again, commanded all his nobility and others to depart, and avoid the chamber, saving the chief secretary and one other of the Council, and willing me to approach near unto him, with my interpreter, said unto me these words:

" 'Anthony, the last time thou wast with us here, we did commit unto thee our trusty and secret message to be declared unto the Queen's Majesty herself, thy mistress, at thy coming home, and did expect thy coming unto us again at the time we appointed, with a full answer of the same from her highness. And in the meantime there came unto us several messengers three times, to whom we sent to know whether thou Anthony were returned home in safety, and when thou shouldst return unto us again. But these messengers, could tell us nothing and did miscall and abuse with evil words both our messenger and thee, whereat we were much offended. . . . And shortly afterwards we were informed that one, Thomas Randolfe, was come into our dominions, by the way of Dvina, ambassador from the Queen, and we sent a gentleman to meet and conduct him to our city of Moscow, at which time we looked that thou shouldst have returned unto us again. . . . We gave the said Thomas access and audience, but all his talk with us was about merchants' affairs. We know that merchants' matters are to be heard, for that they are the stay of our princely treasures. But first Princes' affairs are to be established and then merchants'. . . .*"

The Tsar made a long discourse, interpreted at his will by the interpreter. Probably the Tsar spoke at some length before he paused to be interpreted. The report which the English ambassador put in writing is not verbatim. But it is clear that Ivan's speech was more a remonstrance than a tirade. Randolfe had promised on the Queen's behalf things which had not been fulfilled and the Russian ambassador had been obliged to return from London without achieving anything of the Tsar's personal desires. Jenkinson humbly begged leave to reply. He said:

"Most noble and famous Prince, the message which thy Highness did send by me unto the Queen, her most excellent Majesty, touching thy Princely and secret affairs, immediately, and so soon as I came home, I did

* Hakluyt: *Anthony Jenkinson*, 1571–2.

declare both secretly and truly unto the Queen's Majesty herself, word for word, as thou, Lord, didst command me. Which her Highness did willingly hear and accept, and being mindful thereof, and willing to answer the same, the next shipping after her Majesty did send unto thee, Lord, Her Highness's Ambassador, Thomas Randolfe, whose approved wisdom and fidelity was unto her Majesty well known, and therefore thought meet to be sent to so worthy a Prince, who had commission not only to treat with thy Majesty of merchants' affairs, but also of those thy Princely and secret affairs committed unto me. And the cause, most gracious Prince, that I was not sent again, was for that I was employed in service upon the seas against the Queen's Majesty's enemies. . . .''

Jenkinson made a long reply and although he put princely matters first, it would seem that the longer part of his discourse pertained to merchants' affairs. But he was able to suggest to the Tsar that his Majesty had not rightly understood what Thomas Randolfe had promised when he obtained extension of the trading privileges. "He denieth that he ever did agree, conclude or make any promise in any condition or order, as is alleged, otherwise than it should please the Queen her Majesty to like of at his return home."

In a wheedling courtly way Jenkinson managed to shift the blame from the Queen on to the ineptitude of the Tsar's ambassador Savin and on to "wicked persons of our nation, resident here," that is on to English traders who were not members of the Russia Company. He bore a handsome present as a peace offering and a long personal letter from Queen Elizabeth. Ivan sat rigid, holding his steel-pointed staff in one hand, his bearded face immobile and of fixed expression, his strange eyes watchful but not distraught. He was in a good humour, he liked Jenkinson, whose bearing had some sort of fascination for him. When the English ambassador had concluded his long defence of his sovereign the Tsar seemed to be well pleased and commanded him to sit down.

"And after pausing a while, his Majesty said these words to me:—'It is now a time which we spend in fasting and praying, being the week before Easter, and for that we will shortly depart toward our borders of Novgorod, we cannot give you answer, nor your dispatch here, but you shall go from hence and tarry us upon the way, where we will shortly come, and then you shall know our pleasure and have your dispatch."

This first conversation took place at Alexandrof. The next was appointed to take place some six weeks later at a town on the way from Alexandrof to Novgorod. Meanwhile the Tsar, far from fasting and praying, had decided in the middle of Lent to take Anna Koltovska to bed, but must have the blessing of the Church and call it a marriage. Anna was just a girl who had found favour in his eyes, not even a merchant's daughter, something lower still. The Metropolitan Cyril was dead, but Leonide, the venal Archbishop of Novgorod, managed to obtain the sanction of the Church for this fourth union before a new Metropolitan was appointed. One of the curious terms of the sanction was that the Tsar should enter no church for the rest of Lent and be debarred from the blessings of the Holy Sacrament.

The Church's indulgence was for the Tsar alone and must never be quoted by any of his subjects as a precedent for a similar matrimonial outrage. If, in truth, Ivan had at one time sought the hand of Queen Elizabeth through the intermediary of the English traveller, Jenkinson must have been roused by this marriage to some cynical observations.

But Ivan was undoubtedly in a good humour. The Queen's letter pleased him. Whatever he had against her he forgave. His platonic and sentimental attachment to his sister of England was re-established. Jenkinson had fascinated him. There was something agreeable about the English. Sometime or other he would have an Englishwoman to wife, if not Elizabeth who was in any case getting too old for him, then some beautiful young lady of quality whom his ambassador would select.

On the 8th May Jenkinson had a long parley with the Tsar's secretary and submitted a list of commercial grievances and difficulties. These were put before Ivan and he readily agreed to pardon all the traders who had incurred his displeasure and to restore all the privileges which he had withdrawn. Jenkinson had a great diplomatic success. As regards the Tsar's "secret and princely affairs," Ivan said to him, "We do now leave all those matters, and set them aside for the time, because our mind is now otherwise changed, but hereafter, when occasion shall move us to the like, we will then talk of those matters again."

XXX

DEATH OF SIGIZMUND AUGUSTUS

THE Tsar, with his sons and his favourites and his young consort Anna, continued his journey to Novgorod, there to conclude, if possible, an armistice with Sweden. As Moscow was in danger of another attack by the Tartars he had had a great deal of his treasure removed to Novgorod. He felt safer there, nearer to his army, and evidently anticipated no attempt on his life by the survivors of the population he had massacred. But Novgorod was dead; walls without people. It never recovered. The Church alone flourished, Russia had such a superfluity of monks and nuns that killing a few made no difference. The monasteries and convents soon filled up again. The spoliation of the altars may have been remembered against Ivan, but the Archbishop, Leonide, was his man and would not hold his sins against him. Ivan was more at home among monks and priests than with the laity. Merchants were boors; their absence did not trouble him. Going to Novgorod, Ivan went to make merry in the monasteries and the palace of the archbishop, to dispute the theological points, to supervise the singing of the ecclesiastical choirs. He entered into long arguments with clerics, but as he always carried his staff, these arguments sometimes ended abruptly and unfortunately.

It has been suggested that Ivan, fleeing to Novgorod, was possessed by craven fear, but although it would have been braver to remain in Moscow and face the oncoming Tartars there is little in his behaviour that can be called pusillanimous. He was happy in his new marriage and was on good terms with the world. In his conversation with Jenkinson he had dropped the question of taking refuge in England in case he lost his throne. Though he always pretended to insecurity, he treated the envoys of Sweden and Lithuania with such imperiousness that he must have felt fairly sure of himself and his position. Although possibly he required the whole of his army for the defence of Moscow against the Tartars, his object at Novgorod was to impose peace on Sweden rather than to seek it. And as regards Poland and Lithuania he was not less self-confident.

The latter half of the year 1572 was eventful and was an important period in the reign of Ivan the Terrible. On the 18th July King Sigizmund Augustus died; on the 1st August Michael Vorotinsky completely routed the immense army of the Khan which had advanced to within thirty-five miles of Moscow. The Tsar returned to the capital to give thanks and he abolished the *Opritchina*.

Sigizmund Augustus died in poverty, robbed by his mistress and the various parasites of his court. There was not even the money to bury him properly. It was reported that on his death bed he named Ivan his successor, which is not likely to be true. A number of Polish and Lithuanian nobles were in favour of the dual throne going to Ivan's younger son Fedor. The Tsar said: "If you would be willing to take Fedor why not take me? I should be a stronger sovereign than he." Doubtless some of the Poles and Lithuanians thought he might prove a whit too strong. Ivan wrote a hypo-

critical letter expressing his grief at the death of his
brother Sigizmund and saw himself already King of
Poland and Grand Duke of Lithuania.

If anything was wanting to complete Ivan's good
humour it was supplied by Vorotinsky a fortnight later
when he routed the Tartar. In a very bloody and a
prolonged battle the 120,000 followers of the Khan
were reduced to 20,000. At first it was a mediaeval battle of archery and sword-play, hand to hand, face to
face, an imbroglio of floundering horses and gleaming
scimitars and swords. This dreadful clash was indeci-
sive, but Vorotinsky, feigning defeat, lured the Tartar
into a position where he could be pounded by the Russian artillery. Tartar horses and men could not stand
the Russian fireworks. The Muscovites counter-attacked
them in their amazement and started a rout which soon
became almost massacre.

The Russian victory was a great one. It greatly enhanced the prestige of Muscovite arms and the authority of the Tsar. The Khan was completely humbled.
His chance of restoring Kazan and Astrakhan had
faded completely. The Sultan bowed to Fate. Vorotinsky's army of 70,000 men, flushed with victory, was
ready for new enterprises. Ivan was strengthened in all
his dealings with the west. He could treat the King of
Sweden with a greater contempt and at once proceeded
to do so. But of course there was no call for a show of
aggressiveness to Poland and Lithuania. His ambassadors must point out how much more desirable the Tsar
had become as a prospective sovereign, since he had disposed of his greatest enemy in the field. The Russian
army was no longer a menace, but a guarantee of peace.

Ivan was now disturbed by the evil repute his executions and massacres had obtained for him abroad. The Polish monarchy was elective and many would undoubtedly vote against Ivan because of his barbarity. Kurbsky, who stood to lose his head if Ivan became King, was an indefatigable propagandist against him. Not that Ivan's cruelties aroused universal indignation! It was a cruel age, and this same August, 1572, in which Ivan decided to turn over a new leaf, saw in Paris the terrible massacre of St. Bartholomew. Ivan's barbarity was interpreted more as dangerous strength of character than as inhumanity. Many Polish and Lithuanian nobles thought they would rather have a weaker and more pliable lord. And it may be surmised that none of them wanted the introduction of the *Opritchina* into their country. The lawlessness of this large force was a greater blot on the Tsar's rule than all his personal acts of violence.

It may well be thought that Russia rejoiced at the abolition of the *Ópritchina*, all of Russia except the *Opritchina* itself. The great bodyguard was reduced in rank and shorn of authority and estate. The Tsar was able to do this leaning on Vorotinsky and his victorious army. He could not have done it but for the new sense of security he had obtained. But that he did it is also testimony to his unquestioned authority and the tremendous dominance of his will and character. It may be that many stood aghast at Ivan's vices, but he was more feared than any monarch in the land had ever been before. We would do wrong to see him as a mad Tsar staggering from vice to vice. He was in Moscow in 1572 the supreme, unquestioned, magnificent potentate, selfconscious of proximity to the "Divine Substance, triune, unique, indivisible, Father, Son and Holy Ghost," to quote from the preface to his title.

The *Opritchina* was disbanded and the *Zemschina* resumed the position which the former had usurped. Paisy, the abbot of Solovetsk, who had given false evidence against the Metropolitan Philip, was punished. Many hateful personalities hitherto close to the Tsar were banished from court. Boris Godunof began to find favour in the Tsar's eyes. Godunof, a distant kinsman of the Tsar, was ambitious, but he was the first man of real ability to share Ivan's counsel since Alexey Adashef. It is thought possible that the abolition of the *Opritchina* was his idea. The young and handsome Boris, though unscrupulous in politics, had many moral scruples. He was opposed to violence and bloodshed, and though he had been at court for some years, he had managed to keep unsoiled by blood. He had not been among those who ran to fulfil some murder which the favourites thought Ivan wanted. It showed no mean capacity in him to be able to keep out of violence and yet keep in favour.

Boris Godunof advised moderation and craft. All the autumn and winter Ivan plied Poles and Lithuanians with honeyed speeches: "How sad that Sigizmund Augustus should die leaving no children behind him to pray for his soul," and the like. Domestic rule was not marked by murder and violence. The army was ordered north-west against the domains of Sweden. Magnus set to work to conquer a kingdom for himself; for he still held the Tsar's promise of Livonia. Boris Godunof must have laughed cynically at Magnus; for he well

knew that the Tsar would never give Livonia to a
Dane. The Tsar returned to Novgorod and thence
went to the Esthonian front where he made war with
great barbarity. City after city fell into his hands or
those of Magnus. The armies conquered and ravaged
the land, slaying or maltreating the males, outraging
almost all the women. In this campaign the Tsar's favourite, Skuratof, was killed. Malyuta Skuratof, drinking companion and murderer, had survived the Tsar's
fickleness of favour and despite the rise of Godunof
had been still the pet roisterer and villain. Ivan was
unreasonably angry when he heard of his death in a
battle. He made a great pile of bound prisoners, Swedes
and Germans, heaped faggots over them and burned
them alive in token of his ire.

The campaign went well for the Russians, though in
the spring of 1573 the Swedes found a capable general
in Akeson, who, with a small force, defeated 16,000
Russians near Lode. The Tsar's attention was diverted
by a mutiny of the tribes near Kazan and the war with
Sweden hung fire.

At this time Ivan decided to dispose of the pretensions of Prince Magnus for whom he had little further
use. He had been promised marriage; that at least
should be vouchsafed to him. On the 12th April he was
married at Novgorod to Princess Maria, the younger
daughter of the deceased Vladimir Andreyevitch. It
was a very gay wedding. Swarms of German guests
were invited. After the wedding feast there was much
dancing and Ivan constituted himself master of ceremonies. Then there was singing by the monastery
choirs. Ivan, staff in hand, conducted the young monks

and cracked on the head any he thought had made a wrong note. Magnus was pleased. Maria's dowry, the barrels, had been delivered and he believed them to be barrels of gold. And he thought that on the day after the wedding he would be proclaimed King of Livonia. But actually the barrels contained raiment, not gold. And instead of being given Livonia he was fobbed off with a small estate. Ivan remarked that Taube and Kruze had proved traitors and that the Tsar would not be deceived again. Magnus had not the spirit to protest violently. He took what was given him and lived as a poor man, "with three-course dinners," as the chronicler adds. And he went out each day to buy sweets for his wife, who was only thirteen.

At the time of these wedding festivities and disappointments, the Polish Diet in Warsaw was endeavouring to choose a king. There were several candidates: Ernst, the son of the Emperor Maximilian; the King of Sweden; Sigizmund, the son of the King of Sweden; Henri, Duc d'Anjou, the brother of Charles IX, King of France; the Tsar of Russia, Ivan IV. Ivan had not allowed his son Fedor to be named as a candidate.

On the motion of John Zamoisky it was decided that the king should be elected not merely by the Diet but by the nobility as a whole; each noble having the right to cast a personal vote. The king was to be chosen, not by a vote of Parliament but by a referendum. It is thought that this change in procedure was the original idea of Montluc, the French ambassador, who had in advance gathered a great number of votes for the Duc d'Anjou. In the propaganda which ensued Ivan did not take a very active part, proudly assuming that Poland had need of him. He was greatly opposed to the French nominee, because France was friendly with the Sultan, but he could not believe that the Protestant half of the Polish nobility would vote for a man intimately connected with the massacre of St. Bartholomew. The supreme virtue of Poland at that time was her religious freedom. But it so happened there was such division among the interests of the rival candidates that the most unlikely and unsuitable slipped to success, the Duc d'Anjou. He was the only candidate who had a capable election agent. The number of nobles who could be bought was greater than that of any group who were united by conviction. Ivan was disappointed, but if he had taken more trouble he could easily have outbid the Frenchman both in promises and money.

XXXI.

ANNA MEWED UP

IVAN began to slow down. It is not uncommon for Russians over the age of forty to regard themselves as elderly. Longevity, it will be easily understood, was uncommon. Ivan was becoming heavier. His gluttony and sexual indulgence were greater. He soon tired, was stouter, slept longer. As he slept a longer time, executions were naturally fewer. During the years 1574–5 there was a continual squabble at court regarding precedence. This permitted the Tsar to develop again his strange fetishism. He chose to see himself surrounded by dangerous traitors when, in fact, his whole court was not only loyal but abject. The Emperor Maximilian asked the ambassador Sukorsky how it was that Russians could be found to serve a tyrant with such zeal. He replied: "We Russians are devoted to our sovereigns whether they be merciful or cruel." We have the case of a man impaled, suffering untold agony, praising the Tsar, his torturer, with his dying breath. The troubles regarding court precedence and the position of a parvenu like Boris Godunof were capable of adjustment in a peaceful fashion by the Tsar. His word was law. The Tsar had but to decide at once what should be a man's position in the court or in the army and the decision was bound to be accepted. But Ivan let the families argue. Like Peter the Great, Ivan preferred talent to nobility of birth. Second only to the Holy Family, Ivan felt that most of the nobility of birth was locked up in himself and that what was left over was so small as to be difficult to distinguish. And he was not impressed by tradition. He was unimpressed by the argument that the position of a man's grandfather in the army must determine the rank of the grandson. But the Tsar loved both argument and drama. He allowed men to be disobedient in order to hear their defence, make his reply and hand them over to the executioner.

But his belief in men's guilt grew after he had executed them. What had been merely disobedience or obstinacy, became in his mind treachery, and treachery became treason. Ivan wrung his hands in despair and asked: "What am I to do, surrounded by traitors?" At the same time he was deeply convinced of his own wickedness, though he regarded adultery and gluttony as his chief sins. It seems possible that at times he held the view that a Tsar can do no murder. He seldom repented causing a death. He had even a crazy notion that death by him was an honour, or a sacrifice acceptable to God. He had a great contempt for those who fled from martyrdom. The Shakespearean conscience-stricken blood-guiltiness was not his. The ghosts of his victims could only have come back to thank him.

But in those years 1574–5 murder had become petty and habitual. It is an obscure period in Ivan's domestic history because he contrived little that was new. The abolition of the *Opritchina* caused the great conflict as to rank and precedence. But the details of that immense palaver, with its executions, banishments, triumphs, humiliations, are less interesting than the state of the Tsar's mind. Premature old age was creeping upon

Ivan. The conflict between sexual restlessness and the desire to become a monk and renounce the world and the flesh had become more insistent. Ivan still remained a duality. The lustful carnal nature travelled in the company of a frustrated but undying Byzantine fanatic. The fanatic in the Tsar was like the monk living all his life unmoving, stretched in the coffin at the entrance to Sergey-Troitsky Monastery. This black negation of the blessings of living had its counterpart in the thousandfold executions of his reign. As one chronicler of the time says of his victims, "They were sent by the earthly Tsar to the heavenly Tsar." But the same nature which ruled in state, and slew so many, and possessed so many women, was capable, or almost capable, of being a complete ascetic. Actually, his lusts, grown monstrous, proved too strong for him.

Towards the end of 1574 there was evidence of a new sexual restlessness. He had got tired of his young wife Anna. It is said that he was displeased because she had proved barren, though it is not clear of what advantage further children could have been to him. It is more probable that he regarded the barrenness of the union as a sign of God's displeasure with the marriage. He turned upon Leonide, Archbishop of Novgorod, who had made the marriage possible by absolving him from the rule of the Church against a fourth wife. Despite the companionship he had had with this venal prelate, he summoned him to Moscow, tore his vestments from him with his own hands, and had him sewn up naked in a bearskin and delivered to the bearhounds to tear to death.

This apparently happened in the beginning of 1575.

Anna was put away and shorn as a nun, exchanging
the highest glory of a Russian woman for the austeri-
ties of a convent cell. She became Sister Darya, but she
had fifty-one more years to live and she lived them all
in the convent to which she had been banished. What
Ivan said to her for the last time, when she was leaving
him, we do not know. But it is possible to surmise that
he told her he was going to do the same thing, be shorn
as a monk and renounce the world and his throne. He
evidently had that intention and in the following year
compromised it by renouncing the throne, though he
did not become a monk. A strong and unremitting sexuality was a dominant feature of his character and was
an unfailing obstacle to monkery. He had been an abbot with mistresses, but that had not satisfied his craving for black. When he had put Anna away he had another opportunity to enter holy celibacy, but the flesh
was weak. He took another commoner to bed, Anna
Vasilchikof, who is sometimes called his fifth wife,
though the union was consummated without the blessing of the Church. And before he had disposed of Anna
Vasilchikof the Tsar took a beautiful widow called
Vasillissa Melentief. If these are to be considered
wives, Ivan may be said to have been jointly married
to his fifth and sixth wives at the same time. However,
in the same year that he took Anna Vasilchikof the
Tsar made his renunciation of the throne.

One day probably in the late summer of 1575 Ivan
said to one of the Tartar princes in his retinue: "Henceforth you shall be Tsar and I shall be your subject!"
This was the Khan Ssain Bulat. He was a doltish good-
humoured Tartar, christened as Simeon and married to

a daughter of Mstislavsky. There was no solemn abdication and no solemn coronation. Simply the Tsar took his crown from his head and put it on the head of the Tartar and said: "You wear it!"

"He resigned his kingdom," wrote Giles Fletcher at the time, "as though he meant to draw himself from all public doings to a quiet private life."

"He setts in majestie and the old Emperor Ivan comes and prostrates himself," wrote Sir Jerome Horsey. For the first time in contemporary writing Ivan is referred to as an old man. His actual age when making this act of renunciation was forty-five. There is unfortunately little Russian comment on the matter and the Russian historians, great and small, are inclined to ignore the event as if it had no significance or did not take place. English visitors to the court were cynical: they regarded it as a device for raising money.

At first the abdication must have been thought to be one of Ivan's brutal jests, likely to have a tragic sequel. Ivan had made a similar gesture seven years previously, when he had placed his mantle and crown on old Prince Federof and led him to the throne and then killed him. There was a similarity of phrase in Ivan's words on these occasions. To Federof he said: "As I had the power to make thee tsar, so I have the power to bring thee down." Of Simeon he told an envoy of Queen Elizabeth: "I have not so far resigned tsardom but that at my pleasure I can take it again. Tsar Simeon has my crown, but I have seven more crowns and all my treasure also."*

* 29th November, 1575. Vide *State Papers of the Reign of Queen Elizabeth.*

But there is little doubt that the Tartar sat on the throne and had the formal power of the autocrat for the space of a year. He received all petitions, he signed all documents in his own name and under his seal. "They plead in all courts of justice in his name, coins money, receives customs and casual fines and certain revenues," wrote Horsey. He received as Tsar the Metropolitan, the bishops and nobles and foreign ambassadors. Some of the ambassadors and foreign agents refused to have dealings except with Ivan himself. That certainly applies to the English envoys to Moscow. They sought Ivan and found him in plain dress, refusing to be called Majesty, and were not a little bewildered by the situation which they found. Ivan had very quickly withdrawn his favour once more from the English merchants, laying intolerable fines and taxes on them. He was clearly becoming more avaricious as he grew older. It had been his custom when murdering a family to seize the family treasure and he is not immune from the suspicion of having men executed simply to possess their gold. He was all the time filling his treasure barrels and it went against the grain to see traders making money and shipping it out of the country. Now in 1575–6 he was probably using Tsar Simeon to squeeze the English merchants more. It amused him finally that England never got excited unless her trade were affected. As a result of much parley with the English envoy, David Silvestre, Ivan sent Queen Elizabeth a very rude letter in which he told her that she "flowed in her maidenly estate like a maid" and that he was annulling all the privileges of her merchants. On the other hand there was a rumour that he was preparing to transport his treasure to Solovetsky Monastery on the White Sea with a view to taking passage on an English ship and decamping finally to England. But that may be dismissed as a mad fantasy, a plan which Ivan never intended to follow.

The state of his mind in the year of his renunciation is largely a matter of surmise. What Russian records existed were destroyed in the Moscow fire of 1626. We are inclined to think that the renunciation expressed a recurrent phase of the Tsar's frustrated religiosity. It is true he did not explain it in that way. He said: "I have resigned the estate of my government into the hands of a stranger on account of the perverse and evil dealing of my subjects." On the same plea in December, 1564, he had made a tentative renunciation of the throne when he quit Moscow and made a refuge at Alexandrof. But the recurrent phenomenon of renunciation is more cogent than the reasons given. Later, after he had murdered his son, the thought of renunciation recurred. He was strangely frustrated and, as it happened, was made a monk at last, at the moment of his death in 1584.

Giles Fletcher, however, recounts a sinister aspect of the rule of Simeon and Ivan. "Towards the end of the year (1575) he caused this new king to call in all charters granted to bishopricks and monasteries which they had enjoyed many hundred years before. Which were all cancelled." Then, when Ivan resumed the throne, all the religious establishments were called upon to renew their charters and he used the occasion to rob them of much wealth.

XXXII.

STEPHEN, KING OF POLAND

POLAND strove to make its monarchy not only
elective but constitutional. It had many powerful and influential Protestants imbued with a
desire to curb the authority of kings and safeguard the
liberties of the subject. In advance of election all the
candidates for the throne endorsed the conditions
gladly, each surmising that once he was seated in power
he could ignore or annul the election pact. One cannot
imagine Ivan consenting not to marry or not to seek
divorce without the approval of the Polish Diet. The
King must also swear not to interfere with religious
freedom, which might have been agreeable to Ivan who
was not a heresy-hunter, but was poison to the Duc
d'Anjou, who was an ardent Catholic. The King must
also agree to govern through a cabinet of fourteen,
chosen not by himself but by the Diet. He must recognize that he has no power to nominate a successor to the
throne. Finally, if the elected King failed to observe
the promises he must make on oath, the Diet after due
warning would be free to depose him and elect another.

The Duc d'Anjou was in Paris at the time of his election to the Polish throne and took his oath there. It
was six months before he arrived for the ceremony of
coronation. He was surrounded by nobles of his own
faith, and by zealous ecclesiastics who were eager
enough to have the puritanical clauses of the oath
dropped. Although it must be given again at the coro-

nation, the Frenchman almost contrived to have it omitted. But just as the archbishop was about to place the crown on his head, two members of the Diet came forward and protested and one of them snatched the diadem which he would not relinquish until the oath had been administered in full. The favourite son of Catherine de' Medici thought the Poles most unrefined. The French fop with the very white hands and tinted complexion was weak and unintelligent. Someone looking at him said he did not know whether to call him a woman king or a male queen. He gave in at once and took the oath which seemed to make his royalty almost worthless.

He was soon as discontented with Poland as Poland was with him, perhaps more so, because the Poles believed they could make this weakling govern them as they wanted to be governed. It was a great relief to him in June, 1574, when he heard of his brother's death. Charles IX, at the age of twenty-four, was no more and the Duc d'Anjou was his successor, Henri III. The amusing thing was that the Poles would not let him go home. Possibly they conceived that he could govern France from Warsaw as a sort of Polish possession or colony. In those days as always the Poles were possessed of great national vanity. Henri III had to make a clandestine escape late at night, riding for life, pursued by Polish nobles. He got over the frontier and nothing on earth would persuade him to come back. The Diet formally deposed him in May, 1575.

Poland remained unfortunate. The Tartars, seeking weaker opponents than the Russians, ravaged the Ukraine and took away some 50,000 captives into bondage. The country was badly in need of a real king. The weakness of the Duc d'Anjou had caused the birth of serious faction. The bitterness of faction seemed to augur civil war and when the Senate and Diet came to electing a new king they elected two instead of one. The Emperor Maximilian was elected and likewise Prince Stephen Batory of Hungary. But here Fate was kind: Maximilian was dying and could not come to be crowned. The vigorous young Hungarian came at once to Cracow. He strengthened his position by marriage, taking Anna, the younger sister of Sigizmund Augustus, to wife and they were crowned together as King and Queen on the 1st May, 1576. Maximilian died on the 12th October.

There was now an energetic and capable man on the throne of Poland. The Tsar soon realised that he had a dangerous enemy in him. It is quite possible that it was the necessity of grappling with Stephen Batory that caused him to stop the sham tsardom of Simeon and mount the throne again.

King Stephen had bought peace from the Moslem by paying tribute to the Sultan. But he quickly announced his intention of winning back for Poland on the field of battle all lands which had been taken from her by the Russians. In his first missive to Ivan, appointing ambassadors, he omitted to call him Tsar and left out his titles of Duke of Smolensk and Duke of Podolsk. At the same time he called himself Lord of Livonia. Ivan received the ambassadors in full state in the Kremlin. It was November, 1576. Simeon had disappeared. The Tsar was on his throne, wearing his crown, the Tsarevitch Ivan sitting by his side. All were in cloth of gold. The great square was packed with troops. The desire to impress the emissaries of a mere soldier of fortune, as Stephen was regarded, was manifest. And Ivan gave not the slightest sign of being angry. King Stephen wished to observe the armistice which had been arranged before his accession. He would observe it *until it expired.* Very good. That suited the Tsar very well. But he did not ask the ambassadors to dine with him and that omission showed his coolness.

War with Poland at the expiration of the armistice was inevitable. Ivan decided to make the most of the time at his disposal and make certain at least of holding Livonia and the Baltic coast. The army was in a state of preparedness. The Tartar came bounding north, took one look at the opposition forces and rode back faster than he had come. Ivan, after his year's holiday, seemed much more alert. Nothing was omitted for the protection of Moscow from attack and he was able to proceed to the north-western territory with a feeling of great security.

Hostilities recommenced during the cold and stormy winter of 1576–7. The Russians again laid siege to Reval. King Stephen paid no attention. He was himself besieging Dantzig, which city had been for Maximilian and would fight rather than acknowledge Batory. The King of Sweden had written to Ivan advising him not to attack Reval as he intended selling it to the Emperor, to Maximilian's heir, with whom possibly the Russians could strike a bargain. Nevertheless the Swedes defended the city with great valour, and despite attacks from the side of the ice-bound sea they did more damage to the Russians than the Russians did to them. Misery and hardship had inured the Livonians and they were no longer the soft and effeminate people they had been under the Teutonic Knights. Ivan, despite his victories, spread over a number of years, had made the mistake of not consummating his conquest and making peace. A civil organising power had been required to take over the conquered territory and bind it to the Russian commonwealth. We can see how invaluable Alexey Adashef would have been to the Tsar had he been spared. The Tsar's vicious rule bore certain negative fruits which are sometimes overlooked by apologists for the Terrible. The desire to conquer Livonia and give Russia a Baltic outlet may have been farsighted, but it was in nowise furthered by the terror either in Livonia itself or in Russia. The punishment of Novgorod and the consequent destruction of its commerce caused a severe setback to the Livonian policy. Novgorod was the nearest great Russian city and the link for uniting the commerce of the two countries.

There was no growing common interest. Hatred of the Russians communicated itself even to the lowest Esthonian and Lettish serf, and when the Russians suffered reverses in the field these Esthonians and Letts were not slow to take revenge. Armed peasants led by a man nicknamed "Hannibal" went from success to success in the early months of 1577, burning their own towns and villages to drive the Muscovite out. They captured Wittenstein; they burned Pernau, and, paying Ivan in his own coin, they put many Russians to the torture.

But the Tsar was mobilising very large forces. The

ex-Tsar Simeon, now made Grand Duke of Tver, had a large army to command. Magnus reappeared on the scene with a large force, and the Tsar restored him to favour and he set forth again to win the kingdom he coveted. Actually Magnus was now playing entirely for his own hand and was ready to accept the protection of the King of Poland if he could only be sure of the kingdom. The Tsar sent him to take Wenden, which he did easily without recourse to arms, promising freedom and immunity from Russian tyranny. Then he went on without orders, being hailed everywhere as King of Livonia and saviour.

What direction Ivan's great army would take was not known in Livonia. It was assumed that its first task would be the renewed siege of Reval. It wasted several months in inactivity, in manœuvres, exercises, and parades, the Tsar and his two sons amusing themselves first at Novgorod and then at Pskof. It was not until the 25th July that the advance began, and then it was into Southern Livonia, a district peaceably held by the Poles. Before the expiration of the armistice Ivan plunged into conflict with the new king. The Russians swept forward irresistibly, taking city after city and encountering only the feeblest opposition. Where there was resistance the Tsar took reprisals after conquest. The campaign in its opening stages went well, but Ivan soon received a surprise from the direction of Prince Magnus's heroic parade. The "King of Livonia," asked him to respect the rights of his subjects. Magnus gave a list of towns and cities which recognised him as king, and actually included Dorpat. But he had no sense of humour and perhaps Ivan had less, for he ordered his envoys to be flogged. More than that, he seized the nearest town on the list of the faithful, put Magnus's German soldiers to the sword and listing Magnus's loyal subjects there, sent the whole population, man, woman, and child into bondage. This was the fate of Kokenhusen. The Tsar himself, walking in the streets of the city, fell into conversation with a Protestant clergyman. It is a characteristic picture of Ivan which has come down to us. In the midst of the smoke and ruin of war he was quite ready, nay eager, for a theological discussion. But the conversation did not end reasonably. The pastor would enlarge on the virtues of his hero, Luther, and finally had the temerity to compare him with the Apostle Paul. This was too much for Ivan, who lifted his steel-pointed staff and struck the pastor down. "Go to the Devil with your Luther," said he and strode away.

Ivan wrote a contemptuous letter to "Our Beggar King Magnus," warning him to keep within the scope of orders given him or to take himself off home beyond the seas. Otherwise let him not think he was beyond the reach of the Tsar's arm.

Nominees or partisans of Magnus were in control of several strong places in Livonia. But they fell into the hands of the Russians and were mostly beheaded. Magnus himself crept to the Tsar and made submission. He lay on the ground before Ivan on horseback and grovelled. Ivan could have struck him dead, but instead he bade him rise to his feet. "Blockhead!" said he. "How do you think you could be King of Livonia! Vagabond, beggar, whom I took into my family and married to my beloved niece, you whom I have clothed and shod and kept, how have you dared to be false to your sovereign and patron? Answer me! I heard of your disgusting plans for the future many times, but I could not believe and was silent. Now all is laid bare. You have thought of taking all Livonia into your hands and becoming the servant of Poland, but gracious God has saved me from that and delivered you into my hands. Now justice shall be done on you. You shall give back all that is mine and return to the nothingness you were!"

With that, Magnus and the courtiers who had accompanied him were seized and thrown into a litter of dirty straw in a room of an old house, there to await the Tsar's further action. This happened outside the city of Wenden, which flew Prince Magnus's colours. Magnus sent word to the leading citizens to surrender without parley, make the best terms possible at once and not invite the Tsar's terrible wrath. But panic seized on the minds of all in the city and especially upon those who had been the strongest adherents of Magnus. The market place and main part of Wenden were in the hands of the Russian army, but the panic-stricken, as many as could find place, took refuge in the old castle which dominated the city. Men, women, and children bundled into this old keep with their goods and chattels, resolved in a mad way to defend themselves there. Although there was not the slightest chance of their holding the position the men opened fire with their arquebuses on the advancing Russians and wounded not a few. That was sufficient. It guaranteed their awful fate. The angry Tsar had his victims in a trap. To show them what he intended he took the most distinguished Livonian prisoner, George Wilke, the defender of Volmar, who had recently surrendered, and had him impaled on a stake before their eyes. Then the Tsar's cannon, at close range, were trained on the walls of the castle, and the walls began to splinter and tumble down about the defenders. After three days cannonade, the unfortunate people decided on a heroic and desperate act.

The defenders of the castle filled the vaults with gunpowder, and then all went on their knees in prayer, while one of their number, Henry Boisman, took a lighted torch to blow up the castle and all within it. There was a terrific explosion and the castle and its defenders went sky-high. Everyone perished except Boisman, who lived a short while after his act. Then he died. His dead and blackened body was hoisted on a stake by the Russians, but it was too late to torture him. The Tsar's frustrated rage then fell upon the rest of the inhabitants of the town, who were tortured, cut to bits, burned alive. Rape and murder ran the streets for days.

This cruel chastisement spread the terror of Ivan throughout Livonia. The Tsar was much more cruel than any of his commanders. The Tsar was there in person. The terror of his name was a greater force than armies. He had little trouble in taking over practically the whole of Livonia. Cities and towns surrendered upon the instant when they were summoned. The Tsar went from victory to victory. He avoided besieging Reval and Riga, as the reduction of these cities might take too long. But everything else was in his hands. He gave a great feast in Volmar and was thoroughly well pleased with himself. At Dorpat he pardoned Magnus, who had followed him bound, expecting his death at any moment. It even suited his humour to let Magnus still consider himself King of Livonia, under himself. Ivan stipulated that Magnus should collect and pay into his treasury 40,000 Hungarian guldens; Magnus agreed to anything, but to be free. And Ivan set off for Alexandrof to rest from his labours.

This resting on his laurels was characteristic of Ivan. As at Kazan at the beginning of his military career, he quitted the field too early, before conquest had been adequately safeguarded. Stephen of Poland had not met him in battle because he was as yet unprepared. But he was mobilising an expeditionary force, buying mercenaries, borrowing men, getting men on credit, fooling the Polish Diet and staking his career and future on a clash with the Muscovite power. Ivan was vainglorious. From Volmar he wrote a triumphant letter to his traitor Kurbsky. It was to Volmar that Kurbsky had first fled from the wrath of the Tsar. The capture of the city had reminded the Tsar of an unrequited debt. He looked forward to the time when he would force the Poles to surrender Kurbsky to him and he would have the luxurious revenge of torturing him to death.

"The German cities fell without conflict at the appearance of the Living Cross," he wrote. Evidently he attributed the hurried surrenders to the intervention of God and not to the terror which he had inspired by the chastisement of Wenden. He was deeply convinced that Kurbsky, in fleeing from him, had endangered his salvation. He stated that his purpose in writing to him was to remind him of the need for his soul's salvation. Kurbsky had taken up with the devil in the first place when he lent himself to the machinations of the priest Sylvester and Alexey Adashef and Ivan reminded him of Satan's boast of going to and fro in the earth and from walking up and down in it, and of God's rejoinder: "Hast thou considered my servant Job?"*

All Kurbsky's desire that he, Ivan, should be trampled under his feet and that he should have his will in Russia had been brought to nought. . . . "Had you not separated me from my wife, there had been no victims." It is curious that after so many matrimonial adventures he should thus hark back to Anastasia. Again we have Ivan the old man. His mind is not so much on the field of battle in Livonia as dwelling in the far past. He was happy once, in his first love, before he had sullied his life. At forty-seven years of age, despite his triumph over his enemies and his great successes, he was a lonely and at times conscience-stricken old man.

He was lonely and conscience stricken, but still possessed by his lusts. The red fire had not gone out. It leapt in flames at Wenden. It was an incalculable force, still capable of bursting out at any moment and burning men and women. The dignity of his pose, the charming manner when he was bestowing a favour, the sustained piety of his prayers did not obscure this fire. It is hardly possible that they obscured it from himself. He must have known, when he was writing to Kurbsky as God's favourite and chosen one, that he was capable next moment of torturing innocent people to death.

It was late autumn when Ivan reached Alexandrof,

* *Skazania Kurbskago.*

but the year 1577 did not pass without another surging forth of murderous rage. Writing to Kurbsky and brooding on the past had taken him back in mind to the time when he lay at the point of death and so many of his nobles ranged themselves against him and against Anastasia and his infant son. They had wished to supplant him by his cousin Vladimir Andreyevitch. Prince Vladimir had paid for that; almost everyone else had paid for it. The whole brood of the Adashefs had perished. The families of the traitors had been destroyed and their estates confiscated. But one old man remained, probably the most capable and heroic soldier in his army, Prince Michael Vorotinsky. To him actually belonged the glory of the Tsar's first military enterprise, the conquest of Kazan in 1552. He it was who, flushed with victory, disturbed the Tsar at prayer to say "Kazan is ours." The young Tsar, when he first turned to violence in 1560, banished the prince together with his wife and family to Bielozersk. Five years later, at the inauguration of the *Opritchina* he was restored to favour. It was not to complete favour, he was not appointed to the Tsar's bodyguard, but fell back into the disfranchised Council of Boyars and the *Zemschina*. His fellow nobles and colleagues were subject to the raids of the *Opritchina*, to torture, murder, expropriation. For seventeen years Vorotinsky, faithful servant as he was, could never have been sure on any day that he would not be murdered on the morrow. But he served in simple faith and loyalty with the premiss: "If my sovereign wish to kill me, it is within his right, for I am his to do with what he will." One must understand this type by the saying: "They live best who are always ready to die." The instinct to be born slave of master and lord is something which disappeared in later centuries in Europe and is now almost beyond comprehension. It is not a Teutonic characteristic. In the Slav it is miscalled "fatalism." The possession of it enabled Vorotinsky to serve the Tsar with great brilliance for seventeen years, without precautions for personal safety, without "nerves." His interests were entirely undivided and he won such victories for Russia as could not have been won by a man who was not calm in himself. In his latter years, it was he who finally dispersed the invading Tartars and saved Moscow from being sacked again. He was over sixty years, a good old age in those times. His life was, as it were, steeped in glory, the most celebrated and striking old man of Russia.

It was Vorotinsky who now stood in the Tsar's monstrous mind, between his soul and the light. "*They* poisoned my life and *he* is the greatest of them all." The visionary murderer clutched in air at another victim. He had no peace after victory. He was aware of an evil spell brooding over the palace. The devil had not liked that taunt of God: "Hast thou considered my servant Job?" He was plaguing him. He was using his wretched subjects and they were *practicing* on him. The greatest, Vorotinsky, had got in league with Satan and was using diabolic arts to carry him off.

Vorotinsky was seized and that was the charge against him. Not that the Tsar himself made the charge. It was made by a runaway serf from Vorotinsky's estates, but it was the Tsar's desire. He did not examine the serf. Vorotinsky was arrested and brought before Ivan. He said: "My father and grandfather taught me to serve zealously God and the Tsar but no demon; to bring my sorrows to the altar of the Most High, not to resort to sorcerers. This witness against me is a runagate thief; do not take the word of a miscreant against mine!"

The old general was suspended from a tree and roasted slowly over two fires. It is said that Ivan put the steel point of his staff in the embers and pierced the body of the dying prince with it. Before the old man was dead he was cut down and sent on a litter to the Monastery of Bielozersk, but he expired on the way. His body was brought to the monastery and buried with due honour; for the monks of St. Cyril were much more humane than the Tsar, who sent so many of his victims to them.

This monstrous murder was not the unique outrage of the fall of 1577. Nikita Odoevsky was tortured to death. Michael Morozof, with his wife and two sons, perished. There were probably several others whose names are unrecorded.

At the beginning of 1578 Ivan turned his attention to foreign affairs, being well aware that Poland was undismayed by his victories in Livonia and was steadily preparing to move against him. He sought alliance with Rudolf, the successor to Maximilian and the Holy Roman Empire, but although the young Emperor hated Stephen of Poland he would not enter into a risky alliance which was to give Russia Poland, and himself only Hungary.

Frederick, King of Denmark, then sought alliance with Russia against the Swedes, his idea being to partition Livonia and Esthonia between Russia and Denmark and dispose forever of the Swedish pretensions to the Southern Baltic coast. But Ivan in council with his boyars rejected this proposal, contenting themselves instead with arranging a fifteen years' armistice with Denmark. It is, of course, possible that Danish troops would not have proved of much service and it was not foreseen that Stephen could mobilise a force strong enough to turn the Russians out. But the refusal of Danish help was unwise. The Russians were greedy: they could well have spared the Western territory that the Danes coveted.

Some attempt was made to obtain the co-operation of the Tartars against Poland and Lithuania. Ivan sent largesse of gold to the Khan and his princes and presents to their wives, but King Stephen outbid him.

The Russian garrisons in Livonia, seeing the unwarlike and demoralised condition of their enemies, relaxed their discipline and spent the winter in carouse. King Stephen bided his time. He played Ivan with as much wiliness as if he were himself a Slav, and he did have some Slav blood in his veins. He wrote humble letters and made pacific proposals, even succeeding in arranging an armistice for another three years. His object was to convince the Tsar that he was not a militant sovereign, a man of words but not of action. To what extent the Russians were deceived by him at this time is uncertain. Soon very serious news came to Ivan from Livonia. Magnus, having signed a secret treaty with Stephen, went over to the enemy. And one by one the Livonian cities were falling back into the hands of the Livonians. The Germans sent in barrels of wine to the garrison officers of Duneberg, and when the resultant orgy of drunkenness was at its worst the Livonians broke into the fortress and massacred the Russians. Something much the same occurred at Wenden. The enemy broke in in the dead of night and fell upon the garrison asleep. An attempt was made by Ivan Mstislavsky and his son to win this city back, but they encountered a fierce resistance on the part of bands serving King Stephen.

A Swedish army began to beleaguer Dorpat, entered the suburbs and did great execution among the Russian families there. "Hannibal" with his peasant army began to harass the Russians again. All through the spring and summer the position of the Russians became progressively worse. There were quarrels about leadership and division of counsel. It is obvious that the presence of the Tsar was required. He and he alone could have restored the *esprit de corps* and there is little doubt that his rigorous and ruthless leadership would have enabled him to hold Livonia. Crafty and energetic as King Stephen was, he had not the driving power of personality that Ivan had. But Ivan did the wrong thing. He bullied his commanders with words and threats from Moscow and Alexandrof and that only made matters worse. A large Russian army moved to the siege of Wenden in the summer, but it was ill-commanded. A mixed force of Swedes, Lithuanians, and Livonians aided by Tartars pressed them heavily. Something happened which showed the need of the Terrible. The higher command fled to Dorpat and allowed the army to shift for itself. Deprived of leadership, many fled. In effect, though not planned, the stalwart remainder of the army fought a delaying action while the faint-hearted got to safety. The leaderless army fought well but there was no quarter and it was entirely destroyed, the gunners in despair at the end hanging themselves on their own cannon.

Ivan, understanding that time was required to re-establish discipline, endeavoured to obtain from the King of Poland a cessation of hostilities pending further discussion, but the blandishments of his envoys were unsuccessful. Stephen entertained them, but nevertheless intensified his warlike preparations. The Tsar saw that he must raise a very large new army to replace or reinforce his distraught forces in Livonia, and to carry the war into Lithuania and Poland proper. Russia's preparations for war on a grand scale date from the 5th December, 1578. A new army of 28,000 men was raised and in command were placed the ex-Tsar Simeon, Grand Duke of Tver, Ivan Mstislavsky, Daniel Nogtief and others. Ivan himself decided to go to Novgorod, but it was not till July, 1579, that he set off. Much depended on striking early at Stephen and frightening the Polish Diet, which was much more pacific than the king. In August the Poles and Lithuanians opened the new phase of the war by laying siege to Polotsk.

Thus King Stephen had the initiative. Ivan had contented himself with insignificant operations in Livonia. What with his new army and that already at the front, he must have disposed of nearly a hundred thousand men and could with confidence have advanced on Vilna or even Warsaw, but he preferred to wait and see what his enemy would do and then to reply. He sent an in-

adequate relieving army to raise the siege of Polotsk,
but he had not foreseen the vigour and enterprise of the
Polish king. The garrison of Polotsk fought bravely.
The city was fired by an intrepid Hungarian band followed by a general assault but in fire and smoke it
drove the enemy back. In contrast to Ivan's policy of
terror Stephen offered freedom and safe-conduct to the
Russian frontier for all who would surrender. The defenders, however, knew that if they surrendered they
would incur the anger of the Tsar; their counsels were
divided. But the army of relief was incompetently
handled. Within six weeks of the first attempt to storm
it, Polotsk fell into the hands of the king and was restored to Lithuania. It had been eighteen years in the
possession of Russia. The new king had already justified the expenses and the risks of his great enterprise.

The greater part of the relief force shut up in the
little fortress of Sokol was then destroyed by a Lithuanian army. Ivan, as if paralysed by these defeats, remained idle in the city of Pskof and ordered no counter-attack. "Where are your victories now?" wrote
Kurbsy in mockery to the Tsar. Ivan did not answer
but instead sued weakly for peace.

At the end of the year fortune smiled on the Russians in their campaign in Livonia. The redoubtable
"Hannibal" was routed. He himself was captured,
taken to Pskof and put to death. But victories in Livonia did not affect the general course of the war. Ivan
went to Moscow. The Polish reply to his proposal of
peace was a rude demand for the cession of Novgorod,
Pskof, Luki, and the adjacent territories. King Stephen
had some difficulties of his own, for his mercenaries

were claiming wages and his treasury was empty, but he was a gifted borrower, bluffer and promiser. The hobby of his life was soldiering and he had no mind to settle down to peaceful administration, politics and economics. He had raised himself up to crush the power of Ivan in the west and would not give way until he had accomplished that end.

The year 1580 was not particularly eventful, but in the late summer King Stephen led his army into Russia, advancing due east at a point considerably south of Novgorod, reached the considerable city of Veliki Luki and laid siege to it. The history of this siege was not dissimilar to that of Polotsk. The city was taken first and the relieving army under Prince Khilkof was routed afterwards. Throughout the operations the Tsar's envoys cringed pitifully, asking still for peace. Other Russian cities were taken and in Livonia the Swedes began to be victorious at every point over the demoralised Muscovites. The greater part of the imperialistic success of Ivan's reign was being rapidly undone. The Tsar grew much older, stooped. It was an old man who was ruling now in Russia. Was it a sign of his old age that he became more mild and did not even visit with his displeasure the commanders who failed him in the field? "Carry on as God shall guide you," he wrote feebly. "My hope is centred upon God's help and your zeal."

The Tsar, having disposed of his fifth and sixth wives, now took a seventh, Maria Nagaya. Her surname means "naked." This daughter of a court dignitary was not, however, led to the altar, the difficulty of obtaining the approval of the Church being obvious. It is therefore open to the historian to call Maria his mistress, though the establishment was that of wife and Maria was treated as a legitimate consort. The Tsar's younger son was at the same time married to Irina, the sister of Boris Godunof.

King Stephen, hailed as a great hero in Poland, profited by the Tsar's hypochondria. He never had to deal with a real fighting Russia. Ivan's envoys followed him about from place to place, humbling themselves in the dust before him. King Stephen was a hero, but he obtained an exalted notion of his mission, which was no less than to overrun the whole of Russia and annex it to Poland. The Tsar's self-abasement had so fed his ambition that he admitted to himself the most exaggerated pretensions. His Hungarian and German mercenaries, on whom he chiefly depended, were not capable of realising Stephen's plans. By invading Russia he was making war not so much on Ivan as on the Russian people as a whole. Despite the pusillanimity and hesitation of the Tsar vast new armies were soon swarming to the defence of the Fatherland, as against a new inroad of the Horde. They moved inward from the south and the east, and it is reckoned that in 1581 as many as 300,000 men were advancing against the enemy in the west. King Stephen laid siege to Pskof and met with a heroic resistance which quickly broke the morale of his nondescript army. At Pskof he learned the lesson that Russians fighting on their own territory are ten times more to be feared than when fighting beyond their natural boundaries. The great dream of annexing Russia to Poland faded. The King at last began to consider the advisability of consolidating his success in a reasonable peace. The Russians had been chased out of both Lithuania and Livonia. He must rest content to restrict them by treaty from any renewed encroachment on these countries.

This was the greatest humiliation of Ivan the Terrible during his reign. An army of 300,000 fine soldiers lacked the *esprit de corps* to cope with some 26,000, mostly mercenaries. The well-conceived imperial plan of extending Russia to the Baltic proved a chimera and was postponed in history to the stirring times of Peter the Great. But coincident with this complete failure in the west, glorious exploits were being performed in the east. Beyond the Volga a mere handful of Cossacks and stragglers, under the heroic command of Ermak, first gave the Tsars of Russia the territorial title of Siberia. Russia entered the empty northern half of the continent of Asia for the first time and showed the way for countless pioneers. And the exploit was commenced without the Tsar's permission. Indeed the story of the first conquest belongs more to a history of Ivan's reign than to his biography, for he had little part in it personally.

It is the story of the heroic Ermak who chose to give up banditry and serve the "White Tsar." He began his invasion with less than a thousand men, mostly Cossacks, and gained his first victory on the 22nd July, 1581. He obtained valuable aid and reinforcement from numbers of liberated Lithuanian and German prisoners and some Tartars. The main portion of his little army was composed of Don Cossacks. At the news of the first disorders on the frontier, Ivan was enraged at those responsible for the unauthorised outrage and gave orders for Ermak to be seized and sent to Perm, but the Cossacks' successes liquidated the Tsar's wrath. The Urals were crossed and the little army with its arquebuses and cannon met with but feeble resistance while it took over vast territories in the name of the Tsar. By the 26th October, 1581, Ermak had reached the Irtish and taken the important town of Isker or Sibir, where he found large plunder of gold and precious stones, carpets, and furs. His enemies were the Ostiaks, living until then in peaceful paganism and worshipping golden idols.

In the spring of 1582, Ermak continued the conquest of the territory between the Irtish and the Obi, following the former river northward. He reached the river Obi after a series of petty battles in which his gunpowder always gained him an advantage. On the banks of the Obi, Ermak paused, and sent a petition to Ivan, accompanied by such rich gifts that the Tsar was startled and realised joyfully that vast territory had been added to his crown. There were great rejoicings in Moscow. After Ivan's death, the army of invasion was obliged to retire and Ermak himself was drowned trying to swim the Irtish while wearing armor. But a trail had been blazed into the depths of northern Asia and the Russians would return.

XXXIII.

IVAN MURDERS HIS SON

ALTHOUGH Ivan was noticeably quieter during the last years of his life, it would be a mistake to assume that there were not many incidents characteristic of the name of "the Terrible." In 1579 Doctor Elysius Bomel, the Tsar's clever and unscrupulous astrologer, was roasted to death over a slow fire. He had been found to be in secret communication with the King of Poland. Dr. Bomel was a German who had been educated at Cambridge University, a mathematician, a professor of curious lore; he had been imprisoned by Queen Elizabeth for necromancy, but his reputation grew outside prison walls. The Russian ambassador, Savin, had procured him liberty on condition that he come to Russia to serve the Tsar. One wonders did the stars tell Elysius Bomel of this strange twist of fortune.

He came to Russia with his young wife, Ann Richards, and at once obtained favour at the Tsar's court. He became one of Ivan's intimates and had a position almost equal to that of the Tsar's confessor, the counterpart of a confessor on the black magic side. It is said he prepared subtle poisons for Ivan's use, but that is probably a western European invention. The Tsar was not a notable poisoner. He was not a connoisseur of writhings and contortions, but much preferred to see blood on his victims. But one can believe that the doctor was a priest of vice, for he obtained a most evil reputation. As regards his political influence, one can well believe Horsey, who says he was "an enemy always to our nation." The Bishop of London had him in gaol and it is quite possible he might have been burned at the stake in England had he remained. But Horsey must be wrong when he says that Dr. Bomel deluded the Tsar into thinking that Queen Elizabeth was still young and likely to make a cheery wife for him. When Doctor Bomel came first to Russia the Queen was thirty-seven and it was about that time that Ivan's hope of marrying her faded.

The astrologer's horrible end is thus described by Horsey:

"Bomelius upon the rack, his arms drawn back disjointed and his legs stretched from his middle loins, his back and body cut with wire whips, confessed much and many things more than was written or willing the Emperor should know. The Emperor sent word they should roast him. Taken and bound to a wooden pool or spit, his bloody cut back and body roasted and scorched till they thought no life in him, cast in a sled brought through the castle, cast into a dungeon and died there."*

Next year, in 1580, the Tsar called together all of the more important ecclesiastics to tell them of the danger which threatened the Church and Orthodoxy from the invading armies in the west. He had long had an eye on the estates of the monasteries. He wished to emulate the example of Henry VIII of England. Now he found a plausible motive for spoliation, and that

* *Travels of Sir Jerome Horsey.*

was that money and land were required to pay the immense army which had been mobilised against King Stephen. His personal cupidity was great, but also he held that those who had renounced the world should not be so much engaged in the business of farming land and merchandising produce. Sir Jerome Horsey gives part of the Tsar's speech on this occasion: ". . . The nobility and people cry out with their complaints that you have gotten, wherewith you do maintain your hierarchy, all the treasure of the land, by trading in all kind of merchandise, chafferings and taking the benefit of all other men's travels; having privilege to pay no customs to our crown, nor charge of wars; and by terrifying of the noblest and ablest and best sort of our subjects their dying consciences, have gotten the third part, by due computation, of the towns rialties and villages of this kingdom into your possession, by your witchery, and enchantments and sorcery. You buy and sell the souls of our people. You live a most idle life in all pleasure and delicacy: commit most horrible sins, extortion, bribery and excess usury. You abound in all the bloody and crying sins, oppression, gluttony, idleness and sodomy, and worse, if worse, with beasts. Maybe your prayers avail not, neither for me nor for my people. . . . God forgive my partakership with you. . . . Often have I been moved for your dissolution, to the reparation and re-establishing of thousands of my ancient and poorest nobility from whose ancestors most of your revenues came, and to whom it most justly belongs . . . and my rich people and subjects impoverished through your rapine and devilish illusions, and by the contrary a flourishing commonwealth

would be established and sustained; a fair example by
that valorous king, Henry VIII of England; your revenues being much more beside your standing treasury
than your prodigal and luxurious maintenance can ex-
pend."

The Tsar went on to command that the bishops, the
chief of whom at the convocation was Alexander, Archbishop of Novgorod, and the abbots, the Archimandrite
of Troitsky and the rest "should bring us a faithful and
true inventory, what treasure and yearly revenue every
of your houses have in their possessions. . . ."

There ensued one of those ecclesiastical parleys in
which Ivan delighted. He was ready to spend days and
weeks bandying Holy Writ with his churchmen. But he
was serious in his intentions and though he invited opposition he did not brook it. Russian historians do not
make use of Horsey's witness, but there is no reason to
doubt his reliability here, though he did fall into exag-
gerations in other descriptions. According to him the
Tsar picked out the most recalcitrant of the abbots
(friars) and punished them. He "sent for twenty of the
principallest; chargeth them with odious and horrible
crimes and treacheries, upon such pregnant and apparent proofs as was manifestly known and published to
be true, exclaimed upon and condemned of all people
in general. Now come we to the merry tragedy to re-
quite your patience all this while. The Emperor commands his great bears, wild, fierce and hungry, to be
brought out of their dark caves and cages, kept of purpose for such delights and pastimes at Slobiad Velica
[Alexandrof], upon St. Isaac's day, in a spacious place
high walled. About seven of those principal rebellious

big fat friars were brought forth, one after another, with his cross and beads in his hands, and, through the Emperor's great favour, a boar spear of five foot in length in the other hand for his defence, and a wild bear was let loose, ranging and roaring up against the walls with open mouth, scenting the friar by his fat garments, made more mad with the cry and shouting of the people, runs fiercely at him, catches and crushes his head, body, bowels, legs and arms, as a cat doth a mouse, tears his weeds in pieces till he came to his flesh, blood and bones and so devours his first friar for his prey. The bear was also shot and killed with pieces by the gunners pellmell. And so another friar and a fresh bear was singly hand to hand, brought forth, till they were all seven devoured in manner as the first was; saving one friar, more cunning than the rest, bestirred his spear so nimbly, setting the end thereof in the ground, guiding it to the breast of the bear that ran himself through upon it, and yet not escaped devouring, after the bear was hurt, both dying in the place. This friar was canonised for a valiant saint by the rest of his living brothers of Troitsky monastery. The pastime was not as pleasing unto the Emperor and others beholders thereof, as terrible and displeasing to all the rabblement and consistory of friars and monks that were convocated and combined together as you have heard; whereof seven more were promised to be burned."

The Tsar feared nothing from the Church, for the Metropolitan dared not excommunicate him. He had defied the Church by living openly in sin; it is not to be thought that he feared the anger of the landed clergy,

IOVAN
BASILLI
GRÃ DVCA
DI MOSCOVIA
stampato nouamente·

IVAN THE TERRIBLE IN HIS LAST YEARS

if he made a raid on their estates. He had his way, obtained a goodly contribution to his war chest and his personal treasury and moreover persuaded the Church to renounce, for the future, acquisition of estates by purchase or bequest. The renunciation soon became a dead letter. Men and women were too superstitious not to think they could purchase preferment in heaven by beneficence to the Church. Ivan himself, after he murdered his son, paid the Church the largest amount he ever paid, for the saying of eternal prayer.

It is a Christian truth that when you strike others you strike yourself most. Nemesis is inevitable. We now come to a supreme example. Flesh of his flesh, no one was nearer to Ivan than his eldest son, the Tsarevitch Ivan, fruit of the love match, the serene first marriage of Ivan, the union with the never forgotten Anastasia. Yet in the mechanical action of murderous rage Ivan slew him. That same steel-pointed staff which had struck down so many, killed also the beloved heir.

It happened in Alexandrof in the autumn of 1581. It was the culmination of a conversation in which the Tsar was getting more and more irritated. Boris Godunof was present; who else we do not know. There are various stories of the subject of the conversation and possibly all of them possess some truth. Russians are garrulous and possibly Godunof related the circumstances to his acquaintances who in turn gave their version. It is probable that on the morning of the day of the murder, the Tsar and the Tsarevitch had had words over an assault which Ivan had made on his son's wife. Ivan had found the Tsarevitch's wife wearing two petticoats instead of three and that was considered indecent. Although she was with child, the Tsar had begun beating her when the Tsarevitch intervened. There were angry words and the Tsarevitch had accused his father of spoiling his happiness with his first two wives and asked if he wished to do the same to him with his third. It is not probable that the Tsar struck his son then when he was manifestly in the wrong. But the ill-feeling broke out again later in the day, possibly after dinner.

The Tsar in a coaxing maudlin way was boasting to his son of his treasures and the great wealth he would inherit at his death and how glad he was to leave so much to him. But the Tsarevitch sneered. "Valour, such as the King of Poland possesses, will do more than wealth," said he. "What is the use of wealth if thou art not strong enough to keep it?" The Tsar's anger boiled over. We do not know what he rejoined, but he was at the time profoundly aware of the inglorious figure he was cutting in Russia. He knew that there were murmurs, that many thought him craven, even that some were asking why, if the Tsar were too old for campaigning, he had not sent his son to retrieve Russia's honour in the field.

"Why do you not let me lead an army against the enemy and win back what we have lost?" asked the younger Ivan.

This was the most hateful question. Lead an army, win, come back, lead all the malcontents, murder his father perhaps, or force him to abdicate. Rage and distrust filled the old man's eyes with blood. He raised his murderous staff and struck the Tsarevitch several times, finally beating him on the head with the weighted handle.

Boris Godunof who was present tried to stop the hail of blows, but his intervention was ineffectual. The Tsarevitch fell to the ground and the Tsar with his blood-dripping staff stood staring with horror at his own act. His repentance was as swift as his rage. In an agony of woe he bent down to raise his stricken son. "I've killed my son, killed my son!" he screamed, and kissed the white bearded face which he held in his hands, and kissed it again. Then he placed a hand over a deep wound in the body and tried to stop the flow of blood. He cried, shouted to God and man, called for doctors, groaned.

It was too late for help. The younger Ivan was mortally wounded, not dead but dying. When he recovered consciousness he said in a faint voice that he forgave his father. But the forgiveness which the soul of Ivan required was the restoration of his son to life and that was denied him. Doctors could do nothing. Within a short while, on the 19th November, 1581, the Tsarevitch died. Ivan was fifty-one years of age; his son was twenty-seven.

On the 22nd November the court, all in black, proceeded from Alexandrof to Moscow, carrying the hearse with the dead body of the Tsarevitch. There was a great state funeral. Ivan, tearing his hair and groaning, presented such a spectacle of grief as had not been seen since the death of Anastasia. But he did not, as in the previous case, rush from this sorrow to debauch. He was finally broken. He gave large sums for the remembrance of his son before God. He confessed that his own life was meaningless and empty. His thoughts were once again strongly centred upon resigning the throne. But he behaved more like a madman now than at any other time in his reign, was completely distraught, took no trouble about his appearance, which became wild in the extreme. His court avoided him as he avoided everyone. He constantly fell from his bed o' nights. Like a sleepwalker he wandered about the palace, as it were seeking the presence of the child he had killed. He would be found somewhere in the morning, lying on the floor as if he had fallen unconscious at some moment in the night.

In this mood he called the boyars together and announced his intention to renounce the throne and seek peace of soul in some monastery. "My younger son, Fedor, is not fit to rule," said he. "He must be set aside. You must now elect someone to be tsar, and when you tell me of your choice I shall willingly pass on to him my crown and sceptre." But this was too dangerous a proposal. Whatever may have been the secret thoughts of the company they besought the Tsar as with one voice that he, God's chosen, would remain to rule over them for his allotted span of years. The Tsar sighed, and, as it were unwillingly, promised to humour them and to continue his beneficent rule.

XXXIV.

LADY MARY HASTINGS

IN the course of the war with Poland the Tsar again sought the friendly co-operation of England. He wished that he had been able to conclude that offensive and defensive alliance with Queen Elizabeth that he had idly planned. It is strange that he could have supposed that the Queen would send her navy to the discomfiture of the Swedes in the Baltic. England had no material interests beyond the trading privileges which Ivan had accorded. Possibly the Tsar had encouraged the English merchants to use Narva and conquered Livonia in the hope that they might upon occasion be persuaded to lend a hand to its defence, but he never understood the logical business mind of the English, nor that it was England's policy to do just enough to keep him in a good humour but no more. The Queen's nature was pacific; she had no desire to be embroiled with any nation on the continent. The most Elizabeth would do for Ivan was to send him military supplies, such as saltpetre and gunpowder by ship to the north.

The Tsar restored most of the trading privileges which he had previously withdrawn in pique. The business developed steadily, despite the ups and downs of Ivan's career. English travellers and agents continued to be decently received. The Tsar remained Anglophile and as evidence thereof we have his crazy desire to have an English wife before he died. The fact that he had wives living seldom seems to have occurred to his mind as a deterrent when thinking of wives to come. Nor did the fact that he was debarred by the Church from entering a legal union after the banishment of the fourth wife. A fourth had only been granted as an extraordinary indulgence. It was almost an insult to have asked Queen Elizabeth for some near kinswoman to be his bride, though it was not conceived as such nor, indeed, taken as such. If anything it was at first taken as an excellent jest, and when the Queen's swarthy, pockmarked niece, Lady Mary Hastings, was chosen, she was nicknamed "the Empress" at the English court with much hilarity.

The person who had been first entrusted to bring the Tsar's serious jest to England had been Jerome Horsey, who was sent overland across Europe with a secret message contained in a vodka bottle: "Now [when] the Emperor's letters and instructions were ready, himself and Savelle Frollove, chief secretary of state, closing them up in one of the false sides of a wooden bottle, filled full with aqua vita, to hang under my horse's mane, not worth 3d.; appointed me 400 Hungers ducketts in gold to be sewed in my boots and quilted in some of my worst garments."

Horsey had many adventures, making his way across Europe on horseback; they are recounted in his *Travels*, interesting reading, for he was a facetious gentleman. "Coming from Hamborow (Hamburg) into England," he wrote, "I opened my aqua vita bottle; took out and sweetened the Emperor's letter and directions, as well as I could; but yet the Queen smelt the savour of the aqua vita when I delivered them unto her Majesty, declaring the cause for her Highness more satisfaction."

The Queen was pleased with him, made him "sworn Esquire of her body, gave me her picture and her hand to kiss."

The upshot was that Horsey returned to Russia with thirteen tall ships laden with munitions of war. Among the English passengers was Doctor Robert Jacob, specially sent by Queen Elizabeth to her "brother" Ivan to heal his diseases. But in fact this distinguished court doctor had been primed as to Ivan's secret desire to marry an Englishwoman. At least we surmise so, for it seems he could hardly have indicated Lady Mary Hastings to the Tsar on his own responsibility. According to Karamzin, the greatest writer about the reign of Ivan the Terrible, the Tsar first heard the name of Lady Mary from Dr. Jacob.

"Is there in England a bride, widow or virgin worthy of the hand of the Crownbearer?" asked Ivan.

"I know one," answered the doctor. "Mary Hastings, the thirty-year-old daughter of the Earl of Huntingdon, niece of the Queen on her mother's side."

At that time the quasi-Tsaritsa Maria was with child, and the proposal to marry another must have seemed indelicate enough. But it was no idle whim. The Tsar pursued the idea with his accustomed pertinacity. He sent his ambassador, Pissemsky, to London to obtain an interview with Lady Mary and to obtain her portrait, painted on wood or paper. He must observe whether she were of good stature, physically well developed, not dried up, and of good complexion. He wished to know definitely her age and the position of her father at court. He was to tell the Queen that his wife, at that time Maria, had no legal status and could be easily set aside in favour of her niece. But Lady Mary must embrace the Greek Orthodox faith, as must also any of her own people who wished to live in attendance upon her at the Russian court.

It is interesting that in his document, his instructions to Pissemsky, the Tsar named Fedor as his successor to the throne. He had already changed his mind regarding the incapacity of his younger son to govern after him and the necessity to elect a better successor to the throne. Any children which he might have by Lady Mary Hastings would be appanaged, as had been the ancient custom in Russia.

According to Sir Jerome Horsey, Pissemsky was "a noble, grave, wise and trusty gentleman." He set off from Kholmagora on the 11th August, 1582, and arrived in England on the 16th September. As some sort of plague was raging in London, Queen Elizabeth had betaken herself to Windsor and admitted no strangers to her presence. It was many weeks before the Russian envoy was received. At length, in November, he was bidden to Windsor. He was warmly received in the presence of a large assembly of courtiers and merchants. The Queen graciously accepted the presents of many marvellous sables which he brought from the Tsar. She asked after the Tsar's health and probably whether her good doctor Jacob had been of any service. She expressed her sorrow at the grievous accident which had resulted in the death of the Tsarevitch. She smiled her coquettish and challenging smile. Did she inquire concerning the state of Ivan's heart? Pissemsky replied that his master loved the Queen more than any other sovereign in the world. The Queen rejoined that she loved him no less, and that she would dearly like to see him with her own eyes. On the whole, although the project of marrying Lady Mary Hastings was a good jest, the Queen was somewhat piqued that Ivan should think of any other woman when addressing a message to her. She was not prompt in facilitating a union with Lady Mary. Pissemsky must go hunting in Windsor Forest and otherwise enjoy himself while in England. He replied that he had come on business and could not spare the time for pleasure.

Pissemsky had also been entrusted to push once more the project of an offensive and defensive alliance. He spoke as if the war with the King of Poland had not been concluded. It must seem that, although Ivan had accepted a humiliating peace with King Stephen and had evacuated Livonia and abandoned his claim on Podolsk, he thought of renewing the conflict at the earliest possible opportunity. Pissemsky was charged to talk about an alliance and besides negotiating a marriage he had to obtain for his master a very considerable amount of munitions of war. "But the war is over," exclaimed Cecil. "The Pope takes the credit for having made peace between the Tsar and King Stephen." Pissemsky replied: "The Pope may take what credit he likes. The Tsar knows who is his friend and who not."

But the urgent question was the personal one; what sort of a lady was the Queen's niece and could a marriage be arranged. It got to be understood that such a marriage would be good for English commerce, and the Queen's ministers began to take steps to make the jest serious. An opportunity must be given for Pissemsky and his colleagues to be presented to Lady Mary Hastings.

"Her Majesty caused that lady to be attended on with divers great ladies and maids of honour and young noblemen, the number of each appointed, to be seen by the said ambassador in York House garden. She put on a stately countenance accordingly. The ambassador, attended with divers other noblemen and others, was brought before her Ladyship, cast down his countenance, fell prostrate to her feet, rose, ran back from her, his face still toward her, she and the rest admiring at his manner. [He] said by an interpreter it did suffice him to behold the angel he hoped should be his master's espouse; commended her angelical countenance, state and admirable beauty. She after was called by her familiar friends in court the Empress of Muscovia."*

Nevertheless the English made no haste to hand over the "Princess Huntingdonska" to the Tsar. The lady herself was not eager for the honour, and that is not surprising considering the travellers' tales of Ivan which were current at the time. News came through that the Tsaritsa Maria had borne the Tsar a son and that also was a deterrent, for it seemed to substantiate the right of Maria not to be idly put away. Queen Elizabeth was very dilatory about it all, and probably never seriously intended to allow the union. On the 18th January she gave Pissemsky a private audience. She then heard from his own lips that he thought his master would be well satisfied with the beauty and estate of Lady Mary. "But," said the Queen impa-

* Travels of Sir Jerome Horsey.

tiently, "I do not find her beautiful and I cannot imagine that she would be found so by such a connoisseur of beauty as my brother Ivan. She has but lately had the small pox and our painter has been obliged to depict her with a red face, deeply pitted."

Pissemsky's own description of the lady said nothing of a red face. He said she was tall, well built and slender, possessing a pale face, grey eyes and flaxen hair, and that she had long and tapered fingers. He must have known that this lady, by her age alone, could not have pleased Ivan greatly, but in his way he was a psychologist and no fool. He knew that Ivan had set his mind on wedding this English lady and would not easily be dissuaded. He had been sent, not so much to judge of her as to get her. It is probable that he used very considerable tact in carrying out his extremely delicate mission. Annoyed by the delays, he yet never lost his head, and he managed to make himself particularly agreeable to Queen Elizabeth. And, holding in his hand the valuable trading privileges of the English in Russia, he proved very competent in his arguments with her ministers of state. He obtained at least a qualified consent to most of his proposals. There was a great farewell banquet for him at Greenwich, and the Queen expressed for Ivan her tender sisterly love and hoped he would visit her, not as a fugitive from his rebellious subjects, but in affection that she might meet him face to face, "Our England shall be for him a second Russia," she said.

Pissemsky returned to Moscow in the autumn of 1583, bringing with him an envoy extraordinary in the person of Sir Jerome Bowes, who had power to treat on the Queen's behalf, both in respect of the English marriage and the proposed military alliance. But Pissemsky left England under a misapprehension. His chief quest had been an English bride for the Tsar; commerce and foreign politics were but secondary matters in his mission and it is doubtful whether he would have dared return with an explicit denial of Lady Mary Hastings. And he did not know the secret instructions given to Sir Jerome Bowes. These included the following:

"You shall declare to him (the Tsar) . . . touching the matter of marriage, how the lady mentioned is fallen into such an indisposition of health that there is small, or no hope she will ever recover such strength as is requisite for that state, especially considering the long tedious voyage she were to make, in case he should upon the report of his ambassador and view of her picture have any disposition to proceed therein. You shall therefore use all the best persuasions you can to dissuade him from that purpose, laying before him the weakness of the lady when she is in the best state of health, and difficulties that are otherwise like to be stood upon by the lady and her friends who can hardly be induced to be so far separate one from the other. . . . Unless their consent might be procured, which is a matter very doubtful, the match could not in any sort be brought to pass; considering that in those cases, as over the rest of our subjects, we have not authority other than by way of persuasion to make them like such matches as by good apparent reasons, may tend to their advancement."*

* *State Papers of Queen Elizabeth*, Instructions to Sir Jerome Bowes, May, 1583.

SIR JEROME BOWES

It will be seen that the position of Sir Jerome Bowes was by no means enviable. Although he was a man of a mean character, conceited, fussy, corrupt, making enemies at every turn, it may be doubted whether an envoy more honourable and tactful could have fared better than he did at the hands of Ivan.

Sir Jerome Bowes was met on his way from Kholmagora to Moscow and received more attention on that arduous journey than had any previous visitor from England. An equerry brought him "two ambling geldings" from the Tsar. At the confines of Moscow he was met by Prince Sitsky and 300 horsemen, who escorted him to his quarters in the capital. He received welcoming messages from the Tsar, and sumptuous dishes, and after he had rested a few days he was accorded a public reception in the city. "About nine of the clock upon that day, the streets were filled with people, and a thousand gunners, clad in red, yellow and blue garments, set in ranks by the captains on horseback, with bright pieces, arquebuses in their hands, from the ambassador's door to the Emperor's palace. Knez Ivan Sitsky mounted upon a fair jennet, richly clad and deckt, having a fair gelding led before him, well furnished, sent for the ambassador to mount upon, attended with 300 gentlemen on horseback richly furnished also. The ambassador, displeased the Duke's horse was better than his, mounted on his own footcloth, and with his thirty men liveried in stamel cloaks well set forth . . . marched onward to the king's palace."*

It is said that the Moscow populace did not like the

* *Travels of Sir Jerome Horsey.*

look of Sir Jerome and shouted abusive epithets such as "Spindleshanks!" at him. It is clear he had an exaggerated opinion of himself, and was ill suited to the task which had brought him. He found the Tsar old and possibly thought him to be in his dotage. He was the only man who ever tried to browbeat Ivan the Terrible. Bowes in his account of his mission flatters himself that he had a great success, and that when he was in altercation with the Tsar it was merely to defend the Queen's honour and good name. The statement that the Tsar said he did not reckon Queen Elizabeth his fellow and that there were her betters may have been an invention or a misinterpretation. Instead of soothing the old Tsar and seeing what could be done to satisfy his whims and advance the friendship which Ivan desired with his sovereign, Bowes offensively advanced the difficulties. "England is on friendly terms with Poland, Sweden and Denmark," said he. "If my chief enemies are the friends of the Queen, how can we be allies?" exclaimed Ivan.

"The Queen would think me mad if I concluded a treaty of alliance with Russia," said Bowes. But on the other hand he demanded categorically that England should have a monopoly of the northern trade and that the Dutch interlopers should be driven out. The arguments about these matters "divers times raised many jarres." Since Russia had lost her only Baltic port foreign traders were bound to use the northern harbours. Was it to be thought that Elizabeth demanded that Russia should trade with England only?

Had it not been for the fact that Ivan ardently desired to have this English wife, Bowes would have been sent home with ignominy. But at first Bowes pretended he held a high trump card. "Treat me ill and goodbye to all chance of Lady Mary!" Horsey cogently remarks that he could have taken better advantage of Ivan's passion. "If Sir Jerome Bowes had known the measure and taken the opportunity of time, the [Tsar] so inflamed with the effecting of his desire [would have yielded] to anything propounded; yea promised that if this marriage did take effect with the Queen's kinswoman, her issue should inherit the crown."*

On the 13th December, 1583, the Tsar called Bowes to his presence, that he might declare to him and a chosen few of his most intimate courtiers what exactly was the position with regard to the proposed marriage. First of all, the Tsar made a considered statement of his intentions and wishes, which had not altered. But Bowes was cold and impertinent in his reply. He considered that Lady Mary Hastings was an unsuitable choice for the Tsar's hand. She was ill-looking. Her health was weak. As touching her religion, was not Christianity the same everywhere? He did not think she would be willing to enter the Greek Orthodox communion. The Queen had other and more charming kinswomen.

Ivan was very angry. "Then why have you come here?" he asked. "Were you entrusted with a refusal? You come to me with a lot of empty words and with exaggerated demands of things I should do for England. Why should I do so much for the Queen if she will do nothing for me? It must be simply that her ambassador is incapable."

* *Travels of Sir Jerome Horsey.*

Bowes was sent back to his lodgings to think things over and was kept in much less honour. He became as much a prisoner in his own house as Thomas Randolfe had been. The Tsar sent for him again, but made no progress with him. Finally in February, 1584, he decided to send him back to England, though not in disgrace. Ivan would still hope for an English bride; he would send a new ambassador to treat with the Queen concerning an English marriage *and the business affairs* apparently so dear to her heart. Bowes, pleased at the prospect of going home, relented somewhat in his *intransigeant* manner, assuring the Tsar that the Queen would greatly rejoice at the prospect of a blood union with him, that even if Lady Mary Hastings were unavailable there must be at least ten other unmarried kinswomen of the Queen, charming girls, from whom to choose. Also he was convinced that the Tsar could obtain assistance in his wars if the trading privileges were guaranteed. In short, at their last interview, they parted on good terms and the Tsar gave orders for many old debts due to the merchants to be settled forthwith. But something unanticipated intervened. The Tsar appointed no ambassador. For ere the English ambassador obtained leave to depart for England, Ivan fell ill and died.*

* See also Appendix: "Sir Jerome Bowes."

XXXV.

DEATH

SOME time in the year 1583 the Tsar had prepared a list of over 3,000 souls of men and women done to death during his reign and ordered prayers for them at the Monastery of St. Cyril at Bielozersk. All spelt out in rough capital letters, Ivan must have spent a long time with his secretary or his confessor, recalling the names of the innocent dead and, even so, many were overlooked or forgotten. *"Remember before the Lord the souls of His sleeping slaves, of this generation since Adam, fallen asleep."* . . . The first to be mentioned in the list was Princess nun Yevdokia, beside which was a note to say that she had been drowned by the order of Tsar Ivan. That was Euphrosyne, the mother of Vladimir Andreyevitch.*

It must be that before the preparation of this list Ivan had had a presentiment of his death. A rapid physical decay had set in and gave warnings which caused both Ivan and his doctors some anxiety. What he said to his confessor, what fortification he obtained from his religion, we do not know. Dr. Bomel had introduced him to the devil and his mind in his latter years was greatly obsessed by sorcery and magic. He was appalled by a comet which appeared in the sky and blazed over Moscow. He called great numbers of soothsayers to the court. The north of Russia contains to this

* Sinodik Tsarya Ioanna Vasillievitcha Groznago.

day many professional wizards and it was to the north then that Ivan had recourse.

"Three score were brought post to Moscow, placed and guarded, and daily dieted and daily visited. . . . The soothsayers tell him that the best signs and strongest planets of heaven were against the Emperor, which would produce his end by such a day . . . [Ivan] fell in rage and told them they were very likely to be all burnt that day. The Emperor began grievously to swell in his coddes, with which he had most horribly offended above fifty years together. . . ."

"[He was] carried every day in his chair into his treasury. One day the prince beckoned me to follow. I stood among the rest venturously and heard him call for some precious stones and jewels. [He] told the prince and nobles present, before and about him, the virtue of such and such. . . ."

Sir Jerome Horsey heard the stricken Tsar thus discourse on divination. He was seeking to know by augury whether he would live. Horsey, probably with the help of Dr. Jacob, set down afterwards as much as he remembered.

"You all know," said the Tsar, "that the lodestone hath great and hidden virtue, without which the seas that compass the world are not navigable, nor the bounds or circle of the earth cannot be known. Mahomet, the Persian prophet's tomb of steel, hangs in their Rapatta at Derbent most miraculously. . . . This fair coral and this fair turquoise you see. Take them in your hand. Put them on my hand and arm. I am poisoned with disease; you see they change their pure colour into pale. [It] declares my death. Reach out my

staff royal, a unicorn's horn garnished with very fair
diamonds, rubies, sapphires, emeralds, and other precious stones that are rich in value; cost 70,000 marks
sterling of David Gower from the fowlkers of Ous-
burghe. Seek out for some spiders!"

The Tsar caused his physicians to scrape a circle and
he placed spiders one by one within the circle. Each of
them except the last curled up and died. "That is a certain sign," said Ivan. "Nothing can preserve me."

"Behold these precious stones! This diamond is the
Orient's richest and most precious. I never affected it.
It restrains fury and luxury, and makes abstinacy and
chastity. The least parcel of it in powder will poison a
horse given to drink, much more a man." He then
pointed to a ruby. "O this is most comfortable to the
heart, brain, vigour and memory of man, clarifies con-
gealed and corrupt blood." He then pointed to an emer-
ald. "The nature of the rainbow; this precious stone is
an enemy to uncleanness. Try it! Though man and wife
cohabit together in lust, having this stone about them,
it will burst at the spending of nature. The sapphire I
greatly delight in. It preserves and increaseth courage,
joys the heart, pleasing to all the vital senses, precious
and very sovereign for the eye, clears the sight, takes
away bloodshot and strengthens the muscles and strings
thereof . . . All these are God's wonderful gifts, se-
crets in nature and yet reveals them to man's use and
contemplation, as friends to grace and virtue, and enemies to vice. I faint, carry me away till another time."*

There was silence of suspense brooding over the
Kremlin. The boyars remembered with misgiving the

* *Travels of Sir Jerome Horsey.*

time thirty years before when the Tsar had been expected to die and yet recovered. The difference was that
Ivan had then been passive toward Fate, but now
clearly did not want to die. The Tsar was a very sick
man, but he could not believe that he was being called
away. Strong will and passion fought against the treason of his body. The hysteria and insomnia which visited him after he murdered his son were repeated. He
was wheeled out at night to look at the star blazing
over Moscow. His eyes would be fixed for hours upon
the baleful light. Then later, when he was placed on
his couch, he would break into babblings or shout de-
liriously, calling his dead son to him. His attendants
were frightened. But at daybreak he always recovered
from his delirium and it was clear that he remained in
full possession of his faculties. The astrologers had
forecast his death for the 18th March, but he did not
believe them and looked forward cynically to their
execution. He still thought he would survive to marry
an Englishwoman. Had he been convinced that death
was coming, there is little doubt that he would have
called the Metropolitan and been shorn as a monk,
making a complete renunciation of worldly vanities.
Nevertheless he was obsessed by the efforts of his sorcerers and could not attend to affairs of state. No
ambassadors were appointed to England. Sir Jerome
Bowes remained guarded and shut up in his house
awaiting the Tsar's pleasure and Ivan gave him no official *congé*. On the 10th March the Lithuanian envoys
on their way to Moscow to discuss the new settlement
had been halted as the Tsar was too ill to deal with
them. The first sign that Ivan gave that he was really

facing the possibility of death was when he made a new will. He called Boris Godunof and several of the leading nobles to his side and made a new testament in their presence, nominating Fedor as his successor. He also appointed a committee of safety to act as a buttress and protection for his son. It was composed of Prince Ivan Shuisky, Prince Ivan Mstislavsky, Princes Yurief and Bielsky, and Boris Godunof, who was head and shoulders above the others in capacity and personality. Ivan gave the town of Uglitch to his widow and her infant Dimitry. And he thanked all his boyars and generals for all they had done for him in his wars with the Tartars, the Poles and the Livonians.

It is said that everyone prayed for him, even those who had most cause to hate him. All Moscow and Russia took to prayer for a great sinner, but their lord and master. He was not abandoned in his last hour, as one might suppose, and left outside the pale of human sympathy. The sense of his greatness surged up in men's minds, this most astonishing Russian of Russians vouchsafed to be their sovereign.

On the 17th March he felt better and took a warm bath. The Tsar said he was as "heart-whole" as ever he was and commanded the lying soothsayers to be executed on the morrow. But they answered: "The day ends with the setting of the sun." The ides of March have come—aye, Cæsar, but not gone.

The Tsar made merry that day and had his singers in and sang with them. About the seventh hour he called for his chess men and asked Boris Godunof to play a game with him. He set the pieces himself, but his king would persistently fall down, "which he could not make stand in his place upon the plain board." But he started the game with Boris—and then suddenly he had a seizure.

"The Emperor in his loose gown, shirt and linen hose, faints and falls backward. [There is] great outcry and stir; one sent for aqua vita, another to the apothecary for marigold and rose water, and to call his ghostly father and the physicians. In the mean he was strangled and stark dead." The Metropolitan came in and at once commenced the ritual of the renunciation of the throne for a monastic life and the dead Ivan was there and then made a monk and given the name of Johan. Fedor, a weakling with no hope of issue, became Tsar in his place. Boris Godunof became virtually the autocrat of all the Russians and eventually ruled in his own name.

APPENDIX

SIR JEROME BOWES

IT is possible that had the English ambassador been able to promise Ivan the hand of Lady Mary Hastings, the Tsar might not have sickened and died when he did. Or the Tsar, instinctively scenting death, merely clung desperately to the hope of life embodied in a new and brilliant marriage, but would have died any way. We do not know: the stars were against him. After that stormy interview with Bowes, when the ambassador told Ivan that he could not have Lady Mary, the Tsar saw the comet for the first time and began to wonder timorously what it might mean for him.

Sir Jerome must have reflected sadly, after the Tsar's death, that he might have used the monarch's passion to gain more for England and safety for himself. The death of Ivan might have been a welcome relief instead of the most dangerous circumstance of his embassy. He had not managed to get away from Moscow. For a month he had been mewed up in his house, and after Ivan's death he "trembled and expected hourly nothing but death and confiscation, his gates, windows and servants shut up."

The postscript to his mission was ably written by Sir Jerome Horsey who was on good and friendly terms with Boris Godunof and therefore still *persona grata* at court. He wrote the following in his *Travels:*

"I was sent for and asked what they should do with Sir Jerome Bowes; his business being at an end. I told

the lords it stood with the honour of the King and kingdom to dismiss him with all safety and humanity, according to the law of nations; otherwise it would be ill
taken, and perhaps procure such displeasure as would
not be soon pacified; all which I submitted to their
wiser and better considerations. They all reviled at
him, saying he had deserved death, but that the Emperor and Empress were now of a more merciful disposition; they would have sent a message by me to prepare his dispatch, with some other words of displeasure,
which I prayed might be done by some other of his
Majesty's servants.

"The lord Boris Fedorovitch [Godunof] sent for me
at evening, whom I found playing chess with a prince
of the blood, Knez Ivan Glinsky. [He] took me aside
—'Speak little in defence of Bowes, I advise you, the
lords take it ill. Go shew yourself and pacify such and
such. Your answer was well considered of; many per-
suading revenge of his behaviour, I'll do my best to
make all well, and tell him so from me.' I went to
those noblemen accordingly, and did endeavour to
pacify them. They told me my partaking with Sir
Jerome Bowes would do me more hurt than I was
aware of; knowing how things stood and so distasteful
to all, especially those chief officers that had suffered so
much for his arrogance. They could not but love me for
ancient knowledge, and the more because Boris Fedorovitch did favour me so well.

" 'Therefore meddle you little with that business!'—
And yet I did not leave to deal effectually underhand
for him, for his case was very dangerous. I entreated he
might be sent for and dispatched, being coped up and
kept close prisoner, all allowances taken from him. In
the end he was sent for, when other greater affairs of

state was passed over; not attended upon, but with a mean messenger, had into a withdrawing room, where many of the lords were. [They] used him with no respect, charged him with heinous matter practised against the crown and state, would suffer nor spend time for his answer. [He was] railed upon, especially by the two Shalkans and some others who had endured most displeasure and beatings of the Emperor for his complaints and unreasonable and needless finding fault from time to time, so much to disquiet the King and state as never any ambassador did; and told him that it was very requisite for the example of all others who should so much forget themselves, to cut off his legs and cast his withered carcase in the river, pointing out the window under him, but that God had given us now a more merciful Emperor that wills no revenge, whose eyes he should see for Queen Elizabeth's sake."

They then commanded him to surrender his sword, but Bowes, though somewhat of a fool, was no coward. He refused, saying that it was against his orders and his oath. They then cajoled him, saying it was not fitting to come with show of arms into the presence of the young Tsar who was in deep mourning. Tsar Fedor did not receive him rudely as the boyars had done and he was allowed to go home bearing a letter and a present for the Queen. Horsey, at great risk to himself, organised his transport to the waiting ship at the mouth of the Dvina. And Bowes was humble till he got his feet on the timbers of an English ship. But then, says Horsey,

"he used exceeding intemperate, rash and indiscreet words to the gentleman that conducted him thither, cutting both sables [the gift to the Queen] and letters in pieces, and sent many proud and opprobrious words of the Emperor and his council. After he was gone, those great officers of state, the Shalkans, of friends became my mortal enemies, for taking his part."

Bowes naturally fell into disgrace in England and he was not grateful to Horsey for having saved his life. He even framed a charge against him that one day at table Horsey had breathed scandal against the Earl of Leicester, "how he [the Earl] had cast his wife down a pair of stairs, broke her neck and so became the Queen's minion." This, dealt with by the Privy Council, almost caused Horsey's disgrace, but in cross examination Bowes confessed that he had invented the story.

THE NEW TSAR FEDOR DESCRIBED BY FLETCHER

"The Emperor that now is called Theodore Ivan-ovitch is for his person of a mean stature, somewhat low and gross, of a sallow complexion, and inclining to the dropsy, hawk-nosed, unsteady in his pace, by reason of some weakness of his limbs, heavy and inactive, yet commonly smiling almost to laughter. For quality otherwise simple and slow-witted, but very gentle, and of an easy nature, quiet, merciful, of no martial disposition, nor greatly apt for matter of policy, very superstitious and infinite that way. Besides his own private devotions at home, he goeth every week commonly on pilgrimage to some monastery or other that is nearest hand."

Ivan himself said of Fedor that he would make a better bell-ringer than a tsar. Actually he was most fond of ringing church bells.

SCOTTISH MERCENARIES

Ivan the Terrible put many prisoners of war to death as an after-dinner amusement. There was little idea of feeding male prisoners and repatriating them after the conclusion of hostilities. Those who were not sold in the slave market were in a peculiarly evil case, being liable to be brought forth and tortured at the whim of the Tsar or his subordinates. Many unfortunate Poles and Swedes and Livonians and Lithuanians died in this way. But among the prisoners were a number of Scottish mercenaries, and although at that time Scotland was an independent kingdom, the plight of these Scots awakened the sympathy of the English in Moscow. Sir Jerome Horsey recounts:

"There were four score and five poor Scots soldiers left of 700 sent from Stockholm, and three Englishmen in their company, brought among other captives, in most miserable manner, piteous to behold. I laboured and employed my best endeavours and credit not only to succour them, but with my purse and pains got them to be well placed at Bulvan, near Moscow; and although the Emperor was much inflamed with fury and wrath against them, torturing and putting many of those Swedish soldiers to death, most lamentably to behold, I procured the Emperor to be told of the difference between those Scotsmen, now his captives and the

Swedes, Poles and Livonians, his enemies. They were a nation strangers, remote, a venturous and warlike people, ready to serve any Christian prince for maintenance and pay; as they would appear and prove, if it pleased his Majesty to employ and spare them such maintenance, now out of heart, clothes and arms, as they may show themselves and valure against his mortal enemies the Cryme Tartar. It seems some use was made of this advice, for shortly the best soldiers and men at arms of these strangers were spared and put apart, and captains of each nation appointed to govern the rest; Jeamy Lingett for the Scottish men, a valiant honest man. Money, clothes and daily allowance for meat and drink was given them. Horses, hay and oats; swords, piece and pistols were they armed with. Poor snakes afore, look cheerfully now. Twelve hundred of them did better service against the Tartar than 12 thousand Russes. . . ."*

THE BURNING OF MOSCOW BY THE TARTARS

There are several accounts of the great fire, made by English witnesses. The following, which seems to be anonymous, is to be found among the *State Papers of Queen Elizabeth:*

"The houses are covered with wooden slat, which was the destruction of the town. They say there is left no house in the city; churches and steeples are burnt. It was accounted four times as great as London, and some say six times. There are above 200,000 people burnt.

* *Travels of Sir Jerome Horsey.*

They had hope to have saved themselves in certain places, but the force of the fire would not permit it. There was a market place by estimation as great as one six part of the city of London, where was daily market kept, and thither thousands of people did resort for succour, but when the fire had entered the houses about, the people were smothered and burnt ten thick, one lying upon another, a lamentable case to hear."*

* *State Papers of Queen Elizabeth*. Foreign. CXLVI. 12.

BIBLIOGRAPHICAL NOTES

THE Russian sources for the reign of Ivan the Terrible are somewhat scanty owing to the destruction of the archives in the great fire of Moscow in 1626. Also many invaluable documents must have been destroyed during the "confused times" of the pretender Pugachof. The great Russian historians, Karamzin and Solovyof, had recourse to the testimony of foreigners, which they combined with what they pieced together in scraps of information gleaned from the chronicles kept in the large monasteries. The most valuable information from a Russian source was found in the letters of Kurbsky to the Tsar and Ivan's replies and in Kurbsky's writings generally. But even what Kurbsky wrote had to be taken with caution, because the refugee prince was all the while hostile to Ivan and writing in justification of his own treason.

The Germans Taube and Kruze, employed by Ivan, also gave a mass of information about the tyrannies of the reign, but their testimony is also colored by the fact that they went over to Ivan's enemies. The most impartial witness is contained in the writings of English envoys and travellers. One of the chief literary pleasures in writing this biography has been the providing of a complete background for the stories contained in the Hakluyt collection. Interesting as these are by themselves, out of context, they are illuminated and rendered more interesting by relating them to their proper place in the life of Ivan the Terrible.

There are few biographical studies of Ivan the Terrible in the Russian language and these are small and inadequate. One may mention the following:

Ivany Grozny, by C. F. Platonof: Berlin, 1924.

Ivan Grozny, by P. Bipper: Berlin, 1922.

The best account of the reign is to be found in the course of Karamzin's *Istoria Gosudarstva Rossiiskago*. Solovyof's History follows this, adds little to it, but omits many personal details of Ivan's life. Klutchevsky's History likewise adds little beyond a critical examination of the known facts of the reign.

In the English language there exist, to my knowledge, only two biographies of Ivan the Terrible. One is by a Mr. Pember, and is too slight and ill-informed to merit consideration. The other is translated from the French of Waliszeevsky. This contains much information; one cannot but feel that the gifted author must have been in ill health when he wrote it, the form of the book being so clumsy and the detail so muddled.

The chief English sources are:—*Travels of Sir Jerome Horsey;* this in invaluable, though Horsey fell into exaggeration, as when he said that 700,000 people perished in the punishment of Novgorod; *The Russe Commonwealth*, by Giles Fletcher; the Letters of Jenkinson and others contained in Hakluyt's *Principal Navigations*, Vols. II and III; the *State Papers of the Reign of Queen Elizabeth*.

Further research in the monasteries and ecclesiastical archives of Russia might conceivably yield more information. It is also possible that English letters of the sixteenth century might be found to throw more light on the desire of Ivan to be married to Queen Elizabeth.

INDEX

Adashef, Alexey, advancement of, 29; influence on Tsar, 60–61; charged to collect petitions, 62; reforming the Church, 67–68; sent to Kazan, 74; opposes will of Ivan, 106, 107, 148; apparently pardoned, 110; policy of, 121; opposed to Western enterprise, 148–149; sent to Dorpat, 154; fall of, 154; imprisonment and death, 154; career of, 155
——, Daniel, sent to pacify insurgents at Kazan, 116; sent against Livonia, 139; at siege of Narva, 139; defeats Tartars, 145; put to death, 156
——, Fedor, 106, 107, 110
Afanasy, Metropolitan, 180–182, 193
Akeson, 256
Aleka, 116
Alexander of Macedon, 74
Alexandrof (Alexandrovskaya Sloboda), chosen retreat of Ivan the Terrible, 182; life at, 190–191; monastic rule at, 191–192; Vladimir Andreyevitch murdered at, 212; conversation with Jenkinson at, 249; Convocation at, 289; Tsarevitch murdered at, 293–296; funeral procession from, 295
Alexief, archpriest, 12
Altenthorn, 140
Alva, Duke of, vi
Anastasia, chosen bride of Ivan the Terrible, 37; wedding, 41–42; character of, 42, 147; influence on Ivan, 53–54, 60; gives birth to Tsarevitch Dimitry,

90; at state banquet, 96; gives birth to second Tsarevitch, Ivan, 114; sickness, 145, 150; death, 148
Andrew, uncle of Ivan, *see* Staritsky
Anna, fourth wife of Ivan, 249; Tsar tires of, 261; put away, 262
Anna Vasilchikof, fifth consort of the Tsar, 262
Army, 28, 31, 75, 121, 134, 167, 168
Artillery, 134
Assumption, Cathedral of the, 34, 38, 45, 47
Astrakhan, 69, 76, 122; captured, 122; princes of, called Tsars, 126
Augsburg Confession, 194
Augustus, Sigizmund, King of Poland, Grand Duke of Lithuania, will not recognize Ivan's title of Tsar, 125; letter to Queen Elizabeth, 143; demands cession of Smolensk, 144; takes Livonia under his protection, 144; Ivan asks for his sister in marriage, 158; propounds marriage settlement, 160; sends troops to Livonia, 167; invites co-operation of Tartars, 171; tries to foment civil war, 200; health failing, 233; armistice with Ivan, 233; death, 252

Ballads, 96
Baltic, 122, 127, 140, 168, 234, 270
Basmanof, Alexey, at storming of Narva, 142; becomes Tsar's favourite, 180; assaults Metropoli-